THE NEW POLITICAL ECONOMY
OF EMU

THE NEW POLITICAL ECONOMY
OF EMU

edited by
JEFFRY FRIEDEN,
DANIEL GROS,
and
ERIK JONES

ROWMAN & LITTLEFIELD PUBLISHERS, INC.
Lanham • Boulder • New York • Oxford

ROWMAN & LITTLEFIELD PUBLISHERS, INC.

Published in the United States of America
by Rowman & Littlefield Publishers, Inc.
4720 Boston Way, Lanham, Maryland 20706

12 Hid's Copse Road
Cumnor Hill, Oxford OX2 9JJ, England

British Library Cataloguing in Publication Information Available

Library of Congress Cataloging-in-Publication Data

The new political economy of EMU / edited by Jeffry Frieden, Daniel
   Gros, and Erik Jones.
      p.   cm.
   Includes bibliographical references and index.
   ISBN 0-8476-9018-0 (cloth : alk. paper). — ISBN 0-8476-9019-9
(pbk. : alk. paper)
   1. European Monetary System (Organization) 2. Monetary unions—
European Union countries. 3. European Union countries—Economic
conditions. 4. European Union countries—Economic policy.
I. Frieden, Jeffry A. II. Gros, Daniel, 1955– . III. Jones,
Erik.
HG925.N48   1998
332.4'566'094—dc21   98-24158
                                                        CIP

ISBN 0-8476-9018-0 (cloth : alk. paper)
ISBN 0-8476-9019-9 (pbk. : alk. paper)

Printed in the United States of America

♾ ™ The paper used in this publication meets the minimum requirements of
American National Standard for Information Sciences—Permanence of Paper for
Printed Library Materials, ANSI Z39.48-1984.

Contents

List of Tables and Figures   vii

Preface   ix

1. EMU: Economics and Politics   1
Jeffry Frieden, Daniel Gros, and Erik Jones

2. Monetary Union and European Unemployment   13
José Viñals and Juan F. Jimeno

3. External Shocks and Labor Mobility: How Important Are They
for EMU?   53
Daniel Gros

4. Fiscal Deficit Reductions in Line with the Maastricht Criteria for
Monetary Union: An Empirical Analysis   83
A. J. Hughes Hallett and Peter McAdam

5. Monetary Union with Variable Geometry   125
Jean Pisani-Ferry

6. The Political Economy of European Monetary Union:
A Conceptual Overview   163
Jeffry Frieden and Erik Jones

A Note on Data Sources   187

References   189

Index   201

List of Editors and Contributors   205

Tables and Figures

Tables

2.1 Proportion of the Variance of National Unemployment Rates
     Explained by Innovations in the EU Unemployment Rate   21
2.2 Proportion of the Variance of Regional Unemployment Rates
     Explained   22
2.3 Evidence on Real Wage Rigidity and Hysteresis   24

3.1 Unemployment as a Function of Export Performance   59
3.2 Change in *Employment* Rates as a Function of Their Own
     History and Past Changes in Export Volumes   62
3.3 Change in *Unemployment* Rates as a Function of Their Own
     History and Past Changes in Export Volumes   63
3.4 Change in Unemployment as a Function of Its Own History,
     the Change in Real Exports, and the Change in Real Effective
     Exchange Rates   65
3.5 Exchange Rate Variability and the German Labor Market   70
3.6 Migration in the European Union 15   73

4.1 Deficit Ratios, Successful Simulations   93
4.2 Debt Ratios, Successful Simulations   94
4.3 Output Losses, Successful Simulations   95
4.4 Price Deflation, Successful Simulations   96
4.5 The Changes in Tax Rates   97
4.6 Nominal Interest Rates, Successful Simulations   98
4.7 Deficit Ratios, Successful Simulations   104
4.8 Debt Ratios, Successful Simulations   108
4.9 Output Losses   109
4.10 Price Deflation   111
4.11 The Change in Tax Rates   112

4.12   Nominal Interest Rates   113
4.13   Budgetary Retrenchment Experiences, 1974 to 1994   116
4.14   Large-Scale Budgetary Adjustments, 1974 to 1994   119

5.1   Criteria for Membership in Monetary Union   130
5.2   Correlation Ranks for Three Categories of Symmetry Criteria   131
5.3   Required Changes in the Primary Budget Balance   134
5.4   Unemployment Indicators: Differences between EU 13 and
       Germany   137
5.5   Alternative Union Scenarios   140
5.6   Voting on Monetary Union with Unanimity Rule   142
5.7   Decision on Monetary Union with Unanimity Rule   143
5.8   Decision on Monetary Union with Opting Out/Opting In Rule   147
5.9   Decision on Monetary Union with Club Rule   148

Figures

2.1   Unemployment Rates: European Union, United States, Japan   15
2.2   Unemployment in the EU, 1995: Percentage Labor Force   16
2.3   Inflation and Unemployment: European Union, 1995   18
2.4   Variation in Unemployment Rates: European Union with and
       without Spain   19
2.5   Determinants of Unemployment   28
2.6   A Simple Representation of the Labor Market   47

3.1   The Labor Market   75
3.2   Migration and Housing: 1992—Percent of Population   78

5.1   Decision Tree for Monetary Union with Opting In/Out   144

6.1   Support and Suitability   176

Preface

We would like to take this opportunity to thank all those researchers associated with the Centre for European Policy Studies (CEPS) Economic Policy Group and especially Alberto Giovannini, Niels Thygesen, and Francisco Torres for their generous comments on the different chapters in the volume. The first drafts of these essays were commissioned in 1994 and have been the subject of several meetings of the Economic Policy Group and its associates during the past four years. We would like to extend particular thanks to Peter Ludlow, director of CEPS, for his invaluable support of our work. We would also like to acknowledge the generous financial support of the Deutsche Bundesbank, the Sveriges Riksbank, the Banco de España, and the German Marshall Fund, all of whom underwrote the group's activities, of which these essays are only a part.

The Economic Policy Group, and therefore these studies, have also benefited from the hospitality and assistance of a number of individuals and organizations. Carsten Hefeker, Kathleen McNamara, and James Walsh provided essential advice and support on the activities of the Economic Policy Group throughout. Moreover, the group was fortunate to be able to hold a final meeting at the Centro de Estudos Europeus within the framework of the Portuguese Inter-university Group on European Integration. Financial support for that meeting was generously provided by the European Commission, the European Parliament, the Association for a Monetary Union in Europe, and the Luso-Americano Foundation.

Jeffry Frieden, Cambridge
Daniel Gros, Brussels
Erik Jones, Nottingham

1

EMU: Economics and Politics

Jeffry Frieden, Daniel Gros, and Erik Jones

Europe's plan to form an Economic and Monetary Union (EMU) is among the most controversial developments of the 1990s. EMU dominates the economics pages of quality newspapers, it monopolizes the agendas of European Council meetings, it hovers over financial planning in European boardrooms, and it is the ghost at the feast in ministerial cabinets. Elections have been won on the issue, and they have also been lost.

This level of controversy must come as a surprise to the negotiators who sat around the table at Maastricht in December 1991. For them, EMU was the most carefully considered step on the road to European integration since the original decision to form a common market. Not only did they have access to a broad series of background studies prepared by the European Commission, these negotiators also could draw on a deep academic literature and a precise institutional blueprint prepared by the central banks.

Nevertheless, nothing prepared Europe or its EMU plan for the series of controversies that erupted soon after the signing of the Maastricht Treaty. Within a short span of months, ratification of the treaty was in jeopardy and financial markets began to tear down the edifice for exchange rate cooperation in Europe. Since that time, EMU has rocked from pillar to post. And, while Europe appears certain to form an economic and monetary union, there can be little doubt but that many of the concerns raised in the Maastricht plan's short decade will continue well into the next century.

The purpose of this collection of essays is to examine the concerns about EMU. Each of the essays combines a review of the literature with new analysis. The essays are written to address questions that are political as well as economic in nature. Moreover, and to the extent possible, the essays are written in a language that is broadly accessible to noneconomists—particularly with regard to the introductory material and the discussion of results. If there is a single overarching explanation for the controversy surrounding EMU, it is that too few people understand—or can gain access to information about—the real issues at stake.

This introduction has three sections. The first surveys developments since the signing of the Maastricht Treaty in order to highlight the controversies surrounding Europe's plan for EMU. The second focuses attention on the core issues of the debate and outlines our central findings. The third section charts where future research can and should be done. Whether or not EMU actually comes about on time, the controversies surrounding it are certain to continue.

A Difficult Transition

The Maastricht Treaty was initialed in December 1991 and signed the following February. The document has two major components and derives from two sets of negotiations. One part of the document is political and describes how decisions are to be made concerning a range of subjects in the renamed European Union. The other part is programmatic and explains how the European Union will achieve a specific objective: the formation of an economic and monetary union. The political part of the treaty is hesitant, contingent, over-complicated. The EMU part is confident, definite, precise. Article 109 states that EMU will start on 1 January 1999 at the latest with whichever member states may qualify. Moreover, "all member states shall, whether they fulfill the necessary criteria or not, respect the will of the Community to enter swiftly into [an economic and monetary union], and therefore no member state shall prevent the entering into [an economic and monetary union]."[1]

The distinction between the two parts of the Maastricht Treaty provides a useful starting point for this description of recent events. Not only does this distinction establish the time frame—bounded at one end by the initial agreement on the Maastricht Treaty and at the other end by the start of EMU—it also provides a demarcation between areas of prior agreement (EMU) and those still available for discussion (everything else). Unfortunately, however, the distinction between the two parts of the treaty proved to be ephemeral. The boundaries between the political and economic parts of the Maastricht Treaty blurred soon after the ratification process began.

The Danish population rejected the Maastricht Treaty by a thin margin in a June 1992 referendum. Officially, this rejection was directed at the political aspects of the treaty. The Danish government had already secured the right to opt-out of EMU, and the electorate seemed more put off by the obscure language of the treaty provisions than anything else. Nevertheless, the Danish veto raised concerns that EMU was somehow undemocratic and that the economic side of the treaty lacked an important political dimension.

Within hours of the Danish veto, French president François Mitterrand called for a similar referendum in France. There, too, the results were surprising. Although supporters of the treaty managed to secure a narrow majority, the obvious lack of enthusiasm raised more questions than the referendum could resolve. Specifically, the French vote suggested that Europe's populations might not be so committed to the EMU project as their governments would have liked to believe.

In financial markets, the closeness of the French referendum suggested that the political threshold for abandoning exchange rate coordination was low. At the same time, rising unemployment and poor export performance began to undermine confidence in prevailing exchange rate parities under the Exchange Rate Mechanism (ERM) and to heighten the possibility for realignment. In August and September 1992, financial markets challenged the currencies within the ERM, ultimately forcing several European governments to abandon the defense of their currency pegs. This currency crisis confirmed beliefs that the political will to support fixed exchange rates was lacking.

The 1992 exchange rate crisis also raised suspicions that the Maastricht plan for EMU might be technically flawed. The transition period allowed too much leeway for financial speculators, and the convergence criteria placed tight constraints on economic policymakers. Faced with rising unemployment, national politicians were unlikely to support exchange rate targets with high real interest rates. On the contrary, such politicians were likely to look to devaluation as a means to facilitate domestic adjustment.[2]

The markets struck again in the summer of 1993 and delivered a severe blow to the European Monetary System, forcing Europe's leaders to widen the fluctuation bands of the ERM from 2.25 percent to 15 percent. This second exchange rate crisis added weight to the controversies about the technical adequacy of the Maastricht plan for EMU and reinforced beliefs that the plan was somehow structurally flawed. Not only did it prohibit exchange rate re-alignments, it also constrained the use of monetary and fiscal instruments. As a result, the Maastricht plan seemed to deprive Europe's economies of the means to facilitate real economic adjustment. Soon thereafter, however, two developments pushed the debate about EMU in seemingly opposite directions—toward a strict observance of the convergence criteria and toward a greater focus of attention on the problems of growth, competitiveness, and employment.

The first was an October 1993 German High Court decision indicating, among other things, that the German government cannot make an automatic transition into EMU as described in the Maastricht Treaty. The same ruling also held that the enforcement of price stability in a European currency is a German constitutional right, and not merely a preference (Reeh, 1994; Kaufmann-Bühler, 1994). Therefore, any failure to observe the convergence criteria at the European level could form the basis of a judicial ruling prohibiting the German government from participating in EMU. Taken together, these decisions implied not only that Germany must adhere to a strict interpretation of the convergence criteria but also that the rest of Europe must accept German interpretations in these matters. There could be no EMU without German participation, and no German participation without a strict adherence to the Maastricht convergence criteria.

The second development was the publication of a European Commission white paper, "Growth, Competitiveness, Employment" (CEC, 1993). The intention behind this document was to acknowledge that unemployment should be at the center of political attention. Moreover, the paper suggested that EMU will facilitate all three objectives mentioned in the title—growth, competitiveness, and employment. Nevertheless, the result of the paper was to heighten concerns that any increase in competitiveness would come at the expense of the working classes and of the welfare state. Such concerns drew force from the pressure that the fiscal convergence criteria added to already necessary welfare state reforms. Thus, rather than putting to rest fears about the relationship between EMU and a competitive Europe, the 1993 white paper gave rise to fears about the relationship between EMU and social Europe. And, at the center of those fears lay the tension between Maastricht-style convergence and the necessary reform of the welfare state (Standing, 1997).

The competitiveness debate continued in Europe through the first half of 1994, as did concerns about convergence and the welfare state. The forthcoming accession of Austria, Finland, and Sweden, however, promised to strengthen the social democratic character of the Union and added weight to assertions that Europe would continue to adhere to its particular pattern of social and economic development. Meanwhile, the predominant considerations were not developments within the Union, but those outside in the transition countries of Central and Eastern Europe. Europe's politicians began preparations for a 1996 Intergovernmental Conference (IGC), originally scheduled to ensure the smooth functioning of the Maastricht reforms but modified to adapt Europe's institutions for an eastward enlargement. With some relief, these statesmen suggested that the Maastricht plan for EMU was one part of the treaty that need not be renegotiated (CEPS, 1995).

EMU returned to the center of debates about Europe's future with the September 1994 publication of a "reflection paper" by the parliamentary faction of the ruling Christian Democrats in Germany. The paper echoed warnings of Bundesbank President Hans Tietmeyer that only a few countries were qualified to enter EMU on the first round, and it argued that European integration should proceed according to a concentric circles approach centered on a hard core of those countries prepared and willing to make the greatest effort (Tietmeyer, 1994; Lamers, 1997). The controversy was about what effects EMU would have on countries outside the monetary union. For a concentric circles pattern of integration to function, the hard core must exert a centripetal force on the periphery. If EMU were to exert a centrifugal force on those economies outside the Union, the result would be to exclude them from the more political forms of integration as well.

The danger of a centrifugal union became politically salient within months. Jacques Chirac won the 1995 French presidential election on a platform dedicated to helping the unemployed and socially excluded. For many, this suggested that Chirac would favor a more relaxed approach to fiscal policy and so speculative pressures mounted in financial markets. Such pressures fed on concerns that those countries ejected from the ERM during the 1992 and 1993 crises were benefiting at the expense of those still inside. Close exchange rate coordination, it seemed, did exert a centrifugal force. However the effects of that force were stronger at the core than at the periphery. The exchange rate crises of 1995 confirmed this interpretation for many and suggested that some revision of the convergence criteria was imminent.

The response to renewed exchange-rate instability was unaccommodating. German Finance Minister Theo Waigel proposed a reform of the convergence process in September 1995. However, Waigel argued that the criteria should be strengthened rather than weakened. For EMU to succeed, Waigel insisted, Europe required stability. French President Chirac agreed and signed up with Waigel's proposed stability pact in what many regarded as a reversal of his electoral emphasis on unemployment and the socially excluded. As a result, and in response to a tightening of fiscal reform measures, France erupted in a series of strikes against the government's policy and, by extension, against EMU.

Meanwhile, not only had EMU come to dominate the domestic politics of member states, the reverse was also true, and the domestic politics of member states has begun to dominate the discussion of EMU. From Tony Blair's triumphant victory over John Major, to the disastrous defeat of Alain Juppé (Jacques Chirac's prime minister) at the hands of Lionel Jospin, to Helmut Kohl's running battles with Edmund Stoiber in the coalition and Gerhard Schröder outside, EMU appears to hang in the balance of politic contests at the national level. However, rather than developing in systematic fashion, domestic debates over EMU have evolved idiosyncratically from one member state to the next.

The Central Concerns

Our approach is to tackle five key issues surrounding EMU, one at a time. In Chapter 2, José Viñals and Juan Jimeno focus on Europe's unemployment problem and any possible relationship between that and EMU. Many opponents of EMU maintain that unemployment is the number one problem of Europe today and that EMU would make it worse or, at best, be only a distraction from the essential task of fighting it. Chapter 2 therefore lays out the stylized facts about unemployment in Europe and analyzes the mechanisms by which EMU might affect it.

Viñals and Jimeno suggest that EMU will probably have little affect on unemployment. They base this conclusion on three elements. First of all, even a superficial look at the evolution of unemployment in Europe shows that it is a structural problem. Unemployment has been increasing almost every year since the early 1970s. This is in contrast to the United States where unemployment has gone up and down over time without a clear trend over the last decades. Second, Viñals and Jimeno show that there is considerable rigidity in real wages in Europe. This implies that more inflation would not lead to more unemployment (and by the way, it also implies that disinflation does not necessarily increase unemployment). Third, they show that over the past fifteen years, unemployment in Europe already had a strong common element. Looking at its evolution at the regional level, Viñals and Jimeno find that the European component is more important than the national component. If this has been the case over the past fifteen years, with at times highly fluctuating exchange rates, there is every reason to believe that this will also be the case in the future under EMU.

Although there is a strong common element in the evolution of unemployment across member countries, the measures that need to be taken to combat unemployment fall into the competence of national governments. Once governments accept that devaluations are no longer an escape route, they should be more inclined to tackle the distortions of labor market that are at the root of the European unemployment problem. In this sense, Viñals and Jimeno conclude, EMU could actually help to alleviate the unemployment problem.

Chapter 3 turns to the core argument that appears in any discussion about the potential economic cost of EMU. The question is whether the nominal exchange rate is a useful adjustment instrument in the face of external shocks. If it is, then countries that forego using the exchange rate as an adjustment instrument will experience an increase in unemployment if they have to face a negative shock. Most economists contend that exchange rates are useful for facilitating adjustment. However, empirical evidence in support of that contention has never been measured. The chapter by Daniel Gros tries to measure the importance of external shocks and comes up with a startling result: External shocks do not seem to matter much for unemployment. This is even more surprising given the high degree of openness of most member states. Nevertheless, the surprise diminishes in any attempt to find instances in which a clearly identifiable external shock has had a major impact on the economy of a member state of the European Union (EU). The collapse of Finnish exports to the former Soviet Union and the second oil price shock (when the United Kingdom was still a significant energy producer) are the only examples that would fit this category. The implication is that the role of the exchange rate as an adjustment instrument that needs to be used continuously to offset shocks has thus been exaggerated.

Gros also finds that unemployment may be related to exchange rate volatility. Economists usually regard exchange rate variability as an unimportant nuisance because it seems to have little impact on the volume of trade. However, it appears that exchange rate variability is systematically related to the evolution of unemployment in Germany. No similar link seems to exist between unemployment and the level of the deutsche mark exchange rate. This finding could perhaps resolve the puzzle that German industry supports EMU strongly although it is often claimed that German exports are not much affected by a strong deutsche mark.

The next chapter deals with the fear that Maastricht-style fiscal convergence might be a cause of higher unemployment. The Maastricht Treaty stipulates that only countries with a fiscal deficit below 3 percent of GDP and a declining debt ratio can take part in EMU. Since, by 1994 to 1995, most member countries had deficits much above 3 percent and debt ratios that were increasing, it is clear that the Maastricht criteria on fiscal policy imposed a major fiscal adjustment. Does such a fiscal contraction have a negative impact on demand and output, thus increasing unemployment even more? A. J. Hughes Hallett and Peter McAdam present different scenarios in answer to this question using a well-known international macroeconomic model (MULTIMOD).

Hughes Hallett and McAdam find that the convergence-and-employment question is easier to ask than to answer. A clear-cut answer is difficult because any change in fiscal policy changes a lot of other things as well. Moreover, any assumption about what else will change has many and different effects on the results of the analysis. This applies in particular to the behavior of interest rates. For example, under the assumption that a fiscal contraction is not accompanied by any cut in interest rates, the effects of the contraction are likely to be substantial. If interest rates are cut as the fiscal contraction takes place, the effects of the contraction are less important.

Hughes Hallett and McAdam find that the standard impact (or first year) multipliers are around one. This implies that a reduction in the deficit of around 3 percent would lead to a drop in gross domestic product (GDP) of around 3 percent—compared to a baseline of "everything else unchanged." In subsequent years, the negative impact of the fiscal contraction would diminish so that the loss of growth would be substantial, but only temporary. Applying these multipliers to the case of Italy, which started with deficits above 10 percent of GDP in the early 1990s, adherence to the Maastricht convergence criteria would imply a loss of GDP of more than 7 percent. However, while Italy has already cut this deficit by 5 to 6 percentage points of GDP over the past few years, there is no sign that such a massive reduction of domestic product has taken place. The main reason why this has not happened might be that interest rates have also fallen strongly in Italy over the past years.

The Italian case suggests that fiscal policy cannot be considered independently from interest rates. Indeed the conclusion of Hughes Hallett and McAdam is that a fiscal contraction accompanied by a monetary relaxation should result in only minor output losses. It is thus difficult to quantify how small or large the output cost of reaching the Maastricht target of a deficit of 3 percent will be since it is difficult to predict to what extent interest rates will fall in response to a fiscal consolidation. Hughes Hallett and McAdam provide several simulations to this effect. However, it is clear that the scope for reduction in interest rates is largest in the countries that until recently had interest rates much above the German level. Italy, Spain, and Portugal should therefore be able to benefit much more from this effect than a country like France, which already had interest rates close to the German level since 1990. This is indeed what happened from 1996 to 1997. Both the terms of the stability pact and the prospect of enlargement ensure that fiscal consolidation will remain on the agenda well into the next century. Therefore, findings such as these will remain important long after the start of EMU.

Chapter 5 deals with the question of "variable geometry," or more specifically the notion that European integration should proceed on the basis of a hard core of committed countries. The paper by Jean Pisani-Ferry tries to bring some order to discussion about this issue. First of all it is important to distinguish between variable geometry of the transitional kind and variable geometry as a permanent solution. The transitional type of variable geometry is part of the traditional elements of any progress in European integration and has so far led to few problems. For example, it was used even in the European Monetary System (EMS) with the large band for Italy. This might be different in the case of EMU, however, because those member states that are "willing but temporarily unable" to join the monetary union might fear that they will be penalized by financial markets if EMU starts without them. Hence, these countries might oppose the start of EMU altogether if they cannot be part of the first wave of membership.

Variable geometry as a permanent solution for EMU is already foreseen in the Maastricht Treaty and would pose few institutional problems. (This is again in contrast to the other typical areas of EU activities, such as the entire internal market, where permanent exemptions from core aspects would lead to serious institutional problems.) Nevertheless, it is impossible to determine whether the effects of this variable geometry will be centrifugal or centripetal before the fact.

Pisani-Ferry examines the dynamic potential of a monetary union built around a "hard core" using game-theoretic analysis. He finds that two effects predominate: one in which countries are forced into EMU before they are ready, and another where countries choose to remain outside of EMU in order to "free-ride" on the monetary stability of the hard core. Moreover, Pisani-Ferry argues, while the Maastricht Treaty adequately addresses the danger that countries might be forced to join, it fails to address the problem of free riding. Therefore, Pisani-Ferry concludes that while it might be necessary to construct institutions to counter the dynamics unleashed through variable geometry, such institutions should be directed to encouraging outsiders to join EMU, rather than preventing insiders from excluding others as is commonly suggested.

The sixth and final chapter addresses the political economy of EMU. A question underlying much of this book is why EMU is such a political priority. What political forces are sustaining it through all the turbulence of the 1980s and 1990s? An answer to this question must start from an analysis of politics within member states. The EU works through its member states and progresses only if they agree to do so. Moreover, all important political forces are still organized at the national level. Therefore, it is necessary to ask what economic and political factors are behind the positions different countries have taken with respect to EMU? Why do the French and German governments favor EMU, while the U.K. government opposes it? Why is the German population so opposed to EMU, while the Italian population is so much in support?

In Chapter 6, Jeffry Frieden and Erik Jones argue that a number of common elements appear in most countries. For example, the overall balance of cost and benefits from EMU should be one important element in domestic debates. Nevertheless, they find that such common elements—while analytically important—are rarely decisive. Political decisions are always subject to the influence of pressure groups that mainly have their own perceived interests in mind rather than the aggregate analysis provided by economists. For example, in some countries trade unions might favor EMU because they assume it will bring price stability and low interest rates, whereas in Germany trade unions favor EMU, inter alia, because they hope that the European Central Bank will be more accommodating in setting monetary policy than the Bundesbank.

A second important point is that, in politics, the short-term transitional gains or losses can be more important than the long-term ones. For most pressure groups the long-term effects (whether positive or negative) seem to be of secondary importance. Economists would say that this is not too surprising because a lower inflation rate should not, over the long run, lead to a different income distribution. The results concerning the relative unimportance of external shocks presented in Chapter 3 would reinforce this point of view. By contrast, the transition to EMU does typically have important consequences for income distribution. Disinflation is typically associated with lower real wages and high real interest rates, and fiscal adjustment can hit different groups, depending on whether it is achieved through a cut in social security spending or an increase in personal income taxes.

Frieden and Jones conclude that the political economy of EMU depends on a large number of factors from perceptions to economic structures, and from ideology to institutional constraints. Thus, while general analytic frameworks provided a useful starting point for analysis, considerable empirical research is necessary to generate meaningful conclusions. Such work can be found in

two volumes of country studies originally commissioned as background for
the chapter: Jones, Frieden, and Torres (1998); and Pisani-Ferry, Hefeker, and
Hughes Hallett (1997).

Conclusion

Where does this analysis of the economics and politics of EMU leave us? We
would argue that the cases for and against EMU should be explained more
clearly and honestly. We found that many positions on EMU confirm John
Maynard Keynes' dictum about "practical" people being "the slaves of some
defunct economist" (Keynes, 1964: 383).

Better understanding of the economic and political mechanisms that drive
EMU is essential to narrow the gap between the public debates that followed
the signature of the Maastricht Treaty and actual developments. This gap wid-
ened after the turmoil of 1992 to 1993, when the EMU project was largely
written off as dead.[3] Even financial markets seem to have been impressed
into believing that monetary integration would not progress.[4] Meanwhile, the
European institutional machinery continued to work as though nothing had
happened. The European Monetary Institution (EMI) was created on schedule
in 1994, and over the following years, the European Council delivered a series
of important decisions (on the "Stability Pact," the change-over scenario, the
new exchange rate mechanism, and so forth).

The easy way to close the gap between popular perceptions and institutional
preparations is to suggest that Europe's statesmen and technocrats are somehow disconnected from the real world. However, such suggestions ignore two
important aspects of Europe's plan for EMU. The first of these is that ongoing
institutional preparations have been accompanied by the rapid consolidation of
economic performance in countries such as Greece, Ireland, Italy, and Spain.
Whether or not inspired by EMU, these countries have made dramatic adjustments through the 1990s. As a result, Europe is now more capable of creating
an economic and monetary union than it was when the Maastricht Treaty was
negotiated. Official preparations for EMU, whether conducted at the European
level or in the member states themselves, reflect this progress.

The second aspect of Europe's plan for EMU is the alternatives. Such alternatives do exist, but they are too often assumed in popular debates about the
Maastricht Treaty, and too rarely considered systematically. The best of these
alternatives would see the governments of the member states following responsible monetary and fiscal policies and coordinating their macroeconomic
strategies within the context of a broader European Monetary System. In other
words, the best alternative to EMU is EMU, but without the formality of monetary union. The distinction here hardly seems the stuff to rally large crowds
or massive outcries of opposition. If we consider the planned interim period

from 1999 to 2002, during which the countries retain their national currencies, it is doubtful that the distinction between EMU and its best alternative would be noticeable at all.

Nevertheless there is a distinction, and we would argue that research should be directed toward explaining exactly what that distinction may mean for the future. The formality of monetary union may be only the leading edge of the glacier. Over time, the existence of a common currency may facilitate change in uncountable national regulations, may help eliminate differences in tax regimes or fiscal systems, may standardize banking practices, and may streamline payment systems. Such changes will not happen at once. Moreover, they will not happen without reason. Finally, such changes will not happen without debate. It is impossible to predict at present how EMU will affect the interests of specific groups. Nevertheless, it is possible to say that EMU will have a profound impact, both on the possibilities open to policymakers and on the wants and desires of the public. In this sense, EMU may initiate a revolution in public policy, but it will be a democratic revolution with the outcomes of particular struggles still to be determined. The essays in this book explain how the process began.

Notes

1. This citation is taken from the "Protocol on the Transition to the Third Stage of Economic and Monetary Union." The term "an economic and monetary union" is substituted in the citation for the term "the third stage."

2. The 1992 and 1993 exchange rate crises allow for three interpretations: One states that the exchange rate realignments were necessary to facilitate real economic adjustment; another states that market speculators forced the 1993 realignment to happen without regard to economic fundamentals; and a third contends that realignment was necessary, in part, but also the result of a self-fulfilling prophecy (Eichengreen and Wyploz, 1993).

3. A discussion paper circulated by the Philip Morris Institute in April 1994 summarized the popular sentiment in its title: "Is European Monetary Union Dead?"

4. For example, in 1995, financial markets priced long-term government bonds of the Italian, Spanish, and Swedish governments under the assumption that inflation and interest rates would be significantly higher than in Germany for the next decades. About two years later, the long-term interest rate differential had shrunk to close to zero, and inflation rates were roughly at the same level.

2

Monetary Union and European Unemployment

José Viñals and Juan F. Jimeno[1]

During the past two decades, Western European countries have moved forward along the route to economic integration. As a result, the European Union (EU) currently has expanded to fifteen member states, and the creation of an Economic and Monetary Union (EMU) is envisaged to take place before the end of the decade. During the same period, unemployment rates in many of these countries have increased from about 2 to 3 percent, to two-digit figures. Although unemployment has decreased during expansions and increased during recessions, the average European unemployment rate within each cycle has continuously increased. Remarkably, this evolution of unemployment is not shared by other developed countries, such as the United States and Japan.

Persistent unemployment is the most important social and economic problem of EU countries, putting national governments under pressure to fight unemployment precisely at the time when they are trying to establish an Economic and Monetary Union (EMU). Thus, the following questions are being raised: What effect will EMU have on unemployment? What can the Union do to decrease unemployment? Are structural reforms needed to ease the effects of the move to EMU on unemployment? Is it in the interest of countries with a high unemployment rate to take part in EMU as soon as they satisfy the Maastricht convergence criteria, or should they wait until they succeed in bringing down unemployment?

In order to address such questions this chapter is organized in four sections. The first of these describes the current unemployment situation in the European Union, and in particular, highlights those factors that must be taken into account when assessing the likely effects of Economic and Monetary Union on European unemployment. The second section uses the distinction between cyclical and structural unemployment to examine those elements that, in principle, may contribute to explaining the unemployment situation. This section also reviews the economic impact of labor market institutions with a specific European flavor, such as collective bargaining regimes, job security legislation, and unemployment benefits. The third section presents our analysis of the potential impact of EMU on European unemployment, both during the transition period and once EMU is fully established. During the transition period, the main issue is whether the pursuit of nominal and fiscal convergence will help or hinder the achievement of "real" convergence, as measured, for example, by unemployment rates. In addition, we examine what may be the consequences of abandoning the nominal exchange rate as a tool of macroeconomic adjustment over the shorter and the longer run and once EMU is fully established. Finally, the fourth section summarizes the main conclusions and policy implications derived from the chapter.

Unemployment in the European Union: The Facts

This section highlights those facets of European unemployment that must be taken into account when analyzing the likely effects of Economic and Monetary Union.[2] We first consider whether EU countries are in different starting positions on the path to EMU so far as unemployment is concerned. We then break down national and regional unemployment rates into different components in order to ascertain the importance of common shocks across EU countries for explaining the evolution of national and regional unemployment rates.

A "common" unemployment problem?

Most EU countries have shared a similar evolution of unemployment since the mid-1970s. Nevertheless, this evolution is rather unique when compared to the evolution of unemployment in countries like the United States and Japan (see Figure 2.1). In particular, while U.S. unemployment has moved up and down around an unchanged trend rate of between 5 and 6 percent—and Japanese unemployment has remained at extremely low values close to 2 percent—European unemployment has increased from 2.5 percent in the early 1970s to above 10 percent in 1998.

In 1995, unemployment rates range from 3 percent in Luxembourg to 22.7 percent in Spain (see Figure 2.2). However, within this very broad range there are three relatively well-defined country groupings:

1. the "low" unemployment countries (below or at 7 percent): Luxembourg, 3 percent; Austria, 5.9 percent; the Netherlands, 6.5 percent; and Portugal, 7 percent;
2. the "high" unemployment countries (between 7 and 13 percent): Germany, 8.2 percent; Great Britain, 8.7 percent; Sweden, 9.2 percent; Bel-

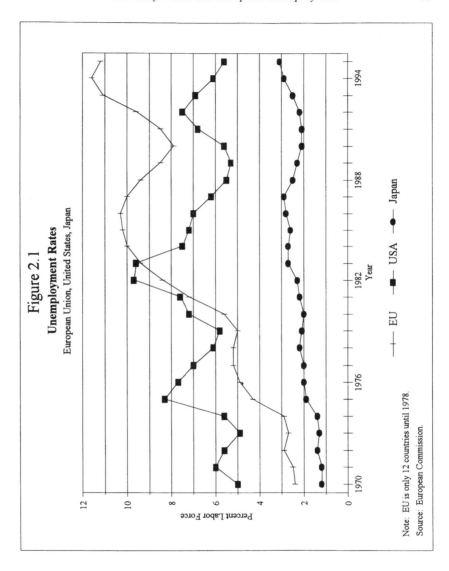

Figure 2.1
Unemployment Rates
European Union, United States, Japan

Note: EU is only 12 countries until 1978.
Source: European Commission.

gium, 9.4 percent; Denmark, 10 percent; Greece, 10 percent; France, 11.6 percent; and Italy, 12.2 percent; and

3. the "very high" unemployment countries (13 percent or above): Ireland, 13 percent; Finland, 17.1 percent; and Spain, 22.7 percent.

All in all, there are four countries in the "lower" unemployment group, eight countries in the "high" unemployment group, and three countries in the "very

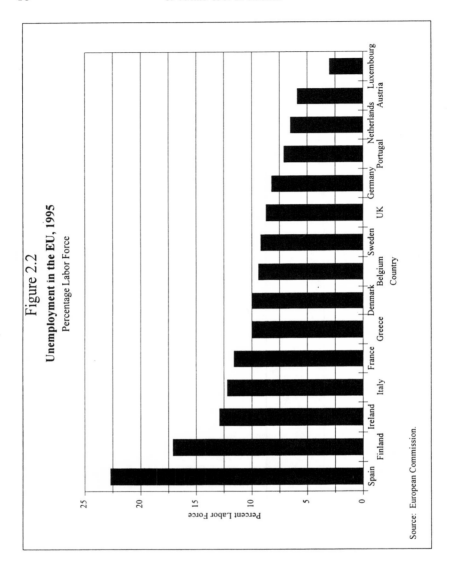

Figure 2.2

Unemployment in the EU, 1995

Percentage Labor Force

Source: European Commission.

high" unemployment group. Thus, while there are significant differences in unemployment situations across the Union, 11 out of 15 countries suffer from either high or very high unemployment rates.[3]

Increasing European unemployment was associated with decreasing inflation from 1975 to 1990, and with rather stable inflation thereafter. A similar development took place in the United States in terms of inflation but with a more favorable unemployment performance. This suggests that the unemployment rate at which inflation is stabilized (the nonaccelerating inflation rate of unemployment, NAIRU, or "natural" rate) is noticeably higher in EU countries than in the United States, a fact confirmed by the available empirical evidence. In sum, while there are undoubtedly differences across European countries, most of them show evidence of strong downward rigidities in the movements of prices and wages: High unemployment rates register only slow disinflationary effects.

Figure 2.3 shows the present situation as regards to both unemployment and inflation in member states and highlights several issues. On the one hand, the countries start from very different positions concerning the state of real and nominal divergences. While only four countries have unemployment rates below the rate that is typically considered to be acceptable (7 percent), eleven countries have already achieved inflation rates of 3 percent or lower, thus coming close to what is typically understood as a reasonable degree of price stability. On the other hand, many of the European countries often referred to as Europe's (geographic) "core" have unemployment rates that are higher than in some countries often regarded as being in the (geographic) "periphery" (for example, Portugal). Thus, the typical notion of what is "core" and "periphery" does not seen to apply in a clear-cut manner when we talk of convergence both in real and nominal terms.

European, national, and regional components of unemployment

The previous paragraphs have illustrated that, in spite of some marked national differences, most EU countries tend to have rather high rates of unemployment, and to exhibit downwardly rigid wages and prices even in the presence of such high unemployment rates. This suggests, in principle, that there is a nonnegligible common element in European unemployment.

In order to assess the likely impact of economic and monetary union on European unemployment, it is important to look at how important European, national, and regional forces are in driving unemployment rates over time. The implied costs of foregoing the nominal exchange rate as a tool for short-term macroeconomic stabilization will be lower or higher depending on which of the three types of forces is more important. For example, if all unemployment rates at the national and regional levels were to be driven by a common European component, then suppressing national currencies would not be costly.

There are several approaches for assessing the relative importance of the different components of unemployment. For example, a descriptive approach consists of measuring the evolution of unemployment dispersion (or variation) across either countries or regions. The standard deviation of unemployment across EU countries (a measure of dispersion) rises continuously from the

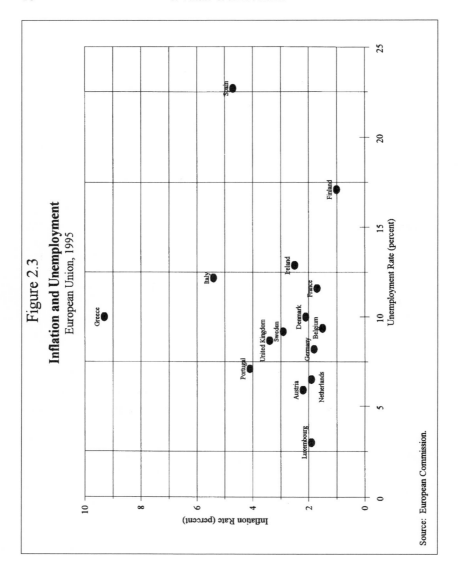

Figure 2.3
Inflation and Unemployment
European Union, 1995

Source: European Commission.

mid-1970s to the mid-1980s, decreases mildly from the mid-1980s until 1990, and surges upward in the early 1990s (see Figure 2.4).[4] However, the evolution of dispersion (and in particular, its rise since 1990), is heavily influenced by the contribution of Spain, one of the very high unemployment countries. Namely, with almost 10 percent of the EU's labor force, the Spanish unemployment rate has roughly doubled that of the EU since the mid-1980s—

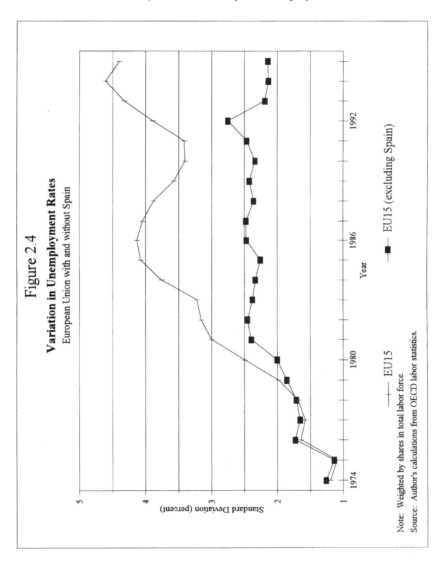

Figure 2.4
Variation in Unemployment Rates
European Union with and without Spain

Note: Weighted by shares in total labor force.
Source: Author's calculations from OECD labor statistics.

shooting up rapidly in the early 1980s and again in 1992 to 1993. Thus, when Spain is excluded we observe an increase in unemployment dispersion of smaller magnitude up to 1981, and no significant trend thereafter.

We have computed a similar index at the EUROSTAT NUTS-1 level of disaggregation in order to capture the regional dispersion of unemployment. Data availability restricts both the period and the number of countries that we can use to construct this measure. Nevertheless, a similar picture arises: There is no significant overall increase in the regional dispersion of unemployment, and it is only in the early 1990s that the regional dispersion increases (and as in the case of dispersion across countries, this increase is largely due to the contribution of Spanish regions).[5]

A second approach toward assessing the different evolutions in the unemployment performance of countries or regions is followed by recent studies focusing on the persistence of unemployment differentials across regions. These studies show that unemployment differentials are not substantially more persistent in the European Union than in the United States (see Blanchard and Katz, 1992, for the United States; Decressin and Fatás, 1995, for the EU). Given the higher interregional labor mobility existing in the United States, this result may appear surprising. Nevertheless, it is explained by the relatively higher procyclical labor participation rate in EU countries. In contrast to the United States, participation rates in European labor markets swell during boom periods and contract as the economy turns down again. Such changes in the participation rate work to counter the effects of lower interregional migration flows, effectively mitigating the persistence of unemployment differentials. There are, however, some European countries where regional unemployment differentials nevertheless show a great deal of persistence: Spain (Jimeno and Bentolila, 1995), Italy (Decressin and Fatás, 1995), and the United Kingdom (Thomas, 1993).

Finally, a more rigorous method for assessing the relative importance of different forces in explaining the evolution of national/regional unemployment rates consists of using econometric models to break down shocks to unemployment into several components; namely, a common component, and a national or regional-specific component. Following this approach, we have estimated a small model for each of the member states (the basic details of which are provided in Appendix 2.2), which allows us to decompose the evolution of unemployment rates into three components—European, national, and regional.[6] In order to summarize our results, Table 2.1 presents the relative importance of European and national shocks in explaining the evolution of national unemployment rates in the European Union, and Table 2.2 shows the relative importance of European, national, and regional shocks in explaining the evolution of unemployment rates in the European regions.

As can be seen in Table 2.1, during the 1971 to 1993 period, EU-wide unemployment shocks explain almost half the variance of unemployment rates within the EU member states across a one-year horizon. This proportion increases to 59 percent, 70 percent, 78 percent, and 83 percent after one, two, three, and four years, respectively.[7] Thus, unemployment developments at the European level seem to play a very important role even in the short run.[8] As a reference point, we have performed a similar analysis on the United States using unemployment rates for the 1976 to 1990 period, recovering develop-

TABLE 2.1

Proportion of the Variance of National Unemployment Rates Explained by Innovations in the EU Unemployment Rate (percent)

Country	Within 1 Year	After 1 Year	After 2 Years	After 3 Years	After 4 Years
Belgium	61	76	82	85	86
Denmark	58	60	64	68	72
Germany	32	54	70	79	83
Greece	36	48	59	68	75
Spain	52	72	86	92	94
France	65	80	87	91	94
Ireland	46	60	72	80	85
Italy	9	26	46	67	79
Netherlands	48	62	73	80	83
Austria	29	54	72	81	86
Portugal	7	26	44	56	64
Finland	60	62	64	67	65
Sweden	13	15	18	20	23
United Kingdom	72	85	90	93	94
European Union	45	59	70	78	83

Note: The percentage of the variance of national unemployment rates explained by innovations to the national rate itself (idiosyncratic shocks) is 100 minus the figures shown in the table.

ments for the whole of the United States and shocks specific to each state's unemployment rate. The resulting breakdown shows that U.S.-wide shocks to unemployment explain, on average, 79 percent of the variance to unemployment rates within states across one year, and between 84 and 85 percent after one to five years.

Interpreting this decomposition of the variance of unemployment between European and country-specific shocks should be handled with caution. Given the simplicity of the model and the length of the time series on unemployment, it could be argued that coordination of monetary policies within Exchange Rate Mechanism (ERM) lies behind these shocks. However, the sample period does not exactly correspond to the period during which the ERM has been in effect. Furthermore, there are countries such as Spain where unemployment rates are mainly driven by Europewide shocks but that only recently joined

TABLE 2.2
Proportion of the Variance of Regional Unemployment Rates Explained

Percent	Within 1 Year	After 1 Year	After 2 Years	After 3 Years	After 4 Years
Innovations to the EU Unemployment Rate (1)					
Belgium	2	28	45	50	50
Denmark	1	3	22	42	49
Germany	5	11	14	14	12
France	19	26	26	23	26
Spain	4	17	24	24	27
Italy	1	6	12	18	22
UK	24	26	21	18	21
Weighted Avg.	11	17	20	21	20
Innovations to the National Unemployment Rate (2)					
Belgium	26	22	17	15	15
Denmark	92	86	64	52	45
Germany	24	23	22	22	22
France	10	6	4	5	4
Spain	10	6	6	5	5
Italy	17	11	15	15	20
UK	48	29	28	31	32
Weighted Avg.	25	18	18	18	16
Innovations to the Regional Unemployment Rate (100 - [(1) + (2)])*					
Belgium	72	50	38	35	35
Denmark	7	11	14	6	6
Germany	71	66	64	64	66
France	71	68	70	72	70
Spain	86	77	70	71	68
Italy	82	83	73	67	58
UK	28	45	51	51	47
Weighted Avg.	64	65	62	61	64

Note: *The figures in this final part of the table are obtained by subtracting parts 1 and 2 from 100.

the ERM. Alternatively, it is possible that international trade and/or (biased) technological progress, combined with wage rigidities in the labor market, have recently been the main sources of shocks to unemployment. Finally, it could also be argued that the Europe-wide shocks that we have identified are nothing but trade and productivity shocks: EU countries are subject to international competition to a similar degree, technological progress is likely to spread simultaneously across these countries, and wage rigidities seem to be common across Europe. Although this may be a likely explanation of European unemployment, our results are not powerful enough to prove it is the right explanation.

Regarding European regional unemployment rates, the results reported in Table 2.2 suggest that region-specific shocks explain between 61 to 65 percent of the variance of regional unemployment rates. Therefore, the combination of EU-wide and region-specific shocks leaves only about 20 percent of the variance of regional unemployment rates to be explained by national shocks.[9]

Overall, taking together the results in Tables 2.1 and 2.2, we conclude that there seems to be a very significant EU-wide component driving unemployment across EU countries. At the national level, this component explains more than half of the variance of movements in unemployment. At the regional level, region-specific shocks and EU-wide innovations to unemployment explain up to 80 percent of the variance in unemployment rates—a similar proportion of the variance in unemployment rates at the national level explained by EU-wide shocks at medium horizons. Moreover, the situation in the European Union regarding the relative importance of common and idiosyncratic shocks in explaining national unemployment rates is similar to that of the United States. Finally, these findings seem to be true not just for the EU as a whole but also for most member states. Thus, it is not possible to draw any clear distinction between the forces driving unemployment in the so-called core and periphery countries.

Real wage rigidity in the EU

One relevant issue for explaining the magnitude and persistence of EU unemployment is the role played by real wage rigidities. As is well known, the higher the degree of real wage rigidity, the higher the "natural" rate of unemployment (NAIRU) and the smaller the impact of monetary and exchange rate policy on real variables, such as unemployment. Thus, finding out how rigid real wages are in Europe is of interest for knowing several things: the extent to which European unemployment is structural (and therefore unrelated to the economic cycle) and likelihood that the loss of the nominal exchange rate—once in EMU—will influence European unemployment. In principle, if real wages are rigid, then unemployment is structural and not cyclical, and so the loss of the nominal exchange rate is unimportant for real macroeconomic performance.

There have been numerous attempts at estimating the degree of real wage rigidity across countries. Some of the most often quoted estimates are in Layard et al. (1991, Chapter 9). These estimates derive from the structural analysis of wage and price equations across Organization for Economic Cooperation and Development (OECD) countries and are reproduced in Table 2.3. However, structural estimations of this kind are sometimes criticized on identification grounds and on the measurement of relevant regressors.

Since the issue concerns the sources of shocks and their transmission to the labor market, an alternative empirical approach can provide interesting insights. This approach consists of estimating the dynamic responses of the main labor market variables after several types of shocks. This technique has

TABLE 2.3
Evidence on Real Wage Rigidity and Hysteresis

	Structural Estimates from Wage-Price Equations			Estimates from VAR $(\Delta(w\text{-}p),\ u)$			Estimates VAR $[\Delta(w\text{-}p),\ \Delta(u)]$
	Real-wage rigidity	Hysteresis	Mean Lag	Real-wage rigidity	Hysteresis	Mean Lag	Real-wage rigidity
Belgium	0.25	0.77	0.70	2.86	0.77	3.44	1.42
Denmark	0.58	0.60	0.45	3.44	0.72	2.55	1.10
France	0.23	0.84	2.72	5.13	0.81	4.20	1.58
Germany	0.63	0.76	2.55	3.76	0.77	3.30	1.48
Ireland	0.27	0.71	3.19	2.92	0.74	2.78	1.68
Italy	0.06	0.69	2.87	4.29	0.82	4.66	1.00
Netherlands	0.25	0.71	2.51	2.11	0.76	3.14	1.52
Spain	0.52	0.59	2.75	4.20	0.78	3.56	1.94
UK	0.77	0.48	1.36	3.43	0.72	2.51	1.16
Austria	0.11	0.53	<0	4.49	0.79	3.69	0.85
Finland	0.29	0.79	4.60	9.55	0.83	5.01	1.71
Sweden	0.08	0.81	1.44	4.92	0.83	4.92	1.41
EU*	0.42	0.68	2.28	4.09	0.78	3.61	1.39
US	0.25	-0.02	1.68	2.39	0.60	1.53	0.73
Japan	0.06	-0.05	<0	2.21	0.65	1.90	0.89

Note: *European average is weighted by shares of the labor force.
Source: Lavard, Nickell, and Jackman (1991) pp. 406–407 for columns 1 to 3.

been used by Bayoumi and Eichengreen (1993), among others, who identified the relative importance of supply and demand shocks in EU countries and the correlation of these shocks across countries. However, they did not investigate the transmission of shocks through labor market variables.

To complement such existing empirical analysis, we pose a simple labor market model (which is a bare-bones version of the model used by Layard et. al., 1991, as extended by Blanchard, 1990) and estimate it following the structural vector autoregression (VAR) approach, as in Bayoumi and Eichengreen (1993).[10] The model of the labor market that underpins our measures of real wage rigidity in EU countries is composed of a labor-demand equation and a real wage equation, according to which real wages depend on current and past (lagged) unemployment. In this setup, real wage rigidity is defined as the increase in equilibrium unemployment that is needed to accommodate a permanent upward shock to wages (wage-push shock).[11]

The results of this exercise are provided in Table 2.3, which distinguishes two cases: one in which real wages react to the level of current unemployment more than to the level of lagged unemployment, and another in which real wages react to changes in unemployment (hysteresis).[12] These results show that the degree of real-wage rigidity and of hysteresis is significantly higher in EU countries than either in the United States or Japan.

European unemployment: What do we know?

We now take stock of the previous analysis and of our reading of the existing literature on European unemployment to draw some tentative conclusions that can be useful in analyzing the potential impact of EMU on European unemployment.

First, while European unemployment has demonstrated some sensitivity to cyclical conditions in the past twenty years, there has been a long-run increase in unemployment that suggests the presence of deep structural causes. This has been confirmed by the available empirical evidence, which although far from conclusive suggests that the long-term increase in actual unemployment rates has been accompanied in many instances by an increase in "natural" unemployment rates, or NAIRUs. The structural nature of European unemployment is nevertheless compatible with both supply and demand shocks having an impact on NAIRUs so long as persistence mechanisms are important enough.

Second, the high unemployment in the European Union relative to the United States and Japan is mainly the result of a fall in the outflow rate from unemployment to employment, rather than the result of an increase in the inflow rate from employment to unemployment (see Layard et al., 1991; and OECD, 1994a). As a consequence, the average duration of unemployment in EU countries is now much higher than it was in the early 1970s, while in the

United States it has not changed significantly.[13] Furthermore, at least until 1985, the Beveridge curve has shifted outward in most EU countries—unemployment rates in EU countries are higher than they used to be for a given vacancy rate—although there seems to have been no further shift since then.[14]

Third, as regards the size and characteristics of national unemployment problems—a key issue in discussions of real convergence—it is far from clear that a neat distinction can be made between central, or "core," EU countries and those in the (geographic) "periphery."

Fourth, unemployment dispersion across EU countries and regions increased during the 1970s and early 1980s. Once the outliers (mainly, Spain) are excluded, however, there has been no further increase in unemployment dispersion after the mid-1980s. In addition, it seems that the evolution of national unemployment rates is driven to a significant extent by common European forces. The uniformly higher unemployment rates in European countries, their persistence, and their broadly similar evolution all suggest that the underlying causes behind European unemployment are common to all member states to a significant extent. Therefore, policies oriented toward reducing European unemployment should be rather similar across countries. Nevertheless, the intensity with which these policies are applied should be particularly high in Spain, Ireland, and Finland, where unemployment rates are the highest.

Finally, real wage rigidity is relatively high in the European Union, and propagation mechanisms are important enough for temporary shocks to have persistent effects on unemployment. Real product wages have increased more in the EU than in the United States, but less than in Japan. The comparison between the EU and United States experiences in this regard suggests the existence of a trade-off between real wage growth and unemployment following the occurrence of adverse supply shocks. In this light, there is well-documented evidence of a productivity slowdown both in the United States and in Europe during the 1970s and the 1980s. Additionally, the adverse oil shocks of the late 1970s and the early 1980s represented a deterioration of the terms of trade. Whereas in the United States these developments caused a slowdown in real wage growth, in EU countries they translated into high unemployment.

In sum, although employment levels may differ, EU countries share a persistent unemployment problem related to the relatively high incidence of long-term unemployment and the low effectiveness of unemployment at bringing down inflation. Furthermore, common European forces seem to play an important role in driving national unemployment rates in member states. However, we still need to explore the causes of the unfavorable unemployment performance in the European Union. This is the purpose of the next section.

The Causes of European Unemployment

The plausible effects of EMU on unemployment cannot be grasped without an understanding of the causes of current European unemployment. In this regard, most models of the labor market distinguish between the natural rate of unemployment, which is the unemployment rate that would prevail in the long run, and cyclical unemployment, which is the short-run unemployment rate caused by transitory shocks that hit the economy. Traditionally, the natural rate was thought to correspond to frictional unemployment, which results from people moving between jobs in an economy working at full capacity and with a stable rate of inflation. Consequently, the natural rate of unemployment was thought to be independent of demand policies and, to a first approximation, constant. However, the European unemployment experience suggests that the so-called natural rate of unemployment is anything but constant, that it should be better called structural or equilibrium unemployment, and that cyclical unemployment may become structural quite rapidly.

The determinants of equilibrium unemployment, summarized in Figure 2.5, are thought to be related to factors affecting wage setting and price setting behavior (see, for example, Blanchard, 1990; Layard et al., 1991; and Phelps, 1994), while actual unemployment may be influenced by nominal shocks that induce price and wage surprises (see Appendix 2.1 for a more detailed presentation of the main conceptual determinants of unemployment). Regarding the determinants of equilibrium unemployment, most labor market models agree that all factors that induce wage pressure on the part of workers (for example, union strength, real wage aspirations, unemployment benefits, and so forth) and price pressures on the part of firms (for example, desired profit margins and so forth) adversely affect the level of equilibrium unemployment.

The adjustment from actual unemployment to short- and long-run equilibrium unemployment may be affected by some of the same variables that determine the equilibrium levels of unemployment. Moreover, long-run equilibrium unemployment may depend on the path followed by actual unemployment (hysteresis). Two sources of hysteresis are usually mentioned. First, insider power in wage determination (resulting, for instance, from high firing costs) and union membership may result in target wages being dependent on the current levels of employment rather than on unemployment (see Blanchard and Summers, 1986; Lindbeck and Snower, 1988). Second, high unemployment usually leads to long-term unemployment. If the long-term unemployed become discouraged and disenfranchised (have a lower job search intensity) or if firms discriminate against the long-term unemployed when hiring (because skills depreciate over time), then the downward pressure exerted on wages by a given unemployment rate will decrease as the proportion of long-term unemployment in total employment increases.

28

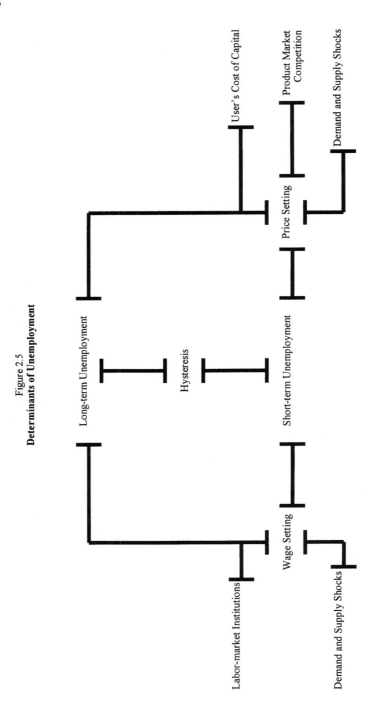

Figure 2.5
Determinants of Unemployment

The conventional wisdom, based on the factors and theoretical arguments sketched above, is that any attempt to explain European unemployment must account for the reasons behind the rise in *equilibrium* unemployment. In principle, there can be two alternative reasons for an increase in equilibrium unemployment: permanent shocks to the equilibrium unemployment rate and transitory shocks, which because of the characteristics of the propagation mechanisms have long-lasting effects on the equilibrium unemployment rate.

There is some debate about the sources of the shocks driving European unemployment and the relevance of the persistence hypothesis. Movements in the price of energy, in the terms of trade, and in real interest rates; demand policy changes; and recently, biased technical progress are often cited as the most relevant shocks that have hit EU economies. As for the degree of persistence, the available econometric evidence is not particularly conclusive in distinguishing between the permanent shock hypothesis and the extreme version of the persistence hypothesis (that is, hysteresis).[15]

There is nevertheless the presumption that labor market institutions affect both equilibrium unemployment and the speed of adjustment after transitory shocks. Thus, most economic policy packages aimed at reducing unemployment often refer to reforming labor market institutions such as wage bargaining, job security legislation, and the unemployment protection system.

The role of labor market institutions

The idea that labor market imperfections are the main cause of unemployment is a recurrent theme. In fact, the main lines of research on the determinants of equilibrium unemployment have focused on the effects of labor market institutions on both the level and the dynamics of unemployment. Nevertheless, as with the sources of shocks to unemployment, different authors attach different degrees of importance to labor market institutions when explaining unemployment in the European Union. For example, the well-known "OECD Jobs Study" (1994a) advocates a complete deregulation of the labor market as the principal measure to fight unemployment. A less extreme case is the 1993 European Commission white paper, "Growth, Competitiveness, Employment," which advocates only very specific changes in labor market regulations and proposes an investment-led demand push and a more employment-intensive growth. There are also skeptics who claim that labor market institutions differ widely across EU countries, and hence, that the similar unemployment evolution observed in these countries must be explained by something else (see, for example, Junankar and Madsen, 1995).

Finally, some authors recognize the specific nature of the labor market and argue that a complete deregulation of the labor market is neither politically viable nor warranted by economic criteria. For them, the correct approach to reforming labor market institutions is to identify inefficiencies in the functioning of the labor market, starting from a recognition of the need to work within the parameters of the existing political economy framework and making incremental changes that work in the "right" direction (Alogoskoufis et al., 1995). In what follows, we give our view on the impact of existing labor market institutions—meaning specifically those for wage bargaining, employment protection, and social insurance—on European unemployment.

The main differences in the wage determination process across EU countries arise from country-specific regulations on collective bargaining, and thus from the role played by unions. However, while specific rules may differ, some commonalities can be found: Although union density in the United States and the proportion of workers covered by collective agreements are similar and low (about 15 percent each), in EU countries union density is higher than in the United States (with the exceptions of France and Spain), and the coverage of collective bargaining is much higher (about 70 to 80 percent).[16]

This disparity between union density and coverage of collective bargaining can be traced back to the fact that collective agreements are reached within single-employer bargaining under a closed shop system in the United States, while in EU countries multiemployer bargaining with an open shop system are most prevalent. Furthermore, while it is true that there are wide variations in collective bargaining practices across EU countries regarding levels of negotiation and the degrees of coordination and synchronization among wage setters, it seems unlikely that these differences account for a large proportion of national intra-EU unemployment differentials.

The mainstream approach to examining the macroeconomic implications of collective bargaining has focused on the concept of centralization. Most authors pay attention to the primary level at which wage negotiations take place—establishment, firms, sectors, nationwide—and to the extent of coordination among wage setters. Drawing on this information, a (subjective) measure of the degree of centralization in collective bargaining is proposed and related to macroeconomic performance. From a theoretical point of view, there are several reasons why centralization of wage bargaining may reduce wage pressure and wage rigidity, thus helping to moderate equilibrium unemployment and persistence. However, there are other reasons by which single-employer firm-level bargaining may be preferred.[17] As a result, there is no conclusive answer about the optimum level of centralization, at least in theoretical terms. And empirical analysis has not settled the issue either, mainly because empirical measures of centralization are not independent of researchers' perceptions of collective bargaining rules.

Although there is no general agreement on the optimal level of centralization, there is some consensus about what the worst collective bargaining procedures might be. In particular, neither the gains from centralization nor the advantages of decentralization are achieved when collective bargaining takes place at several levels, when sectoral agreements establish a layer of minimum wages, and when coordination among wage setters—firms and workers—is low. Thus, under this scenario, equilibrium unemployment is unambiguously higher.

Job security legislation potentially plays an important role as well, and there is a continuing debate on the effects of firing costs on employment. According to some, the main effect of firing costs is to reduce the variability of employment without having much effect on the level of employment. The reason is that firing costs would reduce layoffs during recessions—since they make it more costly to fire workers—and would reduce hiring during expansions—since they increase the shadow cost of labor.[18]

However, this view is subject to criticism once we consider that, if recessions are not short-lived, the difficulties of firms to lay off workers during recessions may finally lead to their closing down, and thus to a more adverse effect on employment than under less costly firing conditions. Under this alternative interpretation, firing costs would negatively affect the average level of employment. In addition to the above, there are other (general equilibrium) unfavorable effects of firing costs on employment. To begin with, firing costs distort the allocation of labor, so that efficiency may decline, pushing the wages that employers can offer down as well. Second, firing costs increase the bargaining power of insiders, so that workers' target wages tend to be higher. As a result of these factors, employment is unambiguously reduced by firing costs.

Firing costs arise from several sources, related both to the regulation on dismissal procedures and to the use of fixed-term (temporary) contracts. Dismissals may be restricted through the requirement of a notice period for administrative approval, severance payments, and the provisions for appeal against unfair dismissals. Fixed-term employment, as an alternative to regular permanent employment, may be restricted by the nature of the work for which fixed-term employees can be hired, minimum and maximum bounds on the length of the period of fixed-term employment contracts, and provisions for renewal.

Most pundits have argued that firing costs are relatively high in continental Europe and that this helps to explain unemployment differentials across countries. That said, it is difficult to come up with a single measure of firing restriction severity to be used for making comparisons across countries. A recent and comprehensive statistical ranking of countries is found in OECD (1994a: Chapter 6). According to that study, there is some variation in the degree of strictness of firing regulations across EU countries, although generally regulations tend to be more strict in EU than in non-EU countries. The exceptions are the United Kingdom, Ireland, the Netherlands, and Denmark—which have the least strict employment legislation across EU countries. The OECD countries with the most strict employment protection legislation are Italy, Spain, Portugal, Greece, and Belgium. Within this group, there are both countries with among the highest (Spain) and lowest unemployment (Portugal) rates in the EU. Our interpretation of this evidence is that firing costs cannot by themselves explain observed unemployment differentials across countries—because there are other factors that need to be taken into account. Nevertheless, they do exert an adverse effect on unemployment in the EU.

When attempting to reduce firing restrictions, most EU countries have turned to partial liberalization strategies based on the allowance of fixed-term employment contracts rather than to reducing firing restrictions across the board for all permanent employment contracts. With hindsight this has proven to be a poor strategy. At least in certain cases, partial liberalization has created artificial incentives for temporary contracts and has led to a segmentation of the labor market, with unfair social consequences and negative economic effects. Insofar as firing costs are regarded as an obstacle to employment creation, the appropriate strategy would be to lower them for all kinds of employment contracts, avoiding the segmentation of employment between permanent and fixed-term workers.

The Spanish experience in this regard is quite remarkable. In late 1984, fixed-term employment was allowed. Currently, more than 30 percent of employees are under fixed-term employment contracts, and the conversion rate of fixed-term employees into permanent ones after their contracts end is rather low (around 15 percent, according to some estimates). This duality of the labor market may have resulted in more wage rigidity (see Bentolila and Dolado, 1994; Jimeno and Toharia, 1993a) since permanent workers enjoy higher protection against dismissals, given the buffer of temporary employees and that wage negotiators mostly represent the interests of the permanent workers. Fixed-term employment also has some negative effects on labor productivity, affecting the effort, choice, and incentives for firms to invest in specific human capital (see Jimeno and Toharia, 1993b). Moreover, excessive reliance on fixed-term contracts spuriously increases labor turnover rates since restrictions on the renewal of such contracts result in the replacement of existing fixed-term employees with new ones when the contracts expire. And higher rotation, combined with generous unemployment benefits, produces an additional burden on the government's budget.

Finally, another source of unemployment is unemployment benefits. While unemployment benefits are justified on social grounds, there are few doubts about their adverse impact on unemployment. To begin with, unemployment benefits increase the duration of unemployment spells by affecting search intensity (ambiguously) and the reservation wage of unemployed workers (unambiguously). Second, benefits make unemployment a less dramatic personal and social experience, thus affecting also employed workers' decision on effort choice and wage setting. As a result, the unemployment benefit system is a determining factor of both equilibrium unemployment levels and unemployment persistence.[19]

EU countries, where social cohesion is a social value, have generally opted for unemployment benefits systems with relatively high replacement ratios and relatively long duration of benefits.[20] However, eligibility rules and the conditioning of benefits on the search for new employment and on the willingness of the recipient to work vary widely across member states. As happens with other labor market institutions, it is quite difficult to obtain an objective measure of generosity to establish comparisons across countries. Nevertheless, it is fair to say that high unemployment countries, where supervision and administration of the social welfare system to link benefits to job search efforts and to the willingness to work is very expensive, and/or perhaps unfeasible, may have no choice but to make eligibility harder and to reduce the duration of benefits. In contrast, low unemployment countries may be able to keep adequate incentives by close supervision and conditional administration of benefits.

The Impact of EMU on European Unemployment

The previous sections have outlined the most salient facts concerning European unemployment and put forward some hypotheses regarding the main causes driving both unemployment in Europe and national unemployment differentials. As a result of the analysis undertaken, we have tentatively concluded that there are significant common roots to the existence of rather high unemployment rates in most member states, and that these roots are, to a significant extent, of a structural nature. Of particular importance seems to be the pervasive role exerted by a number of labor market institutions, developed to extend the welfare state in the 1960s and early 1970s.

Taking stock of our analysis of the roots of the unemployment problem, this section tries to shed some light on how EMU might affect European unemployment. In doing so, we distinguish between the impact of policies to meet the convergence requirements for participation in EMU set by the Maastricht Treaty, and the impact of EMU itself once monetary union is fully established.

Unemployment in the transition to EMU

At the end of the 1990s, unemployment in the EU stands above 10 percent, a rate considered to be higher than desirable on economic and social grounds and the reduction of which is a top policy priority. At the same time, EU countries have had great difficulty meeting all the convergence criteria set out in the treaty to enter into EMU—specifically the fiscal ones, since most countries are far from eradicating excessive deficits. This is exemplified by the fact that, for the EU as a whole, 1995 budget deficits were close to 5 percent of

GDP, and public debt levels close to 70 percent of GDP. The persistence of significant budget deficits and debt levels has required making revenue increases and/or expenditure reductions in order to meet the Maastricht fiscal convergence criteria and to be able to establish the Union by 1999, as envisaged in the treaty. An important question, therefore, is how the needed fiscal consolidation measures will affect European unemployment over the next few years.

From a medium-term viewpoint, insofar as present structural budget deficits are too high, and insofar as their reduction is not carried out through tax increases that raise the degree of "wage pressure," the process of fiscal consolidation should not adversely affect unemployment in the medium term. Indeed, fiscal consolidation may improve employment prospects given that lower budget deficits mean lower real interest rates, which enhance private capital formation and economic growth.

From a short-term perspective, the traditional story is that a fiscal tightening leads to a reduction in the rate of expansion of aggregate demand, which initially affects unemployment adversely. This is corroborated by most empirical macroeconometric models.[21] In addition, insofar as hysteresis mechanisms are at work, the impact on unemployment could persist for some time. While these effects are generally recognized as being valid to a first approximation, in practice the size of the shorter-term impact of fiscal consolidation on unemployment will vary across countries—given their different economic structures and present fiscal situations—and will also depend critically on which kind of measures are implemented, and on how they are implemented.

Unfortunately, many of the existing empirical macromodels are not well suited to handle some of the key factors that influence the final outcome regarding the impact of fiscal consolidation on the economy.[22] In particular, a reduction of budget deficits based on permanent cuts in current government purchases may lead to lower short-term unemployment costs than if deficits are cut by raising taxes or by cutting public investment.[23] The reason is that the reduction in aggregate demand derived from a cut in total public spending would be (at least partially) offset by the beneficial affects on private demand of the credible permanent reduction in current government purchases. Specifically, private consumption would expand as the public revises its expectations of future disposable income upward, in the understanding that budgetary consolidation today reduces future taxes to service the debt. Private investment would also increase once the public responds to the reduction in real long-term interest rates. In European countries, substantial progress toward fiscal consolidation would help reduce the risk premia implicit on interest rates through the reduction of both exchange risk and default risk. For countries with significant interest rate differentials at present, this "interest rate reduction" effect may be all the more important.

In sum, while the differing fiscal positions and macroeconomic structures of the member states suggest that the necessary fiscal consolidation efforts may impact on their economies with differing intensities, the short-term costs of fiscal consolidation will be minimized (or even suppressed) if budgetary adjustments are carried out in an appropriate and credible fashion and especially if accompanied by structural labor market reforms to reduce the degree of real wage rigidity. Furthermore, credible progress along fiscal consolidation would contribute to improving the overall macroeconomic policy mix and thus to reducing the constraints that the pursuit of nominal stability places on national monetary policies, thus allowing lower real interest rates. Finally, given the unfavorable state of public finances in most European Union countries, the reduction of excessive budget deficits is a desirable policy in its own right as it is a precondition for achieving sustainable economic growth—regardless of its importance for the fulfillment of the Maastricht convergence conditions. Even if short-term costs were to arise as a consequence of fiscal consolidation, this would be the necessary price to pay to improve growth potential. The EMU process simply accelerates the implementation of fiscal consolidation measures that would have to be taken in any case.

A further issue regarding the macroeconomic impact of convergence policies during the transition is that the pursuit of convergence may become more difficult—and thus more costly in terms of unemployment—for those countries initially excluded from entering EMU in 1999. This risk will materialize insofar as financial markets turn their backs on the excluded countries' currencies. In such case, countries with "derogation" (meaning unable, or unwilling, to participate in EMU according to the criteria set down in the Maastricht Treaty) will suffer unwanted currency depreciations and higher risk premia. In turn, such premia would affect the domestic inflation rates and budget deficits of those countries adversely, further complicating the fulfilment of the convergence criteria. Moreover, these currency disruptions would also endanger the functioning of the single European market, which might increase unemployment throughout the Union (that is, both in countries inside EMU and with derogation). It is crucial that such problems be avoided. Therefore, it is of the utmost importance that an adequate global framework is established to enable countries with derogation to have a fair chance of meeting the convergence criteria and thus of joining EMU at a later stage.[24]

A separate issue regarding unemployment during the transition to EMU is the concern expressed in some circles that EMU may be difficult to run unless, prior to its establishment, countries achieve a much higher degree of convergence in unemployment rates. It is true that the political acceptability of EMU and, specifically, of the future single European monetary policy, will be wider across member states if their starting unemployment rates are similar. However, as we indicated above, a majority of EU countries already have converged—unfortunately—toward high unemployment (that is, the wrong kind of convergence). Furthermore, the desirability of EMU has much less to do with starting unemployment positions—which relate to the policies and shocks that happened in the past—than with the impact of EMU on unemployment across the Union.

Unemployment in full EMU

Since the beginning of the process of building a monetary union in Europe, there has been a very heated debate on its costs and benefits. In particular, this debate has focused on the consequences of relinquishing the use of the nominal exchange rate as an instrument for macroeconomic stabilization. The main questions are: What will be the impact of EMU on European unemployment in the medium term, and what will be the impact of EMU on European unemployment in the shorter term?

The conceptual model of the labor market underpinning our analysis has rather clear implications regarding the main determinants of unemployment in the medium term. Unemployment will tend to be high if labor market institutions contribute to generating sustained wage pressures and if there are sustained price pressures resulting from insufficient competition in product markets, low total factor productivity, and a high cost of capital (see the theoretical labor market model in Appendix 2.1). Thus, the question to ask is how will EMU effect the main determinants of unemployment over the medium term.

As a first approximation, it can be said that establishing a monetary union is equivalent to having a different monetary policy regime where the nominal exchange rate is no longer variable. Since monetary policy ought to be neutral over the medium term, EMU should have no effect on unemployment over prolonged horizons. However, insofar as EMU leads not only to a different monetary policy regime but also to a more stable economic policy regime, this may also contribute to paving the way for lowering unemployment. For instance, if countries follow more stable economic policies as a consequence of the monetary and the budgetary guidelines included in the treaty, this will contribute to permanently lowering the cost of capital, which would help investment, growth, and unemployment (see, for example, Andrés and Hernando, 1995). Moreover, to the extent that EMU enhances market integration through the consolidation of the internal market, this may well increase the degree of product market competition in the Union, which will lower the medium-term rate of unemployment. Finally, the establishment of EMU may have an impact insofar as the stronger degree of economic integration ends up imposing more discipline on wage setters even if it does not affect the current collective bargaining procedures (which are not conducive to low unemployment). Indeed, as pointed out by Calmfors (1994) and Danthine and Hunt (1994), as economies become more open and integrated, their labor market performance becomes less sensitive to changes in bargaining structure.

The above notwithstanding, it has been claimed that when shocks are very persistent, there is no guarantee that the management of the common monetary policy—once in EMU—will be neutral in the long run, as a result of hysteresis effects. Nevertheless, given the debate over the actual size of those effects, the empirical relevance of this caveat for the Union as a whole is unclear, although it may be of importance in specific countries (see, for example, Blanchard et al., 1995).

While EMU should not adversely affect the medium-term performance of unemployment (and may even improve it), both academics and policymakers disagree about the potential impact of EMU on unemployment over shorter-term horizons (that is, following the occurrence of specific shocks). In particular, there is much debate about the costs that would come from the loss of the nominal exchange rate as a tool for short-term macroeconomic adjustment.

In principle, as is well known from the literature on optimal currency areas, the impact of EMU on the shorter-term evolution of unemployment would depend on the nature of the shocks hitting the economies of the member states and on the existence of alternative tools for macroeconomic adjustment.[25] For example, the loss involved in not making use of the nominal exchange rate as an instrument for short-term macroeconomic adjustment will be smaller, *ceteris paribus*, when shocks require little movement of the real exchange rate to reestablish equilibrium. Normally, this tends to be the case when shocks are symmetric across the Union rather than asymmetric or idiosyncratic. In what follows we define a shock as being "symmetric" when its effects are roughly similar across the Union, and thus no real exchange rate adjustment between the member states is required to restore equilibrium.

In order to infer whether shocks would be symmetrical in EMU, recent empirical analysis has generally looked at the present situation in the EU and has taken the United States as a standard for comparison. The evidence is far from uncontroversial (see Viñals, 1994 and 1996 for recent summaries). Nevertheless, the dominant conclusion seems to be that idiosyncratic shocks tend to be more frequent in the EU than in the United States. Typically, it is also found that shocks are rather similar between the United States and the subset of EU countries that have traditionally maintained closer economic and monetary links with Germany. The implication seems to be that a narrow EMU would work satisfactorily, but that a wider EMU would experience asymmetric shocks and therefore serious national imbalances.[26]

This rather pessimistic conclusion concerning the economic viability of a wider EMU is based on the assumption that national currencies work to serve national labor markets. However, the evidence presented in Tables 2.1 and 2.2 earlier in the chapter—based on the econometric model described in Appendix 2.2—suggests a more favorable prognosis regarding the real costs of EMU. In particular, the finding that the common EU-wide component explains between 59 and 70 percent of the variance of movements in national unemployment rates even over the shorter term (one to two years) is consistent with the interpretation that, in general, the costs, in terms of macroeconomic stability, of abandoning nominal exchange rate flexibility are likely to be rather limited. Furthermore, our results suggest that region-specific shocks explain most of the variance of regional unemployment rates—with national innovations having relatively little effect. This evidence suggests that what would be really costly for Europe is to give up regional currencies (if there were any!) rather than national currencies. That said, and to the extent to which shocks to unemployment continue to be either common or regional shocks, there are no reasons for EMU to worsen the unemployment situation over the shorter term—whether it is a "narrow" EMU or a "wide" one.

Interpreting such empirical results raises an unavoidable problem: regime changes. The results are drawn from comparing the historical performance of a group of countries that have not yet formed a monetary union with that of U.S. regions, which have been long-standing members of a union. In short, the analysis could be biased because it might be the case that certain patterns of behavior now observed in the EU would tend to evolve toward those in the United States as economic and monetary integration advances.

Consider the case of financial and monetary policy shocks. At present, these are country-specific shocks that result from imperfectly coordinated national monetary policies, currency substitution, and exchange rate movements. This source of asymmetries will disappear instantaneously once EMU is formed and the single monetary policy implemented. Estimates by the European Commission (CEC, 1990) and by Canzoneri, Vallés, and Viñals (1996) indicate that this effect is likely to be significant. Looking at the real side of the economy, the main issue of concern is whether the deepening of economic and monetary integration will be associated with a tendency toward productive diversification or specialization in the EU. As Kenen (1969) argued years ago, the more diversified the industrial structures of countries are, the more likely it is that industrywide shocks will not translate into countrywide shocks. In this respect, there are two opposing forces to be considered. On the one hand, since most intra-EU trade takes the form of intraindustry trade, this implies that member states exchange very similar goods. Thus it is foreseeable that deeper integration may contribute to further diversifying national production structures within the EU, lessening the role of asymmetric or countrywide shocks. On the other hand, work by Krugman (1993) suggests that the EU could move in the direction of the United States, with higher regional specialization. Indeed, the existence of increasing returns to scale and "thick-market" externalities could lead to a regional concentration of production, making industrywide shocks regionwide shocks as well.

While we think that the point made by Krugman regarding the tendency toward regional specialization as monetary integration proceeds is, in principle, a very important one, Bayoumi and Prasad (1995) have recently questioned the empirical validity of the supposedly more specialized regional productive structure in the United States. Indeed, Bayoumi and Prasad find that once total output is considered—and not just industrial output—it is no longer the case that the United States is regionally more specialized than the European Union. In addition, even if there were a tendency in EMU toward regional specialization rather than diversification, regional and national specialization need not be the same thing. In particular, while a given industry may concentrate in a specific geographic region, that region might very well spread across several countries. In that case, industrywide and regionwide shocks may coincide with each other, but diverge from countrywide shocks. Once again, the appropriate alternative to EMU is not national currencies, but regional ones.

We conclude from this discussion that it is likely that common, Europewide symmetric shocks will prevail in EMU. Nevertheless, and to be on the safe side, since real asymmetric shocks may still happen from time to time—and since they could be big—it is important that adjustment mechanisms are found to deal with them in EMU. This will be of particular importance in those countries with relatively more differentiated production and trade structures.

Among the adjustment mechanisms available to cope with real asymmetric shocks in a future EMU—labor mobility, fiscal policy, and relative wage flexibility—it is unlikely that labor mobility will play an important role since the numerous historical, cultural, and linguistic differences across European countries constitute a formidable barrier to international migration. Furthermore, the Maastricht Treaty grants only a limited role to national fiscal policies to cushion the impact of real asymmetric shocks. But what about relative wages?

When shocks have asymmetric effects across countries, a movement of the real exchange is required to restore macroeconomic equilibrium and avoid adverse effects on unemployment. If relative wages were to adjust without cost, they would induce a prompt re-equilibrating response of the real exchange rate and there would be no loss from forgoing the present degree of nominal exchange rate flexibility. Unfortunately, both the evidence presented above and experience show that structural rigidities in national labor markets make wages respond slowly to worsening economic conditions. As a result, unemployment tends to persist.

While wages may not be flexible enough in the EU to cope with asymmetric shocks, the absence of residual exchange rate flexibility may improve the behavior of wage setters and so EMU might reinforce the degree of wage flexibility. While accepting that EMU may improve the degree of competition in labor markets over the medium run—as previously discussed—we are not very optimistic on the actual magnitude of this disciplinary effect over the shorter run. The experience of the ERM suggests generally modest disciplinary effects on national labor markets. In addition, the experience in Germany following unification illustrates that there may even be a perverse "wage catching-up" effect, which at least initially could undermine the downward flexibility of real wages. Consequently, restoring a higher degree of wage (and price) flexibility in EU countries is likely to require both a firm and balanced anti-inflationary macroeconomic policy stance, and the implementation of wide-ranging supply-side policies aimed at improving the workings of labor (and goods) markets. Such labor market liberalization might include, for example, the reform of job security legislation and unemployment benefits systems (and also the improvement of competition in service sectors). If such policies are pursued—and the sooner the better—EMU will amplify their beneficial effects on wage (and price) flexibility.

Let us assume for a moment, however, that the necessary structural reform policies do not take place. How costly is EMU then likely to be over the short term in terms of unemployment for particular countries?

To answer that question, it is necessary first to consider how effective the nominal exchange rate actually is in facilitating real exchange rate adjustment in European countries. Clearly, we are not referring to a situation where the nominal exchange rate is used in an activist and systematic way by the authorities. As it is widely acknowledged, the systematic use of monetary or exchange rate policy will not be very effective in altering real variables once private agents take into account the behavior of the authorities in their decisions, and may even lead to an inflationary bias.

The effectiveness of the nominal exchange rate in facilitating macroeconomic adjustment has often been approached from the point of view of how open the economy is, and of how rigid real wages are. In this respect, it has been argued that the growing economic openness among EU countries within the internal market makes use of the nominal exchange rate to restore or improve competitive positions increasingly effective in economic terms, and increasingly more difficult in political terms.[27] Furthermore, evidence of a significant degree of real wage rigidity in European labor markets suggests that nominal exchange rate movements may be ineffective in moving the real exchange rate in the desired direction.[28] Finally, and perhaps most importantly, the usefulness of the nominal exchange rate as a tool for macroeconomic adjustment is questionable in a world of free capital movements where foreign exchange markets are often subject to self-fulfilling speculative crises, which take the exchange rate away from where fundamentals suggest it should be during prolonged periods.[29] In these circumstances, there are serious reasons to doubt that the authorities can successfully resort to nominal exchange rate adjustments to restore macroeconomic balance in the presence of real asymmetric shocks.

Canzoneri, Vallés, and Viñals (1996) investigate empirically whether European nominal exchange rates actually address macroeconomic imbalances, or rather are basically driven by financial considerations that may or may not be related to such imbalances. The conclusion of the paper is that in many EU countries—both large and small, more or less open, and with different economic structures—nominal exchange rates do not seem to be acting like the efficient "shock absorber" described in the literature on optimal currency areas. However, it must be taken into account that while these results apply to "average" shocks, they do not apply to those big real assymetric shocks that come, say, once in a decade and that may require an adjustment of nominal exchange rates.

In sum, it is most likely that EMU will not, in general, adversely affect European average unemployment or national unemployment differentials given the likely dominance of symmetric shocks. Nevertheless, given the limited role of intra-European labor mobility and of national fiscal policies in restoring macroeconomic balance, it is possible that some countries with more differentiated economic structures may suffer if and when sizable real asymmetric shocks take place. This possibility notwithstanding, the growing degree of integration among European economies within the internal market and the increasingly important role of financial disturbances in driving exchange rates would, in any case, make the resort to the nominal exchange rate as a tool for macroeconomic adjustments increasingly less effective in economic terms and more difficult in political terms, even if EMU did not take place. Consequently, the only way to cope successfully with important real—symmetric or asymmetric—shocks and to avoid their unwanted effects on unemployment—inside or outside of EMU—is by increasing the degree of relative price and wage flexibility through the reform of those regulations and institutions that prevent an adequate functioning of national goods and labor markets.

Conclusions and Policy Implications

This chapter has reviewed what we believe are the most important features of the unemployment situation in the EU in order to examine how the establishment of an economic and monetary union could affect European unemployment. We also considered how Europe's unemployment problem can be fought best. The main conclusions and policy implication obtained from the chapter can be summarized as follows:

First, although there are significant differences in unemployment situations across the European Union, most countries have in common rather high rates of unemployment and a significant resistance of inflation to come down in the presence of such high unemployment rates. The contrast between the persistently high and drifting European unemployment rates and the much lower and stable rates observed in the United States and Japan suggests that there is a nonnegligible common element in European unemployment. This impression is confirmed by the empirical evidence provided in the chapter, which shows that common European forces seem to have been very important in explaining the behavior of national unemployment rates in the last decades. Furthermore, it is not possible to draw a clear distinction between the so-called core and periphery countries as concerns the main determinants of national unemployment rates.

Second, the persistent nature of European unemployment over many years suggests that it is mostly of a "structural" rather than of a "cyclical" nature. While a high rate of structural unemployment can be, in principle, effected both by supply and demand shocks and policies, our discussion seems to suggest that several labor market institutions may have been responsible for the less than satisfactory performance of European labor markets, both by contributing to sustained wage pressures and by slowing down the speed with which wage growth decelerates in the presence of worsening economic conditions. Among the labor market institutions discussed, three stand out: collective bargaining, job security legislation, and unemployment benefits systems. It is also important to bear in mind that cyclical unemployment may become structural, given the strong persistence mechanisms observed in European labor markets.

Third, the pursuit of the convergence criteria established in the Maastricht Treaty for entering into EMU requires implementing sound economic policies that are desirable in their own right and that would need to be introduced even in the absence of EMU. The treaty simply advances those policies. Furthermore, such policies need not be inconsistent with making progress on the unemployment front. Namely, while in some cases there may be short-run costs in terms of unemployment, these ought to be more than offset by the long-term benefits obtained. Finally, short-term costs may be lessened—and sometimes even eliminated—if convergence policies are credibly implemented and, where applicable, accompanied by structural reforms in national product and labor markets.

Fourth, as concerns the impact of EMU on European unemployment, our analysis suggests that insofar as EMU leads to more stable monetary and nonmonetary policies and to a higher degree of economic integration, this might have, if anything, a favorable impact on unemployment performance across the Union in the medium term. Nevertheless, since the size of these effects is uncertain, it is stressed that—quite apart from EMU—the fight against unemployment must necessarily involve removing the structural obstacles to the good functioning of national labor markets, and the sooner the better.

We have also explored how EMU might affect unemployment performance over the shorter term given the unavailability of the nominal exchange rate to restore macroeconomic balance. Our tentative conclusion is that the fears that an EMU may result in higher unemployment and/or higher national unemployment differentials are grossly exaggerated for several reasons. On the one hand, as explained in the chapter, common shocks are likely to prevail once in EMU; on the other hand, the increasing integration of European economies within the internal market, their relatively high degree of real wage rigidity, and the presence of self-fulfilling speculative elements in foreign exchange markets suggest that, in any case, it will be increasingly less effective (economically) and more difficult (politically) to use nominal exchange rate flexibility to stabilize macroeconomic performance. This notwithstanding, it must be recognized that in those countries with more differentiated economic structures, and thus more likely to be exposed to real asymmetric shocks, EMU membership should be accompanied by structural reforms designed to improve the degree of relative wage flexibility so as to avoid future problems. These problems might be, in addition, all the more important if prevailing labor market institutions increase the persistence of the effects of those shocks.

Fifth, while we do not find justification for the argument that unemployment convergence should become an additional explicit or implicit requirement for entrance into EMU—as demanded by some—it is quite clear that countries with badly functioning labor markets, in addition to having worse growth and unemployment performance, will have more difficulties in meeting the nominal convergence criteria established in the treaty since wage and price inflation will be stickier in a downward direction. As a result, it can be said that the convergence criteria in the treaty already take into account, to some extent, the concerns of those who worry about starting EMU with wide unemployment differentials, and thus that no explicit or implicit amendment to the criteria should be made for this reason.

Finally, although there is a significant common European element in the national unemployment situations of member states, policies to reduce unemployment are—and are likely to remain—mainly the responsibility of the national authorities. Nevertheless, Europewide institutions can and should play a role in ensuring an adequate coordination of national efforts to fight unemployment within the framework already established to move toward EMU. As we have argued throughout the chapter, the pursuit of nominal convergence need not be incompatible with furthering real convergence if the coordinated implementation of sound monetary and fiscal policies, aimed toward achieving nominal stability, is accompanied by the introduction of appropriate structural reforms. In this regard, the further deregulation and liberalization of nontraded goods and services sectors, when necessary, and the redesign of labor market institutions—such as job security provisions and unemployment benefits schemes—should be among the top priorities.

To conclude, high European unemployment is a most important problem that, with or without EMU, must be fought directly by removing its structural roots. Furthermore, while having unemployment rates above 10 percent should not preclude EMU from being established, the operation of the monetary union will be smoother and its net economic benefits larger if European countries succeed in implementing those structural reforms that are needed for unemployment to go to lower, more reasonable rates.

Appendix 2.1
European, National, and Regional Components of Unemployment Rates in EU Countries

The decomposition of unemployment rates in EU countries and regions is based upon the following recursive model:

$$u_t^{EU} = \delta^{EU} + A_i(L)u_t^{EU} + \epsilon_t^{EU}$$
$$u_t^I = \delta^I + A_2^I(L)u_t^{EU} + B_2^I(L)u_t^I + \epsilon_t^I \qquad (2.1)$$
$$u_t^{IJ} = \delta^{IJ} + A_3^{IJ}(L)u_t^{EU} + B_3^{IJ}(L)u_t^I + C_3^{IJ}(L)u_t^{IJ} + \epsilon_t^{IJ},$$

where δ's are constants, u^{EU}, u^I, u^{IJ} are, respectively, the EU average unemployment rate, the unemployment rate of country I, and the unemployment rate of region J in country I; $A(.)$, $B(.)$, and $C(.)$ are polynomials in the lag operator L (with $A_I(0) = B_2(0) = C_3(0) = 0$), and ϵ are unemployment shocks. Under this model, nation-specific shocks have no effects at the EU level, and region-specific shocks have no effects at the national level.

Since the system is recursive, and we have different sample sizes for national and regional unemployment rates, we estimate the first two equations to decompose shocks to national unemployment into an EU component and a nation-specific component. The decomposition of shocks to regional unemployment rates is based on the estimation of the three-equation system on the panel of EUROSTAT NUTS-1 regions for each country, controlling for regional fixed effects, and imposing the constraint that the coefficients of the third equation (in equation 2.1) are the same across regions within the same country. The results in the text arise from the estimation of the system (2.1) for each of the EU member states (except for Luxembourg and for countries in which regional data are not available during a long enough period). Data on national unemployment rates are for the 1969 to 1993 period. Data on regional unemployment are available from EUROSTAT (REGIO databank) for the 1983 to 1993 period (except for the new member countries, Greece, Portugal and the Netherlands).

Note that this recursive model is a simplification of the following three dimensional Vector Autoregression (VAR):

$$x_t = D(L)x_t + v_t; D(0) = 0. \qquad (2.2)$$

with $x^I = (u^{EU}, u^I, u^{IJ})$ and v_t are innovations to unemployment. We have also estimated this VAR and recovered aggregate, national, and regional shocks to unemployment under the identifying assumptions that both the contemporaneous effects of national shocks on the EU average unemployment rate, and that the contemporaneous effects of regional shocks on national unemployment rates are nil. Under this maintained hypothesis, we cannot reject the (overidentifying) restrictions imposed on the recursive model (2.1).

Appendix 2.2
Real Wage Rigidity in EU Countries:
An Index Based on the Impulse Response of Unemployment to Wage Push Shocks

As noted in the text, the degree of real wage rigidity in the EU member countries is a crucial determinant of both the costs and benefits of EMU. It is often argued that European countries show a relatively high degree of real wage rigidity (when compared to the United States, for example) and, at the same time, noticeable nominal wage flexibility (see Layard et al., 1991; Bean, 1994). This combination produces short-lasting effects of nominal shocks and long-lasting effects of real shocks. The costs of a full EMU are decreasing in the degree of nominal flexibility and increasing in the degree of real wage rigidity. Hence, it is important to assess the magnitude of real wage rigidity across these countries.

Following the theoretical model of Appendix 2.1, we can write a wage and a (long-run) price equation. Assuming constant markup pricing, prices (in logs) are given by:

$$p - w = m + z, \tag{2.3}$$

where p is prices, w is (nominal) wages, m is the markup and z are shocks assumed to follow an $I(1)$ process, and therefore, innovations in z have permanent effects on real wages. Wages are negatively related to unemployment, as in:

$$w - p = -c\,(u - hu_{-1}) + z^w, \tag{2.4}$$

where u is the unemployment rate, c and h are positive parameters, and z^w are shocks to the wage equation when $h < 1$. A measure of real wage rigidity is the inverse of $c\,(1 - h)$. The higher c is, the less rigid real wages are; the higher h is, the more rigid real wages are. Combining these two equations yields that unemployment is given by

$$u = m/c + hu_{-1} + (z^w + z)/c. \tag{2.5}$$

Now suppose that shocks to the price-setting equation are mostly of a "technological" nature with permanent effects on real wages ($z = -e^s$). Shocks to the wage equation include both technological shocks and (stationary) wage push/labor supply shocks, so that $z^W = e^s + e^w$. Then,

$$U = \frac{m}{c} + h\,u_{-1} + \frac{e^w}{c} = \frac{m}{c(1-h)} + \sum_{j=0}^{\infty} \frac{h^j}{c} e^w_{-j} \qquad (2.6)$$

Thus, unemployment is stationary and its initial response to wage push/labor supply shocks is greater the more rigid real wages are. The mean lag of the response to unemployment $(h/(1-h))$ is increasing in h.

If $h = 1$, unemployment follows a random walk with drift, and its short-run and long-run responses to wage push/labor supply shocks are decreasing in c. This simple model suggests that the degree of real wage rigidity is related to some characteristics of the impulse-response of unemployment to wage push/labor supply shocks, which are easily identified. In both cases considered ($h < 1$ and $h = 1$) real wages are $I(1)$ and wage push/labor supply shocks have no long-run effects on the level of real wages. Thus, the empirical exercise to assess the degree of real wage rigidities across countries is very simple. When $h < 1$, estimate a VAR composed of the growth rate of real wages and the (level of the) unemployment rate, and recover the impulse-response of unemployment to shocks that have no long-run effects on real wages. When $h = 1$, estimate a VAR composed of the growth rate of real wages and the first difference of the unemployment rate, and recover the impulse-response of unemployment to the same kind of shocks. Note that the model above suggests that the other type of shocks recovered are technological shocks, which increase real wages in the long run and do not affect unemployment.

Appendix 2.3
A Benchmark Model of the Labor Market

Most models of the labor market identify two unemployment components: the natural rate of unemployment (also called structural unemployment or equilibrium unemployment), which is the unemployment rate that would prevail in the long run; and cyclical unemployment, which is the short-run unemployment caused by transitory shocks that hit the economy. There is a continuing debate on the determinants of equilibrium unemployment and the sources of cyclical unemployment. However, most macroeconomists share a rather common approach when modeling the labor market.

Figure 2.6 provides a simple representation of the labor market that can encompass most models of unemployment determination. Given technological constraints and a fixed stock of capital, there is a short-run price-setting equation (or inverted labor demand equation) that establishes a negative relationship between real wages and employment, l^D_{SR} (in logs), which depends on expected demand. The labor force is given by l^s (in logs), so that a perfectly competitive labor market will yield full employment and (log) real wages equal to $(w - p)^c$. However, wage determination is given by a wage-setting equation that because of several reasons (efficiency wages, union power, and

Figure 2.6
A Simple Representation of the Labor Market

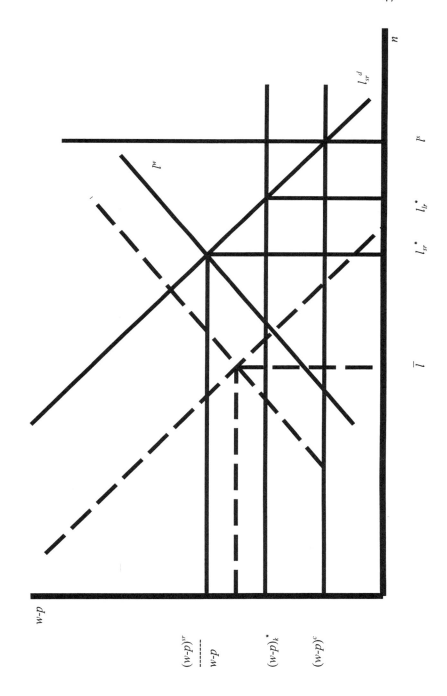

collective bargaining, etc.) establishes a positive relationship between real wages and employment, l^w (also in logs). Assuming correct expectations, the resulting short-run equilibrium unemployment rate is given by $l^s - l^*_{SR}$, and inflation will be constant. Misperceptions on aggregate demand make the actual unemployment rate, $l^s - l$, different from the short-run equilibrium unemployment rate, so that a cyclical unemployment component arises. In the long run, since the stock of capital is endogenous, the price-setting equation is horizontal, l^p_L, at a level that depends on the user cost of capital and on the rate of growth of total factor productivity (see Blanchard, 1990) and under some conditions on the degree of competition in product markets. If the latter variables are roughly constant, long-run equilibrium unemployment is mainly determined by the variables that shift the wage-setting curve, that is, basically the reservation wage and whatever factors may affect the desired markup of actual wages over reservation wages.

The dynamics of the adjustment from actual unemployment to short-run and long-run equilibrium unemployment can be very rich for two reasons. On the one hand, some of the variables that determine the equilibrium levels of unemployment may also affect the speed of adjustment from one equilibrium to another. On the other hand, there may be hysteretic effects, so that long-run equilibrium unemployment may depend on the path followed by actual unemployment (in terms of Figure 2.6, this means that the position and, plausibly, the slope of the wage-setting and price-setting curves, l^w and l^p_{SR}, depend on the path followed by actual unemployment).

Thus, the determinants of equilibrium unemployment can be divided into three categories:

1. Factors that influence wage-setting behavior. In the so-called battle of the markups (Layard et al., 1991), the position of the wage-setting equation depends on the target real wage (or "wage pressure"), while its slope is related to the degree of real wage rigidity. In particular, as the degrees of wage pressure and real wage rigidity increase, so does equilibrium unemployment. Additionally, Phelps's (1994) structuralist theory stresses the role of efficiency wage considerations, so that the position and slope of the wage-setting curve depend on the quitting and shirking behavior of workers. This behavior is affected primarily by the ratio of nonwage income to total income, so that changes in wealth, interest rates, and government transfers are among the variables shifting the wage-setting curve.

2. Factors that influence price-setting behavior. While different variables may effect price setting, in the battle of the markup the employers' desired profit margin—which depends on the degree of competition in goods markets—is the main variable affecting the position of the labor demand curve. In the structuralist story, many other variables may play

a role such as productivity growth, productivity and supply shocks, asset and wealth shocks, interest rate shocks, tax and tariff distortions, and public expenditure shocks.

3. Hysteresis effects. These effects relate the long-run wage setting and labor demand loci to the path followed by actual unemployment. The main sources of hysteresis are insiders' power in wage determination and long-term unemployment, which reduce the downward pressure exerted by unemployment on wages. Thus, shocks to actual unemployment, which do not affect short-term equilibrium unemployment directly, may have permanent effects on long-run unemployment.[30]

Notes

1. We thank Javier Andrés, Samuel Bentolila, Juan Dolado, Jeffry Frieden, Daniel Gros, Abel Mateus, Leonor Modesto, and Javier Vallés for comments, and Sonsoles Castillo and Rosa Duce for excellent research assistance. Juan F. Jimeno acknowledges financial support from DGICYT, grant SEC95-0131. The views expressed are solely those of the authors and thus do not necessarily represent those of the institutions with which they are affiliated.

2. OECD (1994a), Chapter 1, is a comprehensive account of stylized facts on European unemployment. The survey by Bean (1994) also provides the most significant facts.

3. Although there has been some dispersion in labor force growth across countries, it is the different evolution of employment that constitutes the main source of disparities in unemployment across these countries. However, participation rates (labor force as proportion of working population, 15–64 years of age) range from about 60 percent in Spain to about 85 percent in Denmark, with high unemployment countries having relatively low participation rates. This means that dispersion in employment performance across EU countries, measured by employment rates, is larger than the dispersion of unemployment rates. A noteworthy feature of employment creation in EU countries is that it has been mostly concentrated in the public sector of the economy. On the contrary, employment growth in the United States and Japan has been driven by the private sector (see OECD, 1994a: Chart 2.2).

The incidence of unemployment across different population groups also varies across countries. Generally speaking, female unemployment and youth unemployment are relatively higher in southern European countries, where these population groups account for a sizeable proportion of unemployment. However, in most countries there is a close relationship between the evolution of total unemployment and adult male (25–55) unemployment. The difference of the adult male unemployment rates between EU countries and the United States is not as large as the difference of total unemployment, but both show similar patterns and evolve accordingly.

4. Weighted by the share of each country or region in the total labor force.

5. From 1983 onward, and excluding Portugal, Greece, Austria, Finland, and Sweden.

6. Except for Luxembourg and for those countries in which regional data are not

available for a long enough period. Data on national unemployment rates are for the 1969 to 1993 period. Data on regional unemployment are available from EUROSTAT (REGIO databank) for the 1983 to 1993 period for all countries with the exception of Greece, the Netherlands, Portugal, and the new member states. The identifying assumptions have been made that region-specific shocks to unemployment have no effect on national nor European unemployment, and that national-specific shocks to unemployment have no effect on European unemployment. Regional unemployment data are at the EUROSTAT NUTS-1 level.

7. This variance decomposition is somewhat robust to the inclusion of deterministic and stochastic trends in the specification of the unemployment process. We have estimated our model with no trends, a similar deterministic trend for all countries, a segmented trend in 1973, and in differences. In the text we report the results from the estimation of the specification with no trends (see Appendix 2.2). The variance decompositions from the specifications, which include deterministic trends, are very similar to the decomposition reported in the text. When the model is estimated in differences, EU aggregate shocks explain (on average) 41 percent of the variance within the year and 53.6 percent, 57.6 percent, 57.6 percent, and 57.9 percent after one, two, three, and four years, respectively. These results are available upon request.

8. We have estimated Europewide shocks allowing them to have different effects across countries. This means that the same shock influences unemployment more in some countries than in others. Had we restricted Europewide shocks to have symmetric unemployment effects across countries (the common shock increases unemployment by the same amount in all the countries), we would have found that country-specific shocks explain a much higher proportion of the variance of unemployment (roughly 75 percent). There are three countries in which Europewide innovations explain a relatively low proportion of the variance of their respective unemployment rates over the short run: Italy, Portugal, and Sweden. At the other extreme, the United Kingdom, France, and Belgium are the EU member countries where aggregate innovations explain the highest proportion of the variance of national unemployment.

9. Denmark is the only exception to this general pattern.

10. As usual in this type of exercise, the Lucas critique is relevant. We can learn about the sources of shocks and their transmission before EMU is in place. Both the sources of the shocks and their transmission could likely change under EMU. In any case, the current dynamics of real wages and unemployment provide the starting point for EMU.

11. Under the assumption of constant returns to scale and constant mark-up pricing, the initial response of unemployment to a transitory wage-push shock is determined by the response of real wages to current unemployment, while the mean lag of the adjustment path followed by unemployment after such a shock depends on the response of real wages to lagged unemployment (see Appendix 2.3). Thus, the impulse response function of unemployment to wage-push shocks can be used to compute an index of real wage rigidity.

12. In the first case, unemployment follows a stationary process and we estimate a bivariate VAR composed of (the rate of growth of) real wages and the level of unemployment. In the second (hysteresis) case, unemployment follows a process integrated of order one, and we estimate a bivariate VAR composed of (the rate of growth of)

real wages and changes in unemployment. The hysteresis case is plausibly relevant for some EU countries since 1973, where the presence of a unit root in unemployment cannot be rejected. It is not, however, a case that fits the U.S. and Japanese experience in this regard. Nevertheless, we also report the results of the United States and Japan for the sake of completeness.

13. However, the increase in EU long-term unemployment (unemployed who have spent at least one year without a job) took place in the late 1970s and early 1980s and has remained fairly constant since then (with two exceptions, Ireland and Italy, where it has increased). Since unemployment in the EU is mainly the result of a fall in the outflow rate to employment, there is a high correlation between total unemployment rates and long-term unemployment rates. Thus, unsurprisingly, long-term unemployment is especially high in Ireland and Spain (despite the fact that the high incidence of fixed-term employment in Spain has significantly increased workers flows in and out of unemployment since 1987).

14. The Okun curve (the relationship between the unemployment rate and the capacity utilization rate) shows a similar pattern. Instead, in the United States, there are no significant outward shifts either in the Beveridge or Okun curves (indeed, if anything, the curves shift inward). In other non-EU countries an increase in vacancies but not in unemployment has been registered. The shifts of the Beveridge and Okun curves are illustrative not only of the nature of the shocks affecting the economy but also of the degree of mismatch between labor demand and labor supply, and of changes in social protection (see Blanchard and Diamond, 1992). Therefore, the EU experience suggests that, up to the mid-1980s, either the matching efficiency of EU economies has decreased, or the social protection system has improved, leading to changes either in reservation wages or in the search intensity of the unemployed, or both.

15. There are two approaches to distinguishing between the permanent shock hypothesis and the hysteresis hypothesis. According to the first approach, while the permanent shock hypothesis, in its extreme version, implies the existence either of a deterministic trend or of a mean shift in the stochastic process driving unemployment, the hysteresis hypothesis implies the existence of a unit root. The presence of unit roots in the stochastic processes followed by the unemployment rates of most EU countries cannot be rejected (see Elmeskov and MacFarlan, 1994). However, given the number of observations in macroeconomic series, the power of unit root tests is low, and this evidence cannot thus be taken as supporting hysteresis versus a nonhysteretic but slow adjustment process. According to the second approach, estimation of the structural equations contained in the model of the labor market can provide information on the size of some interesting economic effects among the relevant variables. However, structural estimation is subject to some identification problems, and in any case, the usual estimation of aggregate dynamic macroeconomic wage relationships has mostly failed to prove the existence of hysteresis. Therefore, there is no conclusive evidence on the actual relevance of hysteresis at this stage.

16. See OECD (1994b), Chapter 5.

17. See Calmfors (1994) for a survey, and Jimeno (1993).

18. See Bentolila and Bertola (1990), and Bentolila and Saint-Paul (1994).

19. For a very detailed empirical analysis of the impact of unemployment benefits see Bover et al. (1996).

20. See OECD (1994a), Chapter 8.

21. See, for instance, Barrel et al. (1995), and the discussion in Gros (1996a).

22. See European Monetary Institute (1996).

23. See Viñals (1986); Giavazzi and Pagano (1990 and 1995); Argimón, González Páramo and Roldán (1995).

24. See, for example, Viñals (1996) for a discussion of these issues.

25. For the costs (and benefits) of EMU see: CEC (1990), De Grauwe (1992), Eichengreen (1992), Gros and Thygesen (1992), Masson and Taylor (1993), Goodhart (1993), and Viñals (1994).

26. See, for example, Bayoumi and Eichengreen (1993).

27. See, for example, Eichengreen and Ghironi (1995) and Viñals (1996).

28. See Bean (1992).

29. See Flood and Rose (1995) and Rose (1995).

30. In econometric terms, the stochastic process followed by unemployment has a unit root.

3

External Shocks and Labor Mobility: How Important Are They for EMU?

Daniel Gros

The exchange rate is potentially one of the most important policy instruments. It is highly visible and has an immediate impact on some sectors of the economy. The economic effects of exchange rates merit careful attention for two reasons. First, the sectors that are directly affected by the exchange rate will lobby for or against EMU if they perceive that it will affect their interests. Second, the results of overall cost and benefit analysis of EMU done by economists are used by these sectors and might also exert a considerable influence on policymakers in general.

There is no need for economists to second guess the impact of EMU on the exposed sectors of the economy since these sectors have already made clear that their own evaluation is positive. Public pronouncements of industry associations, their lobbying, and the published opinion polls of industrial leaders all point in the same direction: By and large the sectors that trade intensively tend to favor EMU (Pisani-Ferry, Hefeker, and Hughes Hallett, 1997; Jones, Frieden, and Torres, 1998). This chapter therefore discusses only the second issue, namely the overall cost and benefit analysis of EMU. In doing so it focuses on what academic discussions of the economic costs and benefits of EMU usually take as their basis, namely the "optimum currency area" (OCA) approach.

The OCA approach starts from the premise that when an external shock hits the economy, it is easier to adjust the exchange rate than domestic prices or wages. The seminal contribution in this area is Mundell (1961: 657) who puts the problem succinctly: "A system of flexible exchange rates is usually presented, by its proponents, as a device whereby depreciation can take the place of unemployment when the external balance is in deficit, and appreciation can replace inflation when it is in surplus."

Most economists accept the general idea behind this approach, namely that

53

nominal wages are usually sticky in the short run and that it is therefore easier to adjust to external shocks and obtain changes in the real exchange rate or the terms of trade through a movement in the exchange rate. But there is little agreement on how important these "external" shocks are in reality. Will the loss of the exchange rate instrument lead to massive unemployment because large negative external shocks are likely? Or do external shocks play only a marginal role in the evolution of unemployment? The presumption of most economists would be that external shocks should have a significant impact at least for small countries.

The first key issue for an evaluation of the economic case against EMU is whether external shocks (that is, shocks to exports and/or the exchange rate) have a strong impact on (un)employment in member countries. This question anticipates some of the analysis posited in Chapter 2, where Viñals and Ji-meno concede that big asymmetric shocks may occur and ask what is the appropriate response. The approach here is to suggest that even if such shocks do occur, it is necessary to consider whether they have any substantial affect on unemployment. This is an empirical issue that has not been addressed in the literature up to now.

A second key point of the OCA approach concerns the role of labor mobil-ity. In the words of Mundell (1961: 661), "The argument for flexible exchange rates based on national currencies is only as valid as the Ricardian assumption about factor mobility." The latter has two aspects: "that factors of production are mobile internally, but immobile internationally."

The emphasis on the difference between interregional and international labor mobility in Mundell is often overlooked in discussions about EMU. If one were to find that labor mobility is as low within member countries as it is between them, one would have to conclude (yet again!) with Mundell (1961: 660) that "the optimum currency area is the region."

The case for flexible exchange rates based on national currencies is only as strong as the difference between interregional and international labor mobil-ity.[1] This key point is always overlooked in the literature on EMU, which considers only one aspect, namely the low degree of international labor mobil-ity within Europe. It is assumed that mobility within a country is higher than that between countries.

But even if one abstracts from this argument, the larger question remains: How important is labor mobility in theory and in practice? Is the general impression that labor mobility is extremely low in Europe justified? Is more labor mobility desirable for EMU (because it facilitates adjustment)? Or is it undesirable (because it favors concentration), hence increasing the potential for more asymmetric shocks in the future?

The reader needs to be warned that this chapter is somewhat unbalanced. The following section provides a substantial amount of new research results on the (lack of) importance of external shocks and thus suggests that the loss of the exchange rate as an adjustment instrument is not costly. By contrast, the second section is much shorter. It provides little new evidence on labor mobility in Europe, but otherwise relies on previous studies on migration in the United States that do not confirm perceived wisdom. The third section concludes the discussion.

The attentive reader will also notice that there is an inconsistency between the arguments used by trading sectors in favor of EMU and the arguments used by economists against EMU: The trading sectors usually favor EMU because they fear that the alternative to EMU would be a world that was subject to large exchange rate volatility. Economists that oppose EMU implicitly assume that the alternative is a world in which exchange rate can be used as an adjustment instrument to exogenous shocks. This implies implicitly that exchange rates should be rather stable because major economic shocks do not occur daily or monthly. The trading sectors presumably fear excessive volatility because they feel that most exchange rate changes would actually not be due to exogenous shocks, but by changing sentiments in financial markets, which might have little to do with fundamentals. This contradiction cannot be resolved here. Instead, the following analysis adheres to the convention in economic analysis that the alternative to EMU is that the exchange rate can be adjusted (or changes on its own) only in response to shocks that actually require an exchange rate adjustment.

Unemployment and Asymmetric Shocks

The standard line of reasoning in support of exchange rate flexibility is clear: If a shock reduces the demand for the exports of a country, a real depreciation is required to maintain full employment and external equilibrium. The required real depreciation could also be achieved by a reduction in nominal ("money") wages, but this takes time and can presumably be achieved only if there is a period of substantial unemployment. The more wages are downwardly sticky—as suggested in Chapter 2—the longer the period of unemployment. The proper exchange rate policy could thus reduce, and possibly even eliminate, the unemployment problems that arise from "asymmetric shocks." This line of reasoning has become the standard economic objection to EMU. Asymmetric shocks, it is often argued, will invariably ratchet up unemployment.

However, the available studies on the potential cost of EMU do not attempt to test this line of reasoning directly. Rather, such studies usually analyze the degree to which various macroeconomic indicators, such as output, the real exchange rate, unemployment, and so forth, are correlated across countries. A finding of low correlations is usually interpreted as implying that the countries concerned are subject to important asymmetric shocks and that they would sustain large economic costs if they formed a monetary union.

The degree of acceptable correlation is difficult to decide *a priori* because there is no theoretical reason to accept a given correlation coefficient as a baseline or benchmark. Put another way, there is no reason to accept a coefficient of, say, 90 percent as sufficiently high for EMU but reject anything below. This is why the implicit or explicit benchmark is often the United States in the sense that it is argued that if the economies of member countries show a similar degree of correlation among them, as do states or regions inside the United States, EMU should not create particular problems for Europe.

Many previous studies have followed this approach. It is sufficient here to take just one prominent example that can stand for most of this literature. Bayoumi and Eichengreen (1993) are a good example; they compare the correlation of certain shocks to output among eight regions within the United States and among eleven member states within the EU.[2] They distinguish between shocks that have transitory effects, which they assume to be demand shocks, and shocks that have permanent effects, which they assume to be supply shocks. Their main finding is that the supply shocks, thus defined, are larger in magnitude and less correlated across regions in Europe than in the United States, whereas the opposite holds for demand (or transitory) shocks. Moreover, they also confirm that the core of the EU (here Germany, France, Belgium, the Netherlands, and Denmark) constitutes a homogenous subunit. Within this restricted group of countries, supply (or permanent) shocks are of roughly the same magnitude and cohesion as in the United States. Bayoumi and Eichengreen conclude that a core EMU is economically advisable, but a wider EMU is not.

This example illustrates a central problem in the empirical literature on the optimum currency area approach: The correlations in macroeconomic variables found for the past reflect not only the working of true shocks (or "intrinsic" factors like taste and technology) but also, and perhaps mainly, the extent to which monetary and fiscal policy have in the past tended to move together across countries (under different exchange rate regimes).[3] Bayoumi and Eichengreen (1993) try to take this into account by distinguishing between supply shocks (presumably independent of policy) and demand shocks that might come from monetary and/or fiscal policy. However, neither theirs nor other contributions take into account that the OCA is based on the need to adjust the real exchange rate in response to external shocks. No existing empirical analysis of EMU makes the distinction between external and domestic shocks; this is crucial as argued in the following.

A different way to search for asymmetric shocks looks at differences in economic structures, such as differences in the shares of output accounted for by different industries or the product composition of exports. The underlying hypothesis here is that countries that have different economic structures are likely to experience asymmetric shocks. Gros (1996a) provides a number of indicators along this line and shows that they can give quite different results. This approach can in principle provide some information on likely sources of shocks, but it cannot provide evidence on the size of the shocks one should expect in reality. For example, a finding that two countries export different arrays of goods has little implication for the likelihood of shocks to aggregate exports, since shocks to the demand and supply of individual products should average out.

The available literature thus looks only at the potential for asymmetric shocks or measures comovements in macroeconomic variables without showing how external shocks lead to unemployment. The basic question that has not yet been addressed in the literature is whether the "classic" asymmetric shocks—which is to say, shocks to export demand—are actually an important determinant of unemployment. A subsidiary question would concern the role of exchange rate adjustments in containing unemployment generated by shocks to exports. These questions are central for any evaluation of EMU because if the answer to both questions is yes (meaning that external shocks and the exchange rate are important for unemployment) this would mean that the costs of EMU are high.

A direct test of the optimum currency area (OCA) approach

To what extent do external shocks affect unemployment? In principle there are two strategies for measuring this effect: One uses a large macroeconomic model to trace the impact of such shocks (or changes in export demand) through the entire economy under various assumptions about the flexibility of wages and the exchange rate; the other measures "only" the extent to which (changes in) exports have "caused" (changes in) unemployment in the past.

This subsection relies principally on the second method, based on standard "causality tests." The underlying hypothesis is that export supply is rather stable and so it is possible to equate actual changes (or innovations) in exports with changes in export demand. All the results presented here are based on a comparison of two regression equations:

$$\text{due}_t = \alpha + \Sigma_{i=1} \alpha_i \, \text{due}_{t-i} + \text{error term} \quad \text{and} \tag{3.1}$$

$$\text{due}_t = \alpha + \Sigma_{i=1} \alpha_i \, \text{due}_{t-i} + \Sigma_{i=0} \beta_i \, \text{dexp}_{t-i} + \text{error term}, \tag{3.2}$$

where Σ stands for a summation that starts with the element indicated in the subscript, due_t stands for the change in unemployment between period $t - i$ and $t - i - 1$, and dexp_{t-i} stands for the change in exports between period $t - i$ and period $t - i - 1$. Exports (measured by various indicators as explained below) can then be said to "cause" unemployment if the ßs—that is the coefficients on past and contemporaneous exports—are together significantly different from zero. In other words, these tests measure the impact of changes in (various measures of) export performance on changes in national unemployment rates once the autonomous movements in unemployment have been taken into account by including lagged unemployment rates among the explanatory variables. These tests rely on "changes" because the "levels" of both variables are clearly nonstationary. A significant effect (of whatever sign) implies that one can reject at the 5 percent confidence level the hypothesis that exports do not influence unemployment.

Table 3.1 summarizes the results of causality tests using annual data.[4] These results are not interesting in the usual sense that there are some "significant" relationships. On the contrary their interest lies in the absence of a strong and robust link between unemployment and (past changes in) exports. Each entry in this table shows a plus or minus sign if the variable listed at the head of the column has a significant influence on unemployment, for the particular country concerned. The first four columns report the results of tests of the hypothesis that changes in national unemployment rates are not affected by shocks to the following variables:

- Changes in exports in constant 1990 European Currency Units (ECUs);
- changes in intra-European exports as percentage of GDP;
- changes in total exports as percentage of GDP; and
- the contribution of exports to the growth in final uses.

In order to minimize clutter, Table 3.1 has no entry in a cell if one can*not* reject the null hypothesis of no relationship at the 95 percent confidence level. A negative sign implies that one can reject this null hypothesis and that, in particular, an increase in one of these proxies for export performance leads to a fall in unemployment (as one would expect). A positive sign implies the opposite and would be difficult to explain.

A glance at the first four columns shows that the first and the last variables are the ones that have the largest numbers of entries. But even concentrating on the variables that perform "best," it still remains true that for almost half of all member countries, shocks to exports have in the past played no significant role in determining unemployment in the way one would expect from the OCA approach. This was found for a large country like France as well as for a small country like Denmark (where the sign is wrong), for a poor country like Spain and for a rich country like, again, Denmark or France.

For the other member countries shocks to exports had some influence on the evolution of unemployment. However, a closer look at the individual regressions (not reported in the table because of lack of space) shows that this influence was in all cases minor in the sense that shocks to exports could explain only a very small part of the fluctuations of unemployment rates over time. The strongest influence of exports on unemployment can be found in the case of Belgium. The results for this country are presented in detail below

TABLE 3.1
Unemployment as a Function of Export Performance (summary results)

Dependent Variable →	Changes in Unemployment Levels				Changes in Unemployment Differences		Unemployment Differences	
Independent Variable →	*csc	*eec	*etc	*ne	*nd	*tdc	*nd	*td
Belgium	-		-	-			-	
Denmark		+	+					
Germany	-		-					
Greece	-							
Spain						+		+/-
France								
Ireland				-				
Italy						+		
Netherlands	-		-				-	
Portugal	-		-		-	-	-	-
UK	-		-					

Key to Independent Variable List

*csc   Change in constant ECU exports

*eec   Change in intra-European trade as a percentage of GDP

*etc   Change in total exports as a percentage of GDP

*ne   Export contribution to the growth in final uses

*nd   Export contribution to the growth in final uses, difference with European average

*tdc   Change in the difference with European average of total exports as percentage GDP

*td   Total exports as a percentage of GDP, difference with European average

Data source: European Commission

because they can establish an upper limit for the magnitude of the influence of exports on unemployment. The first regression on annual data for Belgium (1960 to 1993) gave the following result (*t*-statistics in parenthesis):

$$due_t = 0.12 + 0.90 \times due_{t-1} - 0.35 \times due_{t-2}$$
$$(1.04) \quad (5.02) \qquad\qquad (1.9)$$

standard error 0.6.

The second regression gave the following result:

$$\text{due}_t = 0.64 + 0.94 \times \text{due}_{t-1} - 0.41 \times \text{due}_{t-2} - 0.08 \times \text{dexp}_t - 0.01 \times \text{dexp}_{t-1}$$
$$(3.3) \quad (5.4) \qquad\qquad (2.6) \qquad\qquad (4.1) \qquad\qquad (0.3)$$

standard error 0.48.

One way to measure the influence of exports is to look at the part of the variability of unemployment that can be explained by export shocks. These results show that the standard deviation of the unemployment rate (after accounting for its own past) is 0.60 percentage points; introducing the best performing measure of exports performance (the change in real exports), it drops to 0.48 percentage points, or by about 21 percent. This means that for Belgium, export shocks had a nonnegligible but still rather small effect on unemployment. The coefficient on the contemporaneous change in exports implies that a 5-percentage-points increase in the growth rate of exports (say from 10 to 15 percent per annum) is, on average, associated with a drop in the Belgian unemployment rate of 0.4 percentage points (for example, from 10 to 9.6 percent). This result is actually quite similar to the impact found in studies that use complete macroeconomic models (see the following).

The Belgian case reveals one of the strongest effects found in the entire sample. For the other countries the contribution of export shocks to unemployment was minor. In the case of Denmark the weak correlation that actually appeared in one case (if one uses the export to GDP ratio) has the wrong sign, which would indicate that increases in export demand are associated with increases in unemployment and not with decreases. This correlation is likely to be spurious.

Table 3.1 also suggests that for most of the core countries (Germany, Belgium, and the Netherlands) trade has a significant influence on unemployment, at least if one looks mainly at the first four columns. At first sight this might contradict the perceived wisdom that these countries are best suited for EMU. However, a look at the individual regression results revealed that all cases give similar results, as the ones for Belgium show in the sense that only the coefficient on the contemporaneous change in exports ($ß_0$) was significant, whereas changes in exports one year earlier did not have an impact on unemployment. This contemporaneous correlation could reflect just the greater correlation in business cycles within this group of countries. The quarterly data used below confirms this interpretation.

The last four columns use two different measures of unemployment performance: The last two columns rely on the difference between national and EU average unemployment rates (to correct for any EU business cycle), and the two columns immediately preceding these use the change in the difference between national and EU-average unemployment because some tests indicate that the differences themselves are not stationary. The measures for export performance used with these dependent variables were then also somewhat different as outlined in the variable list at the bottom of Table 3.1. However, even a cursory glance at the last columns of this table shows that there are even fewer significant entries (and two positive signs) so that changing the dependent variable does not affect the conclusion that the impact of exports on unemployment is weak.[5]

The main problem with the annual data used so far is that the strongest correlation is contemporaneous. Could one obtain better results using quarterly data? In other words, do quarterly data reveal a significant causal relationship between changes in export volumes and changes in the level of employment or unemployment? The quarterly data should at least yield a clearer pattern over time. The following results show that this is true in the sense that the contemporaneous correlation is eliminated. However, in most other respects the results are similar to the ones obtained from annual data.

The first test examines the link between employment in manufacturing (index 1990 = 100, as reported by the IMF) and export volumes (index 1990 = 100, also from the IMF) using data from the first quarter of 1960 to the first quarter of 1994. (Changes were used again since preliminary tests indicated that both variables were nonstationary.) As in the causality tests using annual data, two equations were estimated for each of the ten countries. The first included (the change in) employment as the dependent variable to be explained by a constant, four lags of the dependent variable and three quarterly dummies. The second equation added eight lags of the change in export volumes to the righthand side.

The result was surprising: There is no evidence at all that shocks to exports influence employment. Only five individual coefficients turned out to be significant at the conventional statistical level of 5 percent. Given that the test involved ten countries and eight lags of the change in exports there were a total of eighty coefficients to be estimated. It is only expected that about four of them should turn out to be significant.

Moreover, the coefficients on past export performance—more often than not—take the wrong sign. The correlation between past changes in export volumes and present changes in employment levels should be positive—an increase in past exports should give rise to an increase in present employment. However, in three of the five cases of a "significant coefficient," one finds the reverse: An increase in past exports leads to a decrease in present employment. This is further evidence for the hypothesis that the significant coefficients are just due to chance.

Such a "non-" result is difficult to present. Table 3.2 summarizes the regression statistics for both equations, but only for those five countries for which at least one coefficient on lagged export growth is significant.[6] All the other countries do not even show a single significant coefficient on exports and an F-test did not lead to a rejection of the hypothesis that all coefficients are equal

TABLE 3.2

Change in *Employment* Rates as a Function of Their Own History and Past Changes in Export Volumes

| Country | Adjusted R^2 First Equation | Adjusted R^2 Second Equation | Significant Coefficient on Changes in Export Volumes | | | |
			Lag	Point Estimate	Standard Error	F-Test on All 8 Lags
U.S.	0.60	0.64	t-8	−0.018	0.006	2.77*
Japan	0.72	0.72	t-2	−0.014	0.007	1.02
Spain	0.33	0.32	t-8	0.015	0.006	1.13
France	0.51	0.53	t-5	−0.041	0.021	1.33**
NL	0.25	0.27	t-2	0.038	0.019	1.61*

Note: *significant at the 1 percent threshold; **significant at the 25 percent threshold.
Data source: IMF.

to zero. This result is even more surprising than the previous one concerning (economywide) unemployment since the manufacturing sector is usually equated with the tradable sector. Thus, it would seem that the "other factors" that affect changes in employment rates, beyond the autoregressive element coming from the past, are collectively far more important than shocks to exports.

The same approach was repeated using a (much shorter) series of quarterly (economywide) *un*employment data (reported by the European Commission) as the dependent variable and five lags of export performance. Five lags were sufficient since in no case was a lag beyond five significant when this dependent variable was used. This time, however, only the nine European countries for which data was easily available were considered: Belgium-Luxembourg, Denmark, Germany, France, Ireland, Italy, Spain, Portugal, and the United Kingdom. Table 3.3 reports the summary statistics for the only two countries that revealed a statistically significant relationship: France and Portugal.

These results are difficult to interpret because the sign of the coefficients is not what one would expect. A past increase in export volumes is followed by an *increase* in unemployment and not by a decrease. Moreover—with the exception of Portugal, for which we had only twenty-six observations—the increased explanatory power generated by adding lags of export performance is very small. Hence one should also consider these coefficients as representing spurious correlations (or put the theory of optimum currency areas on its head). Moreover, it perhaps bears repeating that in the case of the seven countries not included in Table 3.3 (Belgium-Luxembourg, Denmark, Germany, Ireland, Italy, Spain, and the United Kingdom) the F-statistics for the test of significance of lagged exports is equal to or below 1, indicating that there is

TABLE 3.3

Change in *Unemployment* Rates as a Function of Their Own History and Past Changes in Export Volumes (1983:1 to 1993:4)

Country	Adjusted R² First Equation	Adjusted R² Second Equation	Lag	Significant Coefficient on Changes in Export Volumes		
				Point Estimate	Standard Error	F-Test on All 5 Lags
France	0.93	0.94	t-3	0.023	0.010	1.13
Portugal	0.44	0.61	t-4	0.042	0.015	1.58**

Note: **significant at the 25 percent threshold.
Data source: IMF, European Commission.

no strong relationship (or, to be more precise, that one cannot reject the null hypothesis that changes in exports have no impact on unemployment).

All in all these results suggest that for most member states shocks to exports have not been a major factor in determining the evolution of unemployment (and employment) in the past. It is always very difficult to prove that a certain relationship does not exist, but given the similarity of the results using a number of different indicators of export demand, this finding is rather strong. Moreover, there is little reason to believe that this will change in the future. Hence there is little reason to believe that shocks to the demand for exports will lead to significant unemployment problems in member countries under EMU.

The influence of the exchange rate

The absence of a relationship between export earnings and (un)employment could be explained in a number of ways. A first objection would be that actual export shocks are determined by shocks to supply as well as demand. However, it is difficult to see why export supply should be subject to large shocks that act within one year or one quarter. The capital stock and even labor inputs move only slowly and technology does not make jumps. By contrast it is much easier to imagine reasons why export demand should be unstable: The business cycle abroad can move rapidly or tastes can change suddenly.

European labor markets are widely regarded as rigid, and this volume presents some evidence on their behavior in Chapter 2. This suggests that the nonresponsiveness of employment to external shocks is unsurprising: Employment may not respond to any shock if it is too difficult to hire and fire. Nevertheless, a simple test demonstrates that this interpretation is unwarranted. Belke and Gros (1997a) show that employment reacts strongly to investment shocks (as opposed to export shocks) when investment is substituted for exports in the estimated equations. Hence, it appears that labor markets are not too rigid to react to short-term shocks. Labor markets do react. It is just that their reactions to export shocks are too small to show up in the aggregate data.

Another argument could be that the absence of a clear relationship between unemployment and export shocks is due to a consistent strategy that systematically offsets the impact of export shocks by using some policy instrument, for example the exchange rate (or fiscal policy, see the following). In principle this policy effect could be taken into account, although the degree to which the exchange rate was used as an adjustment instrument varied enormously over the past thirty years. (The degree of wage flexibility might also have varied considerably, but—as is argued in Chapter 2—it is difficult to find any succinct measure of wage rigidity. This aspect was therefore not used in the empirical analysis presented here.) However, the crude tests on the annual data reported next suggest that the systematic use of the exchange rate or fiscal policy cannot have been responsible for the results so far.

Exchange rate adjustments should be incorporated in the analysis in order to accommodate for the possible objection that during part of the period used in this investigation (1963 to 1993) exchange rates were flexible. One way to test this conjecture is to add changes in the real exchange rate among the determinants of unemployment. Table 3.4 reports the results with annual data obtained using a similar approach as the one used to measure the importance of shocks to exports: The change of the real exchange rate is included among the variables, explaining changes in unemployment.

A general result is that innovations in the (real) exchange rate have not had a noticeable impact on unemployment. After taking past unemployment into account, the real exchange rate has a significant impact on unemployment only for the United Kingdom and Germany. In both cases a depreciation leads to a fall in unemployment, as one would expect. (The signs are different because the exchange rate of the pound is not reported as usual in terms of the number of the amount of domestic currency for one unit of foreign currency.) These results were obtained by adding actual changes in the real exchange rate as one of the determinants of unemployment. Using the nominal exchange rate would yield the same result, because for the time horizons and low inflation countries considered here, namely quarters and years, the nominal and the real exchange rate are highly correlated.

The use of actual exchange rate changes in this analysis measures more than the relevance of the exchange rate as a policy instrument. Under floating rates, exchange rates are determined by many factors and do not always move in the direction wanted by policymakers. The fluctuations of the Italian lira starting in 1992 are only one example. The results reported in Table 3.3 thus indicate that in general exchange rates are not a major policy instrument that has had a major impact on unemployment in the past. The argument that the exchange rate instrument was used until now to offset shocks to export de-

TABLE 3.4

Change in Unemployment as a Function of Its Own History, the Change in Real Exports, and the Change in Real Effective Exchange Rates

Country	Constant	Δ(Unemployment)		Δ(Real Exports)		Δ(REER)	
		1st lag	2nd lag	Contemp.	1st lag	Contemp.	1st lag
Belgium	0.6 (0.19)	0.91 (0.18)	-0.40 (0.16)	-0.08 (0.02)			
Denmark							
Germany		0.70 (0.19)		-0.05 (0.02)	0.05 (0.02)	-0.03 (0.02)	
Greece		0.86 (0.22)	-0.42 (0.02)	-0.03 (0.02)			
Spain		0.85 (0.23)					
France	0.44 (0.23)						
Ireland	1.25 (0.06)	0.57 (0.19)			-0.08 (0.05)		
Italy							
Netherlands	0.79 (0.34)	0.63 (0.21)		-0.14 (0.04)			
Portugal	0.52 (0.24)	0.44 (0.21)			-0.05 (0.02)		
United Kingdom		0.74 (0.18)			0.13 (0.05)		0.09 (0.03)

Note: This table summarizes results from regressions on annual data (1963 to 1993); only significant coefficients at the 5 percent level with a critical t-value of 1.71 are reported. The empty boxes indicate that the corresponding coefficient is not significant. Standard errors are in parentheses.

Data source: European Commission.

mand that would otherwise have resulted in unemployment is thus not supported by actual experience.

The small influence of exchange rates on unemployment is understandable if one takes into account that the ratio of exports to GDP in the larger EU member countries is between 20 and 25 percent and that many econometric estimates of the price elasticity of the demand for exports yield values around one half. These two numbers imply that a 10 percent depreciation (in real terms) increases GDP by approximately 1.25 percent. If one takes into account "Okun's law," which says that one needs around 3 percent growth in real income to reduce unemployment by 1 percentage point, it turns out that the reduction in unemployment that could be achieved by a 10 percent devaluation is only 0.3 to 0.45 percentage points. The model-based simulations reported in the next section confirm this order of magnitude. Unless they are very large, exchange rate changes are unlikely to have a strong impact on unemployment.

For smaller countries, the ratio of imports to GDP is usually much higher (except for Greece) so that a devaluation of the nominal exchange rate is likely to translate much less than one to one in a real devaluation, because the increase in input prices and a quicker pass-through to wages will increase the costs of exporters more quickly for these countries than for the larger countries. What proportion of a nominal devaluation translates actually into prices for tradable goods (which is to say, for export and import prices, as opposed to the consumer price index or wages) is actually very difficult to predict. During 1993—that is, after the 1992 devaluations—export prices of Italy and Spain expressed in a common currency fell relative to those of Germany by about 8 and 4 percent, respectively, although the nominal depreciation against the deutsche mark was in both cases about 20 percent. In the case of the United Kingdom, which also devalued by almost 20 percent, export prices actually increased relative to those of Germany by about 3 percent! It is thus not too surprising that the devaluation of the pound had little affect on the British current account whereas the Spanish and Italian current accounts improved strongly.[7] Even if the price elasticity of demand for exports were much higher than 0.5 percent there would thus be no guarantee that this would lead to a much larger effectiveness of the nominal exchange rate instrument if exporters chose to increase their prices by the amount of the depreciation.

Model simulations

The approach followed in this chapter has been totally astructural. Another strategy would be to impose as much structure as possible by using a large model of the economy that allows one to calculate exactly the impact of a shock to export demand on output and other variables.

One example of this approach can be found in CEC (1990). They use a large econometric model of the European Community (called Quest) that incorporates short-run wage rigidity, which is at the base of the theory of optimum currency areas. Simulations with this model suggest that a 5 percent shock to French export demand causes French output to fall by about 1.3 percent in the first year (it returns to baseline only by year seven) if exchange rates are fixed. Under flexible exchange rates the initial fall in output amounts to 0.6 percent. But since the subsequent recovery is slower, the difference in present values of the GDP loss between fixed and flexible exchange rates is about 1.3 percent. Recent simulations with the MULTIMOD model of the IMF confirm the result in the sense that the fall in output resulting from an exogenous fall in exports of 5 percent is about 0.5 percent of GDP higher under fixed exchange rates than under flexible ones.

The OCA approach (and this chapter) focuses on the impact of external shocks on unemployment as opposed to output. However, these two variables are closely linked. For most countries the standard Okun curve-type relationship translates a fall in GDP of 1 percent into an increase in unemployment of about 0.3 to 0.5 percent (in the short run).

Is a fall in export demand of 5 percent a realistic magnitude for an external shock? Emerson et al. (1990) report that the standard deviation of export demand shocks is about 2.5 percent. If they were normally distributed (as usually assumed in econometric work) a 5 percent shock (up or down) should occur only once every twenty years.[8] Hence this magnitude can be taken to represent a shock that would be large by historical standards and not too frequent.

This implies that the difference between flexible and fixed rates for a rather large shock would be an increase of 0.2 to 0.3 percentage points in the unemployment rate (during the first year). Is this large? Compared to unemployment rates of above 10 percent in the EU at present this would be an increase in the number of unemployed of only 2 to 3 percent. External shocks would have to be unusually large under EMU to have a substantial impact on unemployment.

Types of shocks and the "beggar thy neighbor" effect of the exchange rate

The results so far indicate that the standard shocks considered in the OCA literature (that is, shocks to export demand) do not have a major impact on the evolution of unemployment in Europe and that fixing exchange rates is not likely to make a large difference in this respect. Are there other types of shocks, which are empirically more important for unemployment, that could be better managed with flexible exchange rates? For example, shocks to investment apparently have strong effects on employment, and it is often argued that a major asymmetric demand shock like German unification did require an exchange rate adjustment.[9]

This argument goes beyond the "optimum currency area" as it has been discussed so far. In particular one has to keep in mind that exchange rate adjustments for demand management purposes shift demand from one country to another and are thus always, at least partially, "beggar thy neighbor." In order to decide whether it is in the interest of "Europe" to use (intra-European) exchange rates to offset domestic demand shocks, one has to take this aspect into account. The real issue is thus the optimal exchange rate policy from the point of view of the welfare of the system. This issue cannot be addressed with the usual one country models (which prescribe an exchange rate adjustment in response to any internal shock, demand, supply, or other). One has to use a two-country model.

Gros and Lane (1994) use a standard two-country model with short-run wage rigidity to analyze optimal exchange rate policy in the presence of supply and demand shocks. They find that the Pareto optimum (which happens to coincide with the Nash equilibrium) is to let the exchange rate move in response to both shocks, but only if there are foreign shocks. This result implies that if two countries have a similar structure, so that shocks to the relative price of the goods they produce are unlikely, asymmetric shocks to domestic demand or supply are not a reason to keep exchange rates flexible. Different models might lead to slightly different results, but the basic intuition is likely to be robust to changes in the particular model used: From the point of view of the system, there is no need to use exchange rates to distribute the impact of local shocks to demand if countries produce and consume the same goods.

This argument that at the global level the effects of exchange rate changes on demand net out to zero does not apply to shocks that affect trade directly. If demand shifts from one country to another, an exchange rate adjustment is required from the point of view of both. Hence fluctuations in exports are the main source of shocks that should be taken into account to ascertain the importance of exchange rate flexibility from a global point of view. Other legitimate sources of shocks would be external shocks (like an oil price change) that have differential effects because of differences in the importance of energy.

By contrast, one could imagine the case of a country that experiences a sudden fall in domestic demand because households suddenly save more. A depreciation would shift demand toward domestic goods and increase exports, thus reducing the unemployment that would otherwise result from the drop in demand. However, the "gain" in demand of the country experiencing the shock would come at the expense of the rest of the world. The country that depreciates would only export its unemployment problems. From a global point of view, little would be gained from exchange rate flexibility in this case.

But where do macroeconomic shocks come from? It is likely that policy itself is a source of shocks. Policy shocks—which is to say changes in fiscal or other economic policies—affect overall demand and thus also the exchange rate, as could be observed in the case of the U.S. dollar during the 1980s. However, policy shocks are not unavoidable, and as argued above, it is not always clear that in this case an exchange rate adjustment is a desirable consequence from a global point of view.

It is difficult to imagine in concrete terms economywide shocks that are driven by sudden changes in technology or tastes. While there might be sudden changes at the sectoral level, experience indicates that these fundamental determinants of the economy tend to change slowly at the aggregate level, which should give prices and wages enough time to adjust to maintain equilibrium. For example, the rise in the importance of the automobile industry or the decline of railways took decades. These secular changes certainly caused severe adjustment problems, but the argument that adjustments in the real exchange rate can be achieved quicker through changes in the nominal exchange rate loses its significance for trends that work over a decade or more.

Why care about exchange rates?

If exchange rates cannot be used to cure unemployment problems and if the exchange rate is not really necessary for most member countries to adjust to external shocks, as argued so far, it is necessary to ask: Why do politicians care at all about the exchange rate? As explained in the introduction, exchange rates can remain politically important even if their macroeconomic impact is minor because they can have a strong impact on profits (especially if prices and quantities change little). But EMU could still be important even if the level of the exchange rate is less important than generally believed because of another element, one that is not captured by the OCA approach. The suppression of exchange rate volatility that comes with EMU could also have an impact on the performance of the economy at home. In particular governments are (and will continue to be) held responsible for the state of the labor market, which can be decisive for elections. The position important pressure groups, such as trade unions, take concerning EMU will also depend more on labor market implications of exchange rate variability than on its effect on the volume of trade.

Support for EMU should thus depend on the (perceived) impact exchange rate variability has on employment and unemployment. Given the results found here, one would assume *a priori* that it should be minor. But this assumption is probably wrong, as shown by Belke and Gros (1997b). It is not possible to present the evidence for all member countries, but it is instructive to show the influence of exchange rate variability on the labor market at least for one key country, namely Germany. Belke and Gros (1997b) show that similar results can be obtained for most other countries as well. A simple causality-type analysis shows that exchange rate variability does have a significant impact on unemployment and job creation in Germany. It bears emphasizing that the results reported here suggest that short-term (month-to-month) variability of intra-European exchange rates of the deutsche mark has a negative impact on job creation and tends to increase unemployment. No similar effect was found for the level of the deutsche mark exchange rate.

This final series of causality tests examine the influence of the variability of the deutsche mark exchange rate (against the currencies of the seven other original members of the ERM: Belgium-Luxembourg, Denmark, France, Ireland, Italy, and the Netherlands) on two key labor market indicators: changes

in unemployment and employment growth. Only European exchange rates are
used because only their variability could be suppressed by EMU. These countries also represent the most likely early candidates for membership in EMU.
The initial ERM candidates were used because when the European Monetary
System (EMS) was created, politicians used to emphasize the gains from exchange rate stability.

The results reported in Table 3.5 are again standard causality tests on annual
data. The exchange rate variability of the deutsche mark was measured by
taking, for each year, the standard deviation of the twelve month-to-month
changes in the logarithm of the nominal exchange rate of the deutsche mark
against the currencies of the countries mentioned above. These seven standard
deviations were then aggregated in one composite measure of exchange rate
variability, weighting them by the weights of the countries in the ECU (which
correspond approximately to their weights in terms of GDP).

Since the unemployment rate in Germany was found to be nonstationary,
the analysis was performed using the changes in the unemployment rate. The
nature of the results can be seen by looking at a simple OLS regression of the
change in unemployment on its own past (two lags, t-1 and t-2) and the measure of exchange rate variability during the previous year over the period 1971
to 1995. The results are reported in Table 3.5.

TABLE 3.5
Exchange rate variability and the German Labor Market

Explanatory variables	Dependent variables: (percentage change)	
	Unemployment rate	Occupation
Constant	-0.45 (2.6)	1.66 (5.7)
Lag t-1	0.72 (4.6)	0.79 (5.6)
Lag t-2	-0.52 (3.5)	-0.54 (4.5)
Exchange rate variability (t-1)	0.60 (3.7)	-1.3 (5.3)
Adjusted R^2	0.66	0.78
Mean of dependent variable	0.23	1.34
Standard error of regression	0.41	0.63
Durbin-Watsin	1.71	2.05
F-statistic	16.3	29.22

Note: Standard errors are in parentheses.
Source: Gros (1996b).

These results show that exchange rate variability has a significant impact on unemployment. Given that only one lag of exchange rate variability turned out to be important, the *t*-statistics demonstrate the significance of the effect. The value of 3.7 is highly significant in the sense that there is only one chance in one thousand to find this effect if it does not exist in reality. The point estimate implies that a reduction in the variability measure by 1 percentage point reduces unemployment after one year by 0.6 percent. Formally, one could argue that EMU, which would eliminate (intra-European) exchange rate variability, could reduce unemployment by about 1 percentage point if the starting level of variability is about 1.5 percent per month. Even compared to the German unemployment rate of 9 percent reached in 1995, this is still a significant contribution.

A similar story emerges through the tests on the rate of employment creation (defined as the percentage change in the number of employed persons). A simple OLS regression of this variable on its own past and on exchange rate variability during the previous year produced the results reported in Table 3.5.

Exchange rate variability again has a significant impact on the German labor market since the *t*-statistic on that estimated coefficient is over 5, implying that the likelihood of obtaining this result by chance is less than one in 1000. The point estimate implies that the increase in exchange rate variability in 1995, which increased the standard deviation of the deutsche mark rate from 0.6 in 1994 to about 1.5 in 1995, should lower, *ceteris paribus*, the rate of employment growth in 1996 by almost 1.5 percentage points; this would be equivalent to about half a million jobs lost.

The results presented so far can, of course, be criticized on the grounds that exchange rate variability merely represents some other variable that is the true driving force behind (un)employment. For example, it is conceivable that intra-European exchange rates become variable when the deutsche mark is strong (or when the dollar is weak) so the link between exchange rate variability and (un)employment reflects only a more fundamental influence of the overvaluation of the deutsche mark on the German labor market. Alternatively, it is also possible that variability arises as other EMS countries struggle to avoid matching German interest rate rises. Belke and Gros (1997b) consider a wide range of possibilities by adding a number of control variables to their equation. However, they find that the introduction of such controls does not alter their basic findings: Exchange rate variability retains a statistically significant—and economically nonnegligible—independent impact on employment and unemployment. Moreover, this result can be found for most member countries, and not just Germany.

The results of this section suggest not only that the cost of abandoning the exchange rate instrument have been overrated but also that eliminating exchange rate variability could have substantial positive effects on its own.

EMU and Labor Mobility

The introduction already mentioned the important place accorded to labor mobility in the OCA approach. However, this view looks only at labor flows as a short-run adjustment mechanism and does not take into account that concentration of industry and hence pronounced core periphery patterns are more likely to emerge when labor mobility is high. But since most studies concur that labor mobility is low in Europe—not only across countries but also across regions within countries (Decressin and Fatás, 1995), always compared to the United States—there should be less concentration in Europe than in the United States.

Some authors have used this line of thought to arrive at a sort of Catch-22: So long as labor mobility is low in Europe, EMU is costly because labor mobility is needed to offset asymmetric shocks. However, so the argument goes, if labor mobility were to increase (possibly because EMU comes anyway) concentration would increase and hence the likelihood of asymmetric shocks would also increase, again making EMU costly. The suggested conclusion is that heads, EMU is impossible and tails, it is undesirable. A more proper conclusion would seem to be that labor mobility is perhaps less crucial for EMU than previously thought: Although labor mobility allows for a quicker adjustment to shocks, it also favors concentration of industry and hence increases the potential for asymmetric shocks. However, since labor mobility is usually assumed to be important, it is still useful to take a look at the data, which do not always yield the results that are commonly expected.

International versus interregional mobility

As mentioned in Chapter 2, it is a commonly accepted proposition that labor mobility in Europe is very low in absolute terms and when compared to the United States. A corollary is that the potential costs of EMU should be high. However, this corollary is not entirely warranted. Although an increase in wage flexibility is desirable for all the reasons set down in Chapter 2, the low absolute level of migration between member states does not make wage flexibility any more desirable. As argued above, the key consideration for the theory of optimum currency areas is the difference between interregional labor mobility within countries and labor mobility across countries, and not the absolute levels. This comparison has not been documented systematically because of the absence of reliable statistical material.

That situation is now changing, and the data now available do not confirm the widely held notion of relatively low international labor mobility—where the term relatively means in comparison with intranational (or interregional) labor mobility. In 1992 almost 2.2 million immigrants came to the member states of the EU (equivalent to about 0.7 percent of the population). And it appears (these data are less reliable) that emigration was more than 1 million lower than immigration. This can be compared to the United States where the average net immigration was about 800,000 on average per annum during 1986 to 1991 (about 0.4 percent of population), lower than that of the EU in 1992.

If one wants to judge whether the observed level of migration in the EU indicates a degree of labor mobility that is so low that asymmetric shocks in an EMU will lead to serious problems, interregional migration within member states provides a useful reference point.[10] Table 3.6 therefore shows the most recent available data on immigration from the rest of the world as a percentage of the overall population and the percentage of the population that moved between regions within the country. Given that the data on emigration are much more partial, only the data on immigration will be discussed below.[11]

The total number of immigrants arriving in EU countries, about 2.3 million, is below the number of interregional migrants, about 3.1 million. However, the orders of magnitude are similar. International migration amounts to more than two-thirds of the interregional migration. One can also compare the (un-weighted) averages of the populations that move across national and regional borders. Interregional migration amounted on average to 0.89 percent of population, whereas international migration was equal to 0.67 percent, again more than two-thirds of the intranational level.

Hence it appears that contrary to what economists have so far assumed, interregional and international migration are of a similar order of magnitude in Europe. What conclusions can be drawn from this? While interregional migration within member states is insufficient to make them optimum currency areas, it is possible to conclude that—for a given importance of asymmetric shocks—a monetary union for the EU should not create any more problems than the monetary unions coinciding with existing nation states create at the regional level, provided that international migrants are flexible in the choice of their country of destination.

TABLE 3.6
Migration in the European Union 15

Type of Migration	Percent of population	Thousands of persons
International	0.67	2,356
Interregional	0.89	3,313

Note: International migration is immigration *into* member states; interregional migration is *within* member states. Immigration into Sweden, Finland, Luxembourg, Ireland, Greece, Denmark (all countries for which no data on interregional migration is available) was equal to 186.9 thousands.

Source: Eurostat.

Can labor mobility be a substitute for real wage adjustments?

The usual line of reasoning is quite simple: In EMU unemployment will arise if an external shock hits a given country or region because nominal wages usually do not adjust quickly enough to reestablish equilibrium on the labor market. It is then argued that if all the unemployed leave (and go to the country/region that experiences the mirror image, or positive side of the same shock), there will be no problem. However, this argument is too simple because it neglects the fact that those who leave also reduce the demand for domestic products. Emigration of the unemployed shifts the demand for labor again downward. In other words, there will be a second round of unemployment at the (by assumption) fixed nominal wage.

A simple graph can illustrate this idea easily. Figure 3.1 represents the usual model of the labor market: Labor supply is fixed at N^s (for example, at a constant share of the total population) and labor demand, N^d, is the usual function of the real wage (on the vertical axis). Initially equilibrium is attained at the full employment level N^s. An external demand shock is assumed to shift the labor demand schedule to the left. If real wages cannot adjust, labor demand drops to N' and there is unemployment equal to $N^s - N'$.

Apparently the unemployment problem could be solved if the unemployed emigrated until N^s drops to N'. However, this reasoning neglects that the labor demand curve depends not only on the real wage rate but also on the level of overall demand. Since the unemployed receive unemployment benefits (or some other sort of income) that allow them to maintain their spending close to that of the employed, they also contribute to domestic demand so long as they stay at home. If they emigrate, the domestic demand curve for labor will again shift to the left, thus aggravating the fall in employment that occurred in the first round. At the given wage rate, this leads to more unemployment and hence more emigration. This circle will not continue forever, however, because the induced shift in labor demand should be smaller than the original one.

By how much should the demand for labor curve move down if the unemployed leave? Should it move at all? With the assumption of fixed nominal wages in a Keynesian environment, a lot will depend on other parts of the model, especially the consumption function (including the way in which the government budget constraint is taken into account) and the proportion of consumption of domestic, perhaps nontradable, goods. While the strength of the effect is not clear, it should be clear that labor mobility can magnify the impact of external disturbances on output.

The contribution of labor mobility to adjustment

It is apparent that people move much more often in the United States than in Europe. However, what matters in the context of discussions about EMU is

75

Figure 3.1
The Labor Market

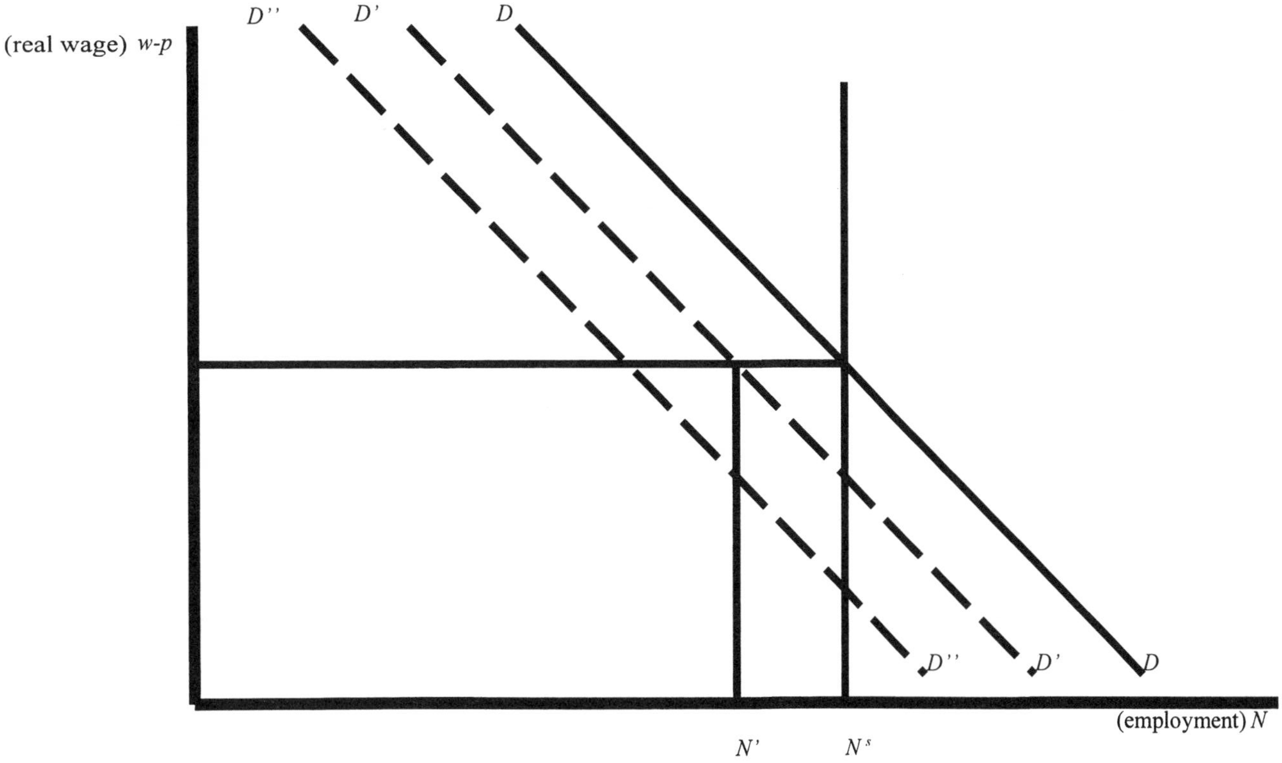

(real wage) *w-p*

D

D'

D''

D

D'

D''

N'   *N^s*

(employment) *N*

the extent to which net movements react to local unemployment. It is surprising to note how little hard evidence exists on this point. The most widely cited study is Eichengreen (1993), who compares the reaction of interregional migration to local unemployment and wages in the United States, United Kingdom, and Italy. He finds that net immigration to any of the nine census regions indeed reacts to unemployment in the previous period, however, the effect is rather imprecisely estimated since the *t*-statistic is only 1.92.[12] The point estimate (-0.37) implies that net immigration would fall only by 0.0825 percentage points if the average unemployment for the United States is 8 percent and if it increases in any region from this level to 10 percent. If migrants have the same family composition and activity rates as the local population, the change in migration would thus be equivalent to 4 percent of the *increase* in unemployment.[13]

Blanchard and Katz (1992) report a much stronger reaction of migration to unemployment. They estimate that a negative shock to employment in any "average" U.S. state is offset within one period by about 60 percent through migration. The problem with their approach is, however, that they do not use any data on migration; instead they calculate implicit migration effects from their data on employment, unemployment, and participation rates.

Blanchard and Katz argue that migration must account for most of the adjustment to shocks to employment in the United States since they find that a 1 percent shock to employment in a given state is followed typically by a 0.3 percent increase in the unemployed and a very small (0.05 percent) decrease in labor force participation. Blanchard and Katz claim that migration must account for the difference, that is, 65 percent of the total adjustment. This interpretation implies that if General Motors fires 100 workers, 65 of them (which is to say, those who do not find a new job the same year) leave the region within one year or substitute for other workers who leave the state (or substitute potential immigrants). This is difficult to believe even for the United States. If it were true, trade unions should incorporate expected migration into their wage demands and so render wages more flexible.

The finding of Blanchard and Katz is also difficult to accept because it runs counter to many other studies on the U.S. labor market, which generally find, as reported in Greenwood (1975, 1985), that unemployment is *not* an important factor in explaining migration flows. This discrepancy might be due to the fact that Blanchard and Katz do not use any direct data on migration, but calculate migration as a residual from data on the labor force, employment, and unemployment. Since these data come from different sources, it is likely that some of their coefficients pick up the inconsistencies in the data (that is, measurement errors) that are strongly correlated with the other variables. Since migration is captured as the residual, the estimated effects of an unemployment shock concern the inconsistencies in the data plus any real migration that takes place.[14]

Reasons for low labor mobility in Europe

It is often argued that international labor mobility is (and will remain) low in Europe because of cultural and social barriers. However, why should inter-regional labor mobility also be rather low? One reason might be the labor market and the fact that once income exceeds a certain threshold, people are no longer willing to incur the psychological cost of moving as suggested by Faini (1994). But this cannot be a full explanation because there is also considerable variation among member states in the rate of domestic migration between regions.

One factor that is often overlooked is the housing market. The most important pecuniary (and perhaps also psychological) cost of moving for most people is that it involves a change of housing. In countries where this market is not flexible, this factor might be decisive. Making the housing market more flexible could thus be as important as a reform of the labor market in preparing for EMU.

For example, Figure 3.2 shows that there are large differences among member countries in the rate of interregional migration—which ranges from 0.4 percent in Italy to almost 1.6 percent in the United Kingdom. What could cause large differences in the rate of interregional migration? The size of regions as defined by Eurostat is similar across countries and should not be a decisive factor.

Differences in unemployment rates and wages should constitute the main incentive for migration. The main obstacle (at least within one country) to mobility should be rigidities in the housing and labor markets. The more flexible such markets are the easier it should be for people to move. However, housing and labor are the most heavily regulated markets in most member states. As suggested in Chapter 2, the overall degree of flexibility of the labor market is almost impossible to measure consistently across countries. For the housing market, the possibility exists by using data on the proportion of households that own their homes. The higher this proportion, the more difficult it will be for people to move, because it is usually much easier and cheaper to change between rented accommodations than to sell a home and buy another one.

Figure 3.2 shows that there is indeed a strong correlation between the rate of interregional migration and the proportion of houses occupied by their owners. The more people own the place they live in, the less significant is labor mobility. This figure also suggests that the United Kingdom constitutes an outlier in the sense that there is more interregional movement in the United Kingdom than one would expect, given the rather high rate of owner occupancy. A regression that included the United Kingdom gave a negative coefficient with a *t*-statistic of 2.5. The regression line shown in the figure does not include the United Kingdom.

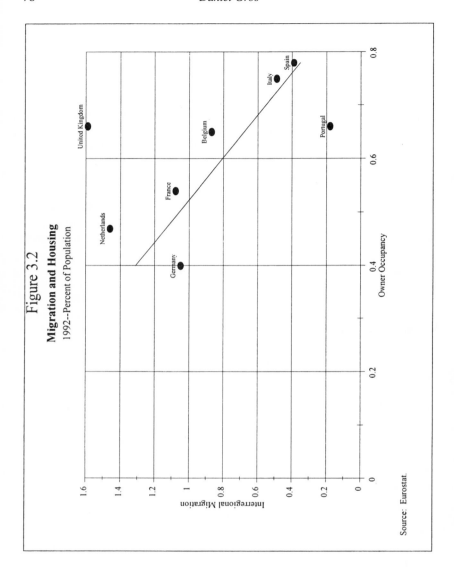

Figure 3.2

Migration and Housing

1992--Percent of Population

Source: Eurostat.

One possible explanation for the higher rates of migration and lower dispersion of unemployment in the United Kingdom might be that the reforms under
Thatcher have made the labor market much more flexible. Until only five years
ago, the dispersion in regional unemployment was much higher in the United
Kingdom (data on migration for the past is more difficult to obtain). Moreover,
the housing market is much more flexible in the United Kingdom than on the

continent, where rules on the proportion of the home value that can be obtained through a mortgage are much tighter and where the real estate sales taxes are typically about 20 percent of the sale value.

Conclusions

The main empirical finding of this chapter is that unemployment in the past was not influenced in a significant way by shocks to export demand and by changes in the exchange rate. This suggests that the standard argument that EMU will lead to more unemployment because asymmetric shocks could no longer be offset through exchange rate changes is empirically less important than often thought.

International labor movements in the EU (especially immigration from third countries) have now increased to a point were they are of a comparable order of magnitude as interregional migration within member countries. EMU should thus not be more difficult to manage than the existing monetary unions in Europe that member states represent. Reducing barriers to labor mobility remains, of course, desirable at any rate. Making housing markets more flexible could contribute considerably to this goal.

All in all, the results of this chapter suggest that the way in which the optimum currency area approach has been used in the literature on EMU is either conceptually or empirically flawed.

Notes

1. The regional dimension is often overlooked in discussions about EMU because it has to be assumed that the alternative to EMU is the continuing existence of national currencies, and not the introduction of regional currencies. However, most European regions are of a similar size as the average states of the United States, which are often compared to member countries.

2. A somewhat different approach can be found in De Grauwe and Vanhaverbeke (1993) who analyze the variability of real exchange rates across regions and countries. The finding that real exchange rates vary significantly more across countries than across regions within a country is difficult to interpret: Is it due to an excess volatility of exchange rates or are there large asymmetric shocks (policy or other) that provoke this exchange rate variability?

3. One could thus argue that the high correlations found for the core countries are probably an underestimate of the correlations that would result under EMU (that is, with a unified monetary policy). Moreover, it cannot be excluded that some of the countries that had lower correlations in the past would actually belong to the core once they also belong to EMU.

4. This table basically reports the result from a fishing trip. For more details see Gros and Jones (1995).

5. In the case of Spain, the notation $-/+$ means an increase in real exports first reduces unemployment and then increases it, with the net effect equal to zero. However, these cases of a significant wrong sign should be discounted—along with some of the weaker coefficients of the correct (meaning, expected) sign. Given the number of regressions that are behind the table (eleven countries using eight proxies for export demand), it is surprising that there are not more cases of spurious correlation.

6. The main result of the causality test on quarterly data of employment in manufacturing can be stated briefly: A significant relationship between (changes in) export volumes and (changes in) *employment* appears for only five of the ten countries examined: the United States, Japan, Spain, France, and the Netherlands. The countries that failed to reveal a significant causal relationship were Germany, Denmark, Italy, Ireland, Portugal, Sweden, Finland, and Austria. Table 3.2 shows the results for the five countries with at least one significant coefficient. The results in Table 3.2 are striking for two reasons. The first is that even for the countries selected for the greatest influence of exports, the adjusted R-squared increases only marginally with the introduction of lagged changes in export volumes among the explanatory variables. For those countries not included in this table (Germany, Denmark, Italy, Ireland, and Portugal), the adjusted R-squared fell when the eight lags of export changes were introduced so that the F-statistic should be below 1. Hence we did not bother to report the details of these regressions.

7. For a more detailed comparison of the effects of the 1992 devaluations see Gros (1996a).

8. For a more general distribution of the shocks, one can still say that the probability of a shock of more than two standard deviations must be smaller than one-fourth.

9. This episode is instructive because it can be used both as an argument for EMU and for greater flexibility of exchange rates. The standard argument is that after 1990, an overheating of domestic demand threatened price stability in Germany, which forced the Bundesbank to adopt a very tight monetary policy. Since other EMS member countries, notably France, did not have the same problem, the optimal solution would have been to have lower interest rates in France than in Germany. This would have been compatible with a step appreciation of the deutsche mark followed by a gradual depreciation (or greater exchange rate flexibility). But one could also argue that if EMU had already existed, the policy of the European Central Bank would have been based on average areawide inflation and its monetary policy would have been less restrictive.

10. The most recent available data on this are for the period from 1990 to 1992, but it appears that interregional migration within member states has been rather stable over the past decade.

11. For interregional movements within member states, emigrants equal immigrants by assumption. One should also keep in mind that the national definitions of what constitutes an immigrant (or migrant) vary greatly.

12. However, the constant term in his equation is rather precisely estimated (t-statistic of 5.76) and indicates that immigration each year amounts to about 1.1 percent of the population of the region if the region has the same wage rate and unemployment rate as the average for the entire United States. The constant term is about ten times higher for the United States than for the United Kingdom.

13. Bayoumi and Prasad (1995) analyze the behavior of sectoral employment in some member states and U.S. regions. They find that most of the shocks to employment are industry specific in both the United States and European countries, but they chose to interpret the same result differently: For the United States this result is taken to indicate a high degree of labor mobility because wages are also mostly affected by industry-specific shocks, whereas in Europe this result is taken as an indication of low labor mobility because shocks to wages are mostly country specific.

14. However, the Blanchard and Katz approach seems to have internal difficulties that become apparent once one applies the same methodology to a European country. As an illustrative example, I replicated the Blanchard and Katz methodology using data from Germany (relative to the EU average). The trivariate system (percentage change in employment, employment rate, and participation rate, of Germany relative to the United States) seems to work well. It yields a sort of "Okun coefficient" of about 0.33, similar to the one found by Blanchard and Katz for the average U.S. state. Moreover, and this is crucial, the reaction of the labor force participation rate to employment shocks is larger than in the United States, but still moderate: A fall in employment of 1 percent leads to a fall in participation of 0.39 percent in the first year. The "implicit" migration would thus be for Germany 0.28 (the result of $1 - 0.33 - 0.39$). This is still too high to be believable. The dynamics of the system implies that after three years, the loss of employment has increased to 2 percent, unemployment has increased only to 0.42 percent (its peak), and labor force participation has fallen by a cumulative 1.2 percent, meaning that 38 percent of the number initially fired should have emigrated in the meantime.

4

Fiscal Deficit Reductions in Line with the Maastricht Criteria for Monetary Union: An Empirical Analysis

A. J. Hughes Hallett and Peter McAdam[1]

The Maastricht Treaty requires participants in a European Monetary Union to achieve, or at least to show satisfactory progress toward achieving, an upper limit of 3 percent of GNP for their fiscal deficits. Similarly participants should achieve a limit of 60 percent for the debt to GNP ratios.

The EU member countries have, until now, shown very little fiscal discipline, whatever the difficulty of their monetary discipline. They are all currently outside one limit or the other, although in the past year they have made increasingly desperate efforts to control their deficits. Nevertheless, in 1995, the average deficit remained at about 5 percent of GNP, with none less than 3 percent, and some as high as 11 percent of GNP.[2] Similarly the average debt level was around 75 percent of GNP, with none lower than 50 percent and some as high as 135 percent. This raises the obvious question: What would happen if these fiscal criteria were enforced? Could a core monetary union ever be formed? How much deflation would be necessary? Would the worst violators also be able to make it into monetary union with a reasonable amount of their economies intact? How would the deficit ratios be reduced? What kind of fiscal policy is needed, and does it need to be coordinated with changes in monetary policy in order to reduce the costs of deflation? And last, but not at all least, is there a danger that countries can arrange to satisfy these criteria so that they may join EMU, but then fail to hold their deficits within the required ratios so that they place that union at risk thereafter? The latter implies a lack of discipline *after* EMU has started, a prospect that worries German policymakers a great deal (De Grauwe, 1996).

It is important to investigate these issues because the fiscal criteria now represent the main precondition (or stumbling block) for entry into monetary union. If they are not satisfied, or if countries cannot accept the adjustment costs of getting themselves into the condition in which they are satisfied, then monetary union may never take place. These criteria are also important because both the German constitutional court and the German parliament have said that they will not permit Germany to enter or participate in EMU if members do not satisfy the fiscal criteria laid down at Maastricht[3]—and one suspects the Bundesbank has said the same. Furthermore, an EMU without Germany is no EMU.

Many commentators have argued that the fiscal criteria are important because excessive fiscal expansions have contributed to Europe's recent economic instability and the collapse of the European exchange rate mechanism (ERM). Governments have become concerned with preventing overexpansion biases, higher interest rates, and the risk of a fiscal bailout within the EMU context. It is therefore important to look at the alternative. This we do by simulating a variety of contractionary fiscal rules, through a multicountry econometric model of the G7 economies, to assess the consequences and importance of attempting to impose the Maastricht criteria. In the past some papers have focused on the implications of imposing the debt criterion, but few have looked at the consequences of meeting the deficit criteria.[4]

By contrast, here we focus entirely on the question of imposing deficit ratios of 3 percent of GNP. Focusing on the imposition of deficit ratios seems sensible since to reduce debt ratios would require a reduction in deficit levels in any case. Moreover the political debate has shifted to (and will continue to focus on) deficit limits, in recognition that achieving the 60 percent debt limit might prove too destructive. We find that the real difficulty actually lies in the transitional cost to *permanently* lower deficits. It is not so hard to get the level of the deficits down if you can accept the associated deflations, but it is often much harder to hold them down when the debt ratio is not achieved at the same time. Such a finding signals a conflict between the two fiscal criteria that can only be fixed by a change in the policy mix, and in tax and revenue policies. The cost of doing this is not so much in output losses and price deflations, but in large increases in the tax burden. That can realistically only be funded through increases in the growth rate.

The Simulation Framework

To explore the implications of greater fiscal discipline empirically, we have relied upon one of the most widely used multicountry econometric models—the IMF's MULTIMOD—which contains linked models for each of the G7 economies (the United States, Japan, Canada, Germany, France, Italy, and the United Kingdom). It also contains fully specified models for the smaller European Community (EC) economies as a bloc (the "rest of the EMS") and for the rest of the OECD as a bloc.[5] There are also models for OPEC and for the developing countries in Africa, Asia, and Latin America. Each of these national or regional models is linked to the others through bilateral trade flows, capital movements, and exchange rates that in turn influence domestic financial markets.

The model

MULTIMOD is an annual multicountry econometric model. The model's specification explains the main expenditure categories and production flows in each country, from which employment, investment, prices, interest rates, and exchange rates are determined. Financial markets, trade flows, and capital movements (including loans and interest payments) are included. Trade is divided into three markets: oil, primary commodities, and manufactured goods. The oil market contains an exogenous real price, demand driven by activity levels in each country, and supplies that clear the market. Perfectly flexible prices clear the commodity markets, where demands are driven by activity levels and supplies by prices and a predetermined capacity. Manufactured goods are produced and traded everywhere. Aggregate demand is then built up from consumption (based on current and expected future earnings, and asset values), investment (based on market evaluations of firms' current and expected future earnings), trade, and the net fiscal position. This determines output in the short run. Note that since assets incorporate the stock of capital and government bonds, as well as net foreign assets, human capital will be constrained to cover discounted future tax liabilities. In this way the credibility effects of fiscal consolidation are included. As a result, the model embodies near-Ricardian equivalence. That said, potential output is determined by a production function so capacity utilization (the ratio of actual to potential output) can vary. Domestic output prices are subject to a Phillips curve, and there is no absolute output constraint. In fact prices change by an amount depending on both the remaining spare capacity and the state of the labor markets. Prices are therefore partly sticky and partly forward-looking, depending on wage contracts, international competitiveness, and capacity utilization. This gives the potential for a trade-off between price flexibility and output losses derived from supply-side responses.

In the government sector, non-ERM exchange rates are determined by open interest parities and *expected* depreciations consistent with a complete model solution. The non-German ERM rates, however, are obliged to stay within a ±2.25 percent band around preassigned parity values. Monetary policy for ERM members, therefore, consists of forcing interest rates to follow a reaction function that targets the given deutsche mark (DM) parity and maintains the currency within its band. For other countries, and for Germany, a preassigned monetary growth rate is targeted, with interest rates set to gradually reduce the gap between actual and targeted money growth. Similarly, tax rates adjust to eliminate the gap between actual and targeted debt levels, subject to an intertemporal budget constraint. Fiscal expenditures are therefore also partly exogenous and partly endogenous.[6] A full description of MULTIMOD's properties and simulation characteristics is given in Masson et al. (1990, 1991), and comparisons with other models in Bryant et al. (1993). Hughes Hallett and Ma (1992) review a number of sensitivity tests of the model's simulation properties.

The baseline information set

The simulations that follow estimate all work from a baseline composed of the historical values of the model's variables, plus projections forward to some terminal period. In this case the projections run forward thirty-one years from our start date of 1995 and are identical to those used in the IMF's annual report *World Economic Outlook* for 1994. The model is solved sufficiently far ahead so as to remove any influence of the terminal conditions from our results. We simulate the period 1995 to 2025 inclusive. In those simulations the forward-looking expectations are solved to be equal to the outcome projected for the relevant future period. This baseline therefore defines our information set, except insofar as we have had to model the unification of Germany explicitly and that the model's assumed deficit/GNP ratios have been replaced by constant 1995 values.[7]

Finally, each ERM country is obliged to accept its official 1990 parity against the deutsche mark and to maintain its 2.25 percent band around that for the duration of the simulation (1993 to 2023). However Italy and the United Kingdom *are* allowed to realign their currencies down during 1992, from DM 1.33 ± 2.25 percent to 0.993 ± 2.25 percent per 1,000 lira, and from DM 2.95 ± 2.25 percent to 2.43 ± 2.25 percent per pound, roughly as happened. But, for the purposes of this chapter, both currencies are required to stay within a narrow band ERM system after 1992. France, of course, is allowed no realignments; we retain 3.35 ± 2.25 percent francs per deutsche mark throughout.

The Simulation Exercises

This exercise is based on five simulations grouped into two categories: one where deficit cuts are made on the expenditure side, and one where the cuts are made by raising taxes. The simulations conducted in this exercise are

A. A baseline simulation with, in place of the IMF's 1994 *World Economic Outlook* projections, budgetary policies set so that the 1995 fiscal deficits persist for the foreseeable future. All other variables remain as in the IMF's 1994 *Outlook*. This constitutes a new baseline for each of the countries. That baseline becomes the reference path against which different deficit reduction rules are compared.

Two contractions involving expenditure cuts

B. A single cut: the same baseline, but each country makes a single cut in government expenditure worth 1 percent of GNP in 1995, and maintains that cut in nominal terms in all subsequent years.[8]

C. The accumulator: Each country makes a cut of 1 percent of GNP in government expenditure in 1995, and an extra cut of 1 percent of GNP each year thereafter until the 3 percent limit is reached. The accumulated cut is then maintained in all subsequent years.

Two contractions involving increases in taxation

D. A stability pact: This simulation combines the baseline of simulation A and a tax function with 60 percent debt targets imposed from 1999. No additional budget cuts are imposed. There are *no* anticipation effects here since we have an *unanticipated* model switch in 1999. Before that year, the forward-looking variables operate through a model that does not show that change happening. Therefore, there is no Ricardian equivalence from the fiscal restructuring. Tax rate changes are then driven by debt targets for a reason that will become obvious.

E. The procrastinator: Simulation D in which the 60 percent debt target is phased in from the first year in which the 60 percent debt ratio is breached, until 2004. Once again there are no actual anticipation effects because the model switch at each increase in the tax function's debt targets is unanticipated. But because each model switch is known after it has happened, these changes simulate what would have happened had the instantaneous imposition of a new tax function in 2004 been anticipated. Therefore, this simulation does imply a Ricardian equivalence solution.

The tax reaction functions

MULTIMOD has an endogenous tax rate, showing that any fiscal perturbation that pulls debt away from its baseline target will be counteracted by a rise in average tax rates:

$$tax\ rate = \alpha_1 \left(\frac{b_{-1} - b^*_{-1}}{p_{-1}y_{-1}} \right) + \alpha_2 \Delta \left(\frac{b_{-1} - b^*_{-1}}{p_{-1}y_{-1}} \right) + (tax\ rate)_{-1} \qquad (4.1)$$

where $b*$ is the target level of debt, p = price level, y = GNP, and α_1, α_2 > 0.[9] Thus the tax rate rises in response to excessive debt (by an amount which is equal in every country) in proportion to the amount that the debt to GNP ratio lies above its target value. Moreover tax rates will continue to rise so long as $b > b*$, even if the debt ratio itself is falling. That deals with the first term. The second term implies that tax rates will also adjust positively to worsening debt to GNP ratios. That means tax rates rise *faster*, at a given debt level, if the debt ratio is worsening; but *slower* if that debt ratio has started to fall. In fact tax rates could even start to decrease if the debt ratio starts to fall fast enough. The latter feature supplies a "soft-landing" effect. Conversely you get extra penalties (in the form of higher tax rates) if the excess debt ratio worsens.

A smooth landing: approaching the criteria at a "satisfactory pace"

Thus the first term of equation (4.1) controls for changes in the ratio from its target value, and the second for the acceleration of those changes. As a result, the rate of increase in the tax rate is reduced the more rapidly the excess debt ratio is coming down, and vice versa when it is going up. Finally, as we near the target debt ratio, the change in the tax rate will be determined largely by the change in the excess debt ratio. That is to say, changes in the tax rate are likely to be negative as we near the target ratio, and possibly earlier if the excess debt ratio is declining fast enough, so that we glide onto our target rather than overshoot. That "smooth landing" should ease the costs of fiscal adjustment in terms of the other policy targets. Notice that this "smooth landing" condition captures the spirit of the Maastricht Treaty. It says that fiscal corrections must be made to regain a lost convergence criterion *unless* "substantial progress," as defined by the first term, is being made "at a satisfactory pace" controlled by α_2 (whereupon the corrections may be smaller, or even suspended, if the pace of correction is fast enough). Indeed the weight to be given to this wording in the Maastricht Treaty can be increased or decreased by increasing or decreasing the ratio of α_2 to α_1. Our α_1 to α_2 ratio puts quite a lot of weight on that aspect of the treaty.

On rules that eliminate excessive debt

The tax reaction function (4.1) can also be justified as an error correction device. Salmon (1982) has shown that to eliminate the discrepancy between the value of a current state variable and its desired or target value, say z_t and $z*_t$, then the *controlled* state variable must follow a difference equation of at least p^{th} order:

$$(1 - L)^p z_t = B(L) z_{t-p} \qquad\qquad (4.2)$$

when z^*_t is following a difference equation of order $p - 1$. B (L) represents a polynominal in the lag operator, L. Hence the controlled state must follow a difference equation of order 1 higher than its target; if it is of the same order, z_t and z^*_t will converge on a constant difference; if it is of a lower order, they will diverge. But the target debt and deficit ratios are constant in the Maastricht Treaty. Hence $p = 1$ in our case.

The rule we have adopted in equation (4.1) is clearly second order in the state variable, $b/(py)$, when incorporated in the underlying model. That implies an element of overkill so far as the Maastricht Treaty is concerned; not only can it achieve the 60 percent debt criterion ($b/(py) = 0.6$), it can *also* reach strict fiscal solvency:

$$\lim_{t \to \infty} \left(\frac{b}{py} \right)_t = 0$$

if b^* is adjusted to zero. So whereas it may be too savage for Maastricht itself, equation (4.1) does ensure long-run fiscal sustainability—a necessary property that is missing from simpler policy rules and from the Maastricht Treaty. Weaker rules such as

$$\text{tax revenue} = (\text{tax revenue})_{-1} * (y / y_{-1}) + \alpha (b - b^*_{-1}) \tag{4.3}$$

or

$$\text{tax revenue} = (\text{tax rate})_{-1} * y + rb \tag{4.4}$$

do not guarantee long-run solvency; although equation (4.3)—being a first order scheme—does allow the Maastricht debt criterion to be reached.[10] In fact equation (4.3) will ensure debt stocks are always bounded, although not that they will tend toward any particular level (whether zero, 60 percent, or any other value). Equation (4.4), by contrast, raises taxes to cover any interest payments but cannot guarantee to meet the Maastricht criteria unless there are no further primary deficits. Hence weaker tax rules are likely to show different outcomes in the short run, and a weaker ability to adhere to the Maastricht criteria in the long run. That difference is unlikely to matter for long-run outcomes if reaching the Maastricht criteria is the only objective. But if we want to guarantee solvency at the same time, then we will have to use a rule like (4.1). The significance of this point is illustrated by the deficit reductions reported by von Hagen and Lutz (1995) where nominal incomes fall so fast (through price deflations and output losses) that fiscal insolvency follows. In the Italian case, output falls 6 percent and prices 30 percent, which puts the authorities into a liquidity crisis and would probably trigger a bailout. That prospect undermines the credibility of their monetary policy.

The initial conditions

We use MULTIMOD with the 1995 deficit-to-GNP ratios imposed on ERM countries indefinitely; that is, the baseline assumes no change in underlying

fiscal policies from their 1995 position. Other policies are also assumed to
remain as in the IMF's 1994 baseline. This set of assumptions is to simulate
what would happen if the fiscal authorities were to continue with their existing
policies, so that the same fiscal deficits were reproduced every year from 1995
onward.[11] We do this, not because we think it produces realistic projections of
what is most likely to happen. It does not. (In fact, one might suppose that the
deficits would automatically improve through growth, but in practice they
have not, despite the growth of the past two decades.) We set our assumptions
in order to show what would have to be done to reduce a fiscal deficit of a
given size over a certain period of time without the aid of favorable shocks.
We then compare this with the results of various restrictions on fiscal policy
designed to reduce the deficit to an acceptable limit. This comparison illustrates the general costs and benefits of a deficit reduction program, *independently* of any announcements of changes in fiscal policies that the authorities
might choose to make, and also *independently* of any specific assumptions
they may (or may not) have made about the endogenous development of their
deficits in the 1990s.

Having imposed these deficit figures, the baseline is a straightforward simulation from 1995 to beyond 2023 (to remove the effects of any terminal conditions) in the usual way. The 1995 deficit ratios used were: 2.4 percent
(Germany), 4.9 percent (France), 7.9 percent (Italy), and 4.8 percent (United
Kingdom).

Phasing in the debt targets

We set the debt targets as follows. Let b = the debt-to-GNP ratio, and b^*
= the target debt to GNP ratio. Then

1. if $b < 60$ percent, $b^* = b_{-1}$ (normal IMF rules); that is, tax rates are
   set to stop any further increases in the debt ratio from the level prevailing
   at the start of each period. But
2. if $b \geq 60$ percent and $t \geq 1999$, $b^* = 60$ percent of baseline GNP; that
   is, tax rates are set to hold the debt ratio at 60 percent of the GNP that
   would have prevailed in the absence of any budget cuts. This defines
   simulation D. Or
3. if $b \geq 60$ percent and $t \leq 2003$, $b^* = [2004 - t]^{-1} (b - 60$ percent of
   baseline GNP). But rule (4.2) applies if $t \geq 2004$, and $b^* = b_{-1}$ if $b <$
   60 percent. This is simulation E, based on Gros (1996a) but with a grace
   period of ten years to demonstrate "sufficient progress" back to the 60
   percent level.

So rules (4.2) and (4.3) both try to reproduce the baseline equilibrium growth
projections but with 60 percent debt ratios or lower.

What Constitutes a Successful Deficit Reduction Program?

Redesigning the tax regime

Before getting into the details of the different budget cutting strategies, we describe a strategy that did work. We need some tax and expenditure combination that will reduce the deficit-to-GNP ratios to 3 percent in all four countries *and* hold them there. That means that, once the fiscal cuts have been made and/or the required deficit ratio reached, any further fiscal controls must be eliminated so that national income is not reduced any further. If income is reduced any further, in an attempt to satisfy the debt criterion as well, for example, the ratio will start to rise again; and in order to prevent that from happening a new tax (or expenditure) regime will have to be introduced once the prescribed criteria have been reached. However, the ability to maintain a deficit ratio of 3 percent turns out to be *very* sensitive to the design of the new tax/expenditure regime.[12] For example, we tried introducing debt targets in 1999 only, in order to generate a sharp tax rise before switching back to normal IMF rules for setting the debt target. That strategy attempts to cut the deficit ratio and then to hold it steady at the new lower level. Unfortunately if the debt ratio is still above target, taxes have to rise further. Incomes then fall again and the deficit ratios drift back up to their earlier levels. The same happens if we phase in the tax rises. Finally adding fiscal expansions back in after the tax increases in 1999 prevents the income fall problem, but again expands the deficit level so that the ratio still does not fall.

The scheme that worked switched to autoregressive tax rates after the fiscal contractions are completed in 1999 (that is, setting $\alpha_1 = \alpha_2 = 0$ in (4.1), for $t \geq 2000$), instead of having them driven by the excess debt ratio. The logic is the same as before. Starting with either "normal IMF tax rules" or expenditure cuts, deficits fall as planned. But thereafter, because taxes follow a simple autoregressive path instead of rising, incomes do not fall much further, and the deficit ratios stabilize at between 2.5 percent for Germany and 6 percent for Italy. That result represents progress since the ratios no longer rise again, but they have not fallen far enough. To bring the ratios down even further, we added our 60 percent debt targeting rule in 1999 and then simply eliminated the tax function thereafter (leaving tax rates constant at their 1999 level). That implies the debt ratio is being reached because national income is being cranked up, rather than the deficit being brought down. In other words, we have to grow out of debt, not contract out of it.

In an earlier exercise where the 3 percent limit only needed to be met after ten years (by 2010), this proved entirely successful. However if the deadline for that limit is 1999, we also have to target a sustainable level of debt since, at that earlier date, debt ratios are still way above target. This illustrates the potential conflict between the deficit and debt criteria. Ideally one should plan to reach both criteria together over a suitable adjustment period, and then switch off the fiscal contractions. But if that cannot be done (because an accelerated time-table has been imposed, for example), then we should aim to achieve the required deficit ratio, switch off the fiscal contractions, and then allow growth under a *sustainable* tax and expenditure regime to gradually tighten and reduce the debt ratio to its limit. If this is not done, fiscal contractions designed to reach the 60 percent debt limit will cost us the 3 percent deficit ratio, since the latter will be reached earlier (debt being an accumulation of deficits). Further income restrictions will cause the deficit ratio to start rising again. In our case the sustainable debt targets turned out to be 60 percent for Germany, 53 percent for France, 52 percent for the United Kingdom and 76 percent for Italy. Thereafter growth and neutral taxes allowed the 60 percent debt ratios to be achieved gradually over the next five years.[13] In other words, the real task is to redesign the tax regime, not to fine-tune the fiscal policies or to force fiscal discipline as such.

The results of this successful simulation are displayed as simulation 1 in Tables 4.1 to 4.6. They show that the required deficit ratios are all met by 1999 and maintained thereafter with the exception of Italy in 2003–2006 (2005 in the table) when the restriction of sustainable debt targets is taken off. On the other hand, the British and French deficits fall to 1.5 percent of GNP or lower, close to the aspirations behind the "stability pact." The 60 percent debt ratios are also all achieved—albeit somewhat later (by 2008).

The output costs of this fiscal restructuring are not small however. There are losses of 0.75 percent per year in France and Britain in 1999, or about 7.5 percent of GNP over the interval 1999 to 2015. The costs are higher in Italy—nearly 2 percent of GNP each year in 1999 to 2000, and 21 percent from 1999 to 2015. That is a recession on the scale of the early 1990s, but spread over a period of fifteen years. Even Germany loses 0.25 percent of GNP. Larger costs, however, appear in terms of price deflation: Permanent price falls of 1 percent to 1.5 percent in Britain or France, and 3 to 4 percent in Italy. Setting these figures against baseline inflation rates of 2.5 to 3 percent shows how fiscal expansions have made inflation control in Europe that much more difficult. The cost here is really in the relative rise (of up to 2 percentage points) in short-term real interest rates. That must be contractionary and, with falling output prices, raises the specter of a 1930s-style liquidity squeeze.

In terms of cost multipliers, these output losses amount to between 0.3 and 0.5 in quantity terms per unit reduction in the deficit ratio, and between 0.3 and 0.4 in price terms. That represents a cost multiplier of about 0.7 to 0.9 in earnings and indicates a fair degree of price flexibility.[14] Thus the impact of fiscal restructuring is a little less than proportional because of the implicit monetary relaxation, but the costs are long-lived and show signs of rising again after fifteen years. Indeed the output costs in quantity terms have fallen significantly by 2015 in France and the United Kingdom; but in cash flow

TABLE 4.1
Deficit Ratios, Successful Simulations (percent GDP)

#	1995	1996	1997	1998	1999	2000	2001	2005	2010	2015
					Germany					
1	2.40	2.40	2.40	2.40	2.45	2.41	2.37	2.40	2.38	2.37
2	2.41	2.41	2.41	2.40	2.42	2.42	2.41	2.41	2.41	2.41
3	2.40	2.39	2.35	2.28	2.26	2.09	2.07	2.39	2.37	2.36
4	2.38	2.39	2.41	2.42	2.47	2.40	2.35	2.38	2.39	2.37
5	2.42	2.41	2.39	2.35	2.35	2.30	2.28	2.46	2.41	2.40
					France					
1	4.90	4.90	4.90	4.91	2.88	2.78	2.69	2.40	2.06	1.69
2	4.90	4.89	4.89	4.89	2.87	2.80	2.72	2.44	2.09	1.87
3	4.90	4.89	4.86	4.80	2.66	2.34	2.08	1.82	1.52	1.19
4	4.88	4.89	4.91	4.92	2.91	2.81	2.70	2.37	2.04	1.73
5	4.92	4.92	4.92	4.91	2.82	2.68	2.51	2.20	1.84	1.49
					Italy					
1	7.90	7.91	7.91	7.95	2.81	2.57	2.64	3.26	2.78	2.42
2	7.90	7.89	7.90	7.89	2.82	2.66	2.75	3.12	2.51	2.27
3	7.90	7.89	7.86	7.81	2.54	2.11	2.09	2.90	2.56	2.23
4	7.88	7.90	7.98	8.03	2.94	2.66	2.65	3.12	2.69	2.43
5	7.93	7.92	7.91	7.90	2.66	2.39	2.45	3.20	2.73	2.39
					United Kingdom					
1	4.80	4.80	4.80	4.82	2.85	2.73	2.63	2.28	1.97	1.58
2	4.80	4.80	4.80	4.80	2.82	2.74	2.64	2.28	1.96	1.77
3	4.80	4.79	4.76	4.69	2.59	2.21	1.92	1.63	1.28	0.89
4	4.77	4.78	4.81	4.83	2.88	2.75	2.62	2.26	1.96	1.65
5	4.84	4.83	4.83	4.83	2.79	2.60	2.40	2.03	1.63	1.24

Key: 1 = basic "successful" simulation; 2 = simulation 1 with price deflation removed; 3 = simulation 1 with monetary relaxation; 4 = simulation 1 with high growth in the United States; 5 = simulation 1 with low growth in the United States.

TABLE 4.2
Debt Ratios, Successful Simulations (percent GDP)

#	1995	1996	1997	1998	1999	2000	2001	2005	2010	2015
					Germany					
1	53.8	57.8	59.5	60.3	61.2	61.6	61.9	61.5	61.8	62.9
2	53.8	57.8	59.4	60.3	61.0	61.5	61.8	61.6	62.0	63.2
3	53.8	57.8	59.3	59.8	60.0	59.8	59.5	59.1	59.9	61.2
4	53.7	57.6	59.2	60.0	60.9	61.4	61.9	61.1	61.6	62.6
5	54.0	58.1	59.8	60.7	61.4	61.7	61.7	61.6	62.2	63.3
					France					
1	56.8	61.5	62.1	62.3	60.7	59.2	57.7	48.8	39.1	30.3
2	56.8	61.5	62.0	62.2	60.4	58.8	57.1	48.7	39.3	31.3
3	56.8	61.4	62.0	62.0	59.8	57.5	54.9	44.1	33.5	23.9
4	56.7	61.3	61.9	62.1	60.5	59.1	57.5	48.6	38.9	30.3
5	56.8	61.6	62.4	62.7	61.1	59.5	57.5	47.8	37.4	28.0
					Italy					
1	115.0	117.0	115.9	115.2	111.8	106.5	101.1	73.1	52.9	38.6
2	115.0	116.9	115.8	114.6	110.5	104.7	98.1	71.4	50.8	36.0
3	115.0	117.0	115.9	114.9	110.5	103.8	96.1	66.8	48.0	34.3
4	114.9	116.8	115.9	115.4	112.6	107.7	101.5	72.9	52.5	38.2
5	115.2	117.4	116.6	116.3	113.0	107.6	101.1	72.2	52.0	37.5
					United Kingdom					
1	47.8	52.6	57.7	60.2	59.8	58.6	57.1	47.9	38.1	29.2
2	47.8	52.6	57.7	60.6	59.4	58.1	56.5	47.8	38.0	29.6
3	47.8	52.6	57.6	59.8	58.6	56.4	53.7	42.4	31.3	21.1
4	47.7	52.4	57.4	59.9	59.6	58.4	56.8	47.6	38.0	29.4
5	48.0	52.9	58.1	60.8	60.3	58.9	56.9	46.6	35.6	25.7

Key: 1 = basic "successful" simulation; 2 = simulation 1 with price deflation removed; 3 = simulation 1 with monetary relaxation; 4 = simulation 1 with high growth in the United States; 5 = simulation 1 with low growth in the United States.

TABLE 4.3
Output Losses, Successful Simulations (percent deviation from baseline)

#	1995	1996	1997	1998	1999	2000	2001	2005	2010	2015
					Germany					
1	-0	-0	-0	-0	-0.24	-0.13	-0.12	-0.15	-0.07	-0.02
2	0	-0	0	0	-0.12	-0.08	-0.06	-0.07	-0.10	-0.16
3	0	0.01	0.14	0.45	0.62	0.95	1.05	0.93	1.08	1.06
4	0.11	0.17	0.24	0.25	0.03	0.18	0.26	0.17	0.22	0.26
5	-0.14	-0.19	-0.25	-0.25	-0.43	-0.27	-0.15	-0.31	-0.20	-0.15
					France					
1	-0	-0.01	-0.01	-0.03	-0.64	-0.59	-0.49	-0.23	-0.35	-0.25
2	0	0	0	0	-0.56	-0.57	-0.51	-0.28	-0.33	-0.50
3	0	0.01	0.06	0.22	-0.02	0.34	0.62	0.70	0.69	0.84
4	0.07	0.07	0.07	0.06	-0.57	-0.52	-0.38	-0.11	-0.22	-0.25
5	-0.10	-0.12	-0.20	-0.25	-0.79	-0.63	-0.37	-0.06	-0.11	0.02
					Italy					
1	-0.01	-0.03	-0.05	-0.11	-1.82	-1.85	-1.67	-0.80	-1.36	-1.60
2	0	0	0	0	-1.68	-1.89	-1.83	-1.18	-1.38	-2.06
3	-0.01	-0.01	-0.04	0.03	-1.24	-0.80	-0.17	0.75	0.34	0.29
4	0.07	0.03	-0.13	-0.28	-2.18	-2.30	-1.91	-0.87	-1.57	-2.09
5	-0.13	-0.18	-0.29	-0.40	-2.03	-1.90	-1.38	-0.36	-0.70	-0.82
					United Kingdom					
1	-0	-0.01	-0.02	-0.04	-0.86	-0.70	-0.50	-0.20	-0.36	-0.15
2	0	0	0	0	-0.76	-0.69	-0.54	-0.23	-0.33	-0.52
3	0	0.01	0.07	0.27	-0.07	0.47	0.87	0.82	0.90	1.15
4	0.16	0.11	0.07	0.03	-0.81	-0.63	-0.37	-0.07	-0.24	-0.20
5	-0.15	-0.17	-0.23	-0.26	-0.96	-0.64	-0.23	0.07	0.08	0.26

Key: 1 = basic "successful" simulation; 2 = simulation 1 with price deflation removed; 3 = simulation 1 with monetary relaxation; 4 = simulation 1 with high growth in the United States; 5 = simulation 1 with low growth in the United States.

TABLE 4.4
Price Deflation, Successful Simulations (percent deviation from baseline)

#	1995	1996	1997	1998	1999	2000	2001	2005	2010	2015
					Germany					
1	0	0	0	-0.02	-0.12	-0.21	-0.46	-0.31	-0.40	-0.77
2	0	0	0	0	0.01	-0.02	-0.04	-0.04	-0.05	-0.09
3	0	-0.01	0.02	0.28	0.49	0.84	1.19	1.82	1.59	1.38
4	0.04	0.22	0.48	0.52	0.37	0.22	0.11	0.18	0.19	0.07
5	-0.08	-0.27	-0.49	-0.73	-1.03	-1.17	-1.20	-1.07	-1.42	-1.72
					France					
1	0	0	0	-0.05	-0.29	-0.64	-1.40	-1.14	-1.12	-1.65
2	0	0	0	0	-0.05	-0.15	-0.22	-0.19	-0.15	-0.23
3	0	0	-0.03	-0.07	-0.16	-0.12	0.13	1.39	0.84	0.27
4	0.01	0.09	0.24	0.23	-0.06	-0.05	-0.85	-0.75	-0.57	-0.96
5	-0.02	-0.12	-0.30	-0.62	-1.13	-1.63	-2.03	-1.69	-1.85	-2.03
					Italy					
1	0	0.01	-0.01	-0.15	-0.86	-1.88	-3.94	-3.51	-3.86	-5.85
2	0	0	0	0	-0.17	-0.46	-0.69	-0.67	-0.58	-0.85
3	0	0	-0.07	-0.32	-0.96	-1.66	-2.00	-0.06	-0.58	-2.29
4	0.02	0.11	0.20	0	-1.00	-2.42	-3.53	-3.54	-3.63	-5.53
5	-0.04	-0.15	-0.39	-0.96	-2.07	-3.42	-4.61	-4.38	-4.75	-6.56
					United Kingdom					
1	0	0	0	-0.06	-0.35	-0.74	-1.52	-1.05	-1.06	-1.44
2	0	0	0	0	-0.06	-0.17	-0.23	-0.14	-0.11	-0.21
3	0	0	-0.04	-0.05	-0.08	0.04	0.46	2.23	1.85	1.83
4	0.03	0.17	0.40	0.39	0.06	-0.42	-0.74	-0.32	-0.18	-0.45
5	-0.06	-0.22	-0.47	-0.87	-1.43	-1.94	-2.25	-1.56	-1.66	-1.72

Key: 1 = basic "successful" simulation; 2 = simulation 1 with price deflation removed; 3 = simulation 1 with monetary relaxation; 4 = simulation 1 with high growth in the United States; 5 = simulation 1 with low growth in the United States.

TABLE 4.5
The Changes in Tax Rates (percent deviation from baseline)

#	1995	1996	1997	1998	1999	2000	2001	2005	2010	2015
					Germany					
1	0	0	0	0	0.05	0.07	0.03	-0.06	-0.20	-0.60
2	0	0	0	0	0.02	0.04	0.04	0.10	0.18	0.26
3	0	-0.01	-0.06	-0.21	-0.46	-0.96	-1.51	-2.62	-2.93	-3.21
4	-0.02	-0.05	-0.04	-0.01	0.12	0.17	0.14	-0.18	-0.12	-0.28
5	0.03	0.05	0.03	-0.04	-0.13	-0.32	-0.56	-0.93	-1.04	-1.33
					France					
1	0	0	0	0	10.8	10.8	10.7	10.6	10.5	10.4
2	0	0	0	0	10.8	10.7	10.7	10.5	10.4	10.4
3	0	-0.01	-0.05	-0.19	10.2	10.2	10.2	10.0	9.9	9.9
4	-0.02	-0.03	-0.02	0	10.9	10.8	10.8	10.6	10.5	10.5
5	0.02	0.04	0.04	0.20	10.8	10.8	10.8	10.6	10.5	10.5
					Italy					
1	0	0	-0.01	0.02	30.8	30.5	29.2	22.9	22.6	22.5
2	0	0	0	0	30.6	30.5	29.2	23.9	23.6	23.6
3	0	-0.02	-0.09	-0.28	29.9	28.7	26.0	18.3	18.1	18.1
4	-0.02	-0.02	0.11	0.22	31.6	31.8	30.3	24.1	23.8	23.8
5	0.03	0.04	0.03	-0.07	31.0	30.4	28.3	21.4	21.2	21.2
					United Kingdom					
1	0	0	0	0	9.5	9.5	9.5	9.6	9.6	9.6
2	0	0	0	0	9.4	8.5	9.5	9.5	9.5	9.5
3	0	0	-0.04	-0.16	8.9	9.0	9.0	9.0	9.0	9.0
4	-0.03	-0.05	-0.04	-0.02	9.6	9.6	9.6	9.6	9.6	9.6
5	0.04	0.06	0.08	0.07	9.6	9.6	9.6	9.6	9.7	9.7

Note: Changes in tax rates are reported as percentages, so that an increase from a 25 percent tax rate to a 50 percent tax rate is reported as a 100 percent increase.

Key: 1 = basic "successful" simulation; 2 = simulation 1 with price deflation removed; 3 = simulation 1 with monetary relaxation; 4 = simulation 1 with high growth in the United States; 5 = simulation 1 with low growth in the United States.

TABLE 4.6

Nominal Interest Rates, Successful Simulations (percent deviation from baseline)

#	1995	1996	1997	1998	1999	2000	2001	2005	2010	2015
					Germany					
1	0	-0	-0	-0	-0.03	-0.05	-0.15	-0.09	-0.09	-0.26
2	0	0	0	0	-0	-0	0	0.06	0.06	0.09
3	-0	-0	0.01	0.08	-0.52	-0.83	-0.91	-0.64	-0.87	-0.98
4	0.01	0.06	0.16	0.21	0.17	0.07	-0.02	0.02	0.07	0.02
5	-0.02	-0.08	-0.17	-0.28	-0.40	-0.48	-0.48	-0.26	-0.47	-0.55
					France					
1	0	0	0	-0	-0	-0.01	-0.07	-0.08	-0.11	-0.24
2	0	0	0	0	0	0	0	0	0.01	0.02
3	-0	-0.01	-0.05	-0.11	-0.49	-0.75	-0.82	-0.71	-0.83	-0.97
4	0	0.04	0.12	0.16	0.16	0.15	0.10	0.05	0.06	0.04
5	-0.03	-0.10	-0.19	-0.28	-0.37	-0.42	-0.42	-0.35	-0.44	-0.55
					Italy					
1	0	0	0	-0	-0	-0.01	-0.04	-0.05	-0.09	-0.23
2	0	0	0	0	0	0	0	0	0	0
3	-0	-0	-0.04	-0.10	-0.45	-0.70	-0.79	-0.76	-0.82	-0.97
4	0.02	0.08	0.17	0.19	0.20	0.19	0.15	0.10	0.10	0.09
5	-0.07	-0.17	-0.27	-0.34	-0.40	-0.43	-0.44	-0.39	-0.44	-0.54
					United Kingdom					
1	0	0	0	-0	-0	-0.01	-0.04	-0.05	-0.09	-0.23
2	0	0	0	0	0	0	0	0	0	0.01
3	-0	-0.01	-0.06	-0.14	-0.49	-0.73	-0.81	-0.76	-0.82	-0.97
4	0	0.03	0.10	0.12	0.13	0.13	0.11	0.09	0.10	0.08
5	-0.02	-0.08	-0.18	-0.27	-0.36	-0.41	-0.41	-0.40	-0.45	-0.55

Key: 1 = basic "successful" simulation; 2 = simulation 1 with price deflation removed; 3 = simulation 1 with monetary relaxation; 4 = simulation 1 with high growth in the United States; 5 = simulation 1 with low growth in the United States.

terms they still run at 0.5 to 0.6 units of lost output per unit reduction in the deficit ratio. And for Italy the cost multiplier has risen above unity (to 1.6 units of lost output revenue per unit reduction in the deficit ratio, of which 0.6 is lost output and 1.0 lower prices). Finally, even Germany has lost 0.8 in earnings.

In each case, therefore, a package of deflationary effects is involved. In fact Tables 4.5 and 4.6 show that these deficit reductions are achieved by a combination of mild monetary relaxation—up to 0.25 percent off interest rates in the long run, shared equally between the four countries (including Germany, despite having no deficit problem)—and a once-and-for-all tax rate hike of 10 percent in France and the United Kingdom and 30 percent in Italy. That increase drifts down to 20 percent after fifteen years; and given the output falls in Table 4.3, tax revenues will rise somewhat less than proportionate. That outcome shows that tax increases, rather than output losses, are the real cost of fiscal restructuring. These increases are the result of near-Ricardian equivalence and the credibility effects of fiscal discipline and imply that deficit reductions in France, the United Kingdom, and Italy could be very expensive in political terms, if not in economic performance. Small wonder that governments have put off correcting their deficits and have used expenditure cuts rather than tax increases when they were forced to act.

Deficit reductions without price deflation (simulation 2)

The rationale for this simulation is that many of our deficit reducing simulations involve large price falls, which put a liquidity squeeze on firms. It might be thought that preventing these price falls would check the falls in output that follow and hence make the fiscal consolidation exercise less deflationary. We do this by adjusting the fiscal feedback rule in taxation to sustain prices along their baseline. Does this affect the scale of the output costs much?

The short answer is that removing the price deflation element of our strategy does not threaten our ability to reach either fiscal criterion. But removing the price deflations of previous simulations does increase average output losses. They double in the long run. The reasons for this are simply that fiscal policy is a good bit more expansionary (particularly for Italy), which helps push inflation back up. Hence Germany, which does not have a deficit problem, has to suffer higher inflation than otherwise. That higher inflation prompts Germany to tighten its monetary stance, so that toward the end of the simulation period German interest rates (and hence those of the non-German ERM) increase by up to 1 percentage point, causing extra output losses. Germany dominates, therefore, but not before the Italian deficit is resolved.

This simulation demonstrates the trade-off between price flexibility and output losses; and given Europe's traditional inflexibility in prices, simulation 2 (rather than simulation 1) is the more likely scenario in practice.

Deficit reductions with monetary relaxations (simulation 3)

Simulations 1 and 2 are both dominated by output losses. We have noted that these contractions can be offset if, for example, they are accompanied by a monetary relaxation. Hence the key question is what is the *minimum* amount of monetary relaxation required to neutralize the output costs shown in simulation 1?

Tables 4.3 and 4.4 show that in order to provide that offset with Italy within the ERM, we have to create extra growth and inflation in Germany, France, and the United Kingdom. Interestingly this expansion does not have to be large—the *minimum* expansion was only 1.5 percent on the baseline monetary target path—but the expansion *does* have to be permanent to neutralize the output costs permanently.[15] We use this approach because, given the narrow bands of the ERM, the non-German countries cannot operate an independent monetary policy; their interest rates are endogenous and must stay close to or above the corresponding DM rates. One solution would be to use wider bands to allow greater monetary relaxations—but those bands would have to be very much wider for a long time. Hence, if the ERM or EMU is to be preserved, Germany has to create the monetary expansion so that interest rates fall system-wide. In other words, Germany has to bail the fiscally indebted countries out—even if only by a small amount. That implies a conflict: *Either* the ERM is maintained and an expansion is achieved via increasing real income balances with price deflation, *or* wide bands are accepted together with a change in policy mix; *or* Germany expands its money supply for the benefit of EU (but not German) targets.

Hence growth, not fiscal contractions, is the key to getting the deficit ratios down. If it is unrealistic to expect Germany to engage in any such monetary relaxation, policy makers must recognize that any change has to be permanent—unsurprisingly given that the tax restructuring policies are permanent. Hence it is the design of the tax system and of the policy mix, not the size of the relaxation, that matter.

The importance of external conditions: high growth versus low growth

We choose fiscal changes in the United States to illustrate the impact of external conditions on deficit reduction programs. We increase and then decrease fiscal expenditures in the United States by 1 percent of GNP.

In the expansion case, simulation 4, Germany receives positive spillovers, and as a result there is a small rise (0.25 percent) in German interest rates for three years to head off extra inflation. Prices in fact rise 0.5 percent. For the other countries there are still heavy deflations (in both output and prices) from their own domestic fiscal contractions. But interest rates have to rise to match those in Germany. So, for them, fiscal discipline within the ERM converts expansion abroad into a beggar-thy-neighbor regime at home.

In the contraction case, simulation 5, Germany gets a negative output and inflation shock, which prompts some easing of German monetary policy (interest rates fall 0.5 percent, a little less than in the monetary expansion of simulation 3). Helpful as that is, it does not offset the domestic contractions in the other countries. However it does leave the output losses smaller than in the base case (simulation 1) from 2000—Germany excepted. The price deflations are rather larger however. The beggar-thy-neighbor effects are now more in prices than output. These two simulations therefore make the point that external conditions can have a significant effect on the *costs* of any deficit reduction program—but rather little on the success (narrowly defined) of those programs.

On the size of the output costs

One conclusion from these simulations is that while the costs involved in reducing these deficit ratios are quite large, they are not impossible. Indeed some might even argue the costs are quite manageable. Why is this? There are two explanations. The first is that fiscal contractions are in themselves partly expansionary, but not so much so as to be *net* expansionary. We deal with this possibility in the following text, and conclude that it is unlikely. A second and much more likely explanation is that accompanying policies have been used to balance the effects of the fiscal contractions, to support aggregate demand and hence the denominator of the deficit ratio. In particular, although we pointed out that real interest rates rise relative to baseline, they fall in absolute terms in simulation 1 (Italy excepted). That means nominal interest rates are falling in the baseline as inflation eases in the transition to steady state growth. In other words, these fiscal contractions have been undertaken against a background of favorable monetary developments.

In more detail, falling nominal interest rates imply a noninflationary expansion of the nominal money supply and an expansion of real money balances. As consumption depends on the expected stock of wealth, and investment on the cost of capital, this scenario has expansionary effects that compensate for (but are not part of) the fiscal contractions. At the same time, falling prices (relative to base) imply a depreciation of real exchange rates in Europe. That strengthens current account balances all around. Net foreign assets therefore rise (relative to base), which again affects wealth and consumption. Those are the demand-side effects.

There are also supply-side effects. Since prices fall relative to base, inflationary expectations must also fall. That fall in expected inflation will increase expected wealth, but reduce the probability of a depreciation of ERM currencies and higher interest rates. Hence expected wealth or asset holdings rise again. Similarly wage bargains will ease (see Bartolini and Symanski, 1993) so that competitiveness increases.[16] The favorable effect of all these changes on costs, and hence the speed with which the deficit ratios fall, makes the case for accompanying supply-side policies to offset the fiscal contractions. In other words, policymakers need to ensure that their fiscal contractions take place against a background of suitably noninflationary growth. Those are conditions that have to be constructed. They do not appear automatically, and without them deficit ratio reductions will be very painful.

On conflicts between the convergence criteria

Another possible cost of these deficit reductions is the fact that they sharpen the conflicts between the convergence criteria for entry into EMU. We have already highlighted the difficulties involved if the debt and deficit criteria are not reached simultaneously, and the following sections show how that conflict arises. We have also found that there may be a conflict between the deficit criterion and the exchange rate criterion. Italy, it appears, is unable to satisfy both criteria simultaneously.

However there appears to be an even more damaging clash between the deficit and the inflation criteria. Our simulations show that, because the deficit criterion is a ratio, it is necessary to find some expansionary forces to accompany the fiscal contractions, since the denominator of the ratio will otherwise fall along with the numerator and prevent the ratio itself from falling. In our case these expansionary effects are supplied by a combination of monetary expansion, price deflations, and competitiveness effects. In simulation 1 this has produced price deflation differentials of 3.5 percent between Germany and Italy in 2001 (and 5 percent in 2015)—the baseline inflation paths being approximately equal in each country. Similar differentials appear in simulations 3, 4, and 5, where there are no constraints to equalize inflation rates.

The attempt to force the deficit criterion threatens inflation convergence as defined in the Maastricht Treaty. In this case, since the deficit reductions are achieved with the aid of price deflations, it is Germany who violates the inflation criterion. But had monetary expansions or currency depreciations been used instead, the country with a deficit problem would have violated that criterion. Perhaps an absolute inflation criterion, instead of a relative one, would be more sensible.

Is It Better to Cut Expenditures or to Raise Taxes?

In this section we compare programs of public expenditure cuts and tax increases for their effectiveness in reducing fiscal deficits. Can such simplified strategies also secure 3 percent deficits?

Deficit reductions

The first conclusion is that none of these strategies are effective in reducing the current fiscal deficits. Only Germany and Italy achieve the required 3 percent limit, and then only in certain cases and only for limited periods of time (see Table 4.7). But these are the only cases where the debt ratios depart significantly from 60 percent, so these are the only cases where there are significant jumps in the tax revenues and significant deficit reductions before 1999.

In fact the only rules that appear to have a serious impact are either a combination of expenditure cuts and debt targeting, or just a debt targeting rule by itself (simulations D or E). A strategy of expenditure cuts alone (simulations B or C) seems to have little effect after the first year. In other words, the expenditure multipliers on output are close to unity and hence about zero on the deficit ratio. That implies rough linearity. But the revenue multipliers on output are by definition nonlinear since tax rates are the instrument. That nonlinearity then gives us an opportunity to get the relevant ratios down. These results are most clearly seen in the deficit ratios of Germany and Italy, but they are also to be seen in the French results for the period 1999 to 2005 when the 60 percent debt targeting rule comes into play. This highlights an important asymmetry: When fiscal policy alone is used, it matters whether you increase taxation or cut expenditures. It appears that tax increases will be the more effective of the two. This result is the opposite of that found by Alesina and Perotti (1995) who point out that, in history, countries who raise taxation tend to raise expenditures again later and so fail to reduce their deficit ratios. Such a compensating rise in expenditures is ruled out here; we presume that fiscal discipline, once imposed, is maintained since the problem of back-sliding is not part of measuring the *potential* effectiveness of those fiscal changes.

Secondly, parametric variations in these rules appear to make little difference. It does not matter much whether a single cut in the budget equal to 1 percent of GNP is imposed and sustained, or whether cumulative 1 percent cuts are made each year. This finding illustrates, once again, that taxes are more effective than expenditure cuts. Nevertheless, given the dynamics of national output following a fiscal contraction, the denominator of the deficit ratio falls a little faster than the numerator, so that for a period (around ten years after an initial expenditure cut) the deficit ratio actually *rises* before settling back to its baseline value. Hence it is *not* true that making a significant cut in the budget deficit, and then maintaining the new smaller budget, will eventually bring the economy back to within its specified 3 percent limit. Something else needs to be done to prevent national income from falling while the fiscal cuts are being made.

It makes little difference whether debt targets are introduced gradually over

TABLE 4.7
Deficit Ratios, Successful Simulations (percent GDP)

#	1995	1996	1997	1998	1999	2000	2001	2005	2010	2015
					Germany					
A	2.4	2.4	2.4	2.4	2.4	2.4	2.4	2.4	2.4	2.4
B	2.43	2.41	2.41	2.40	2.39	2.39	2.39	2.40	2.40	2.40
C	2.43	2.42	2.41	2.40	2.46	2.39	2.39	2.41	2.41	2.40
D	2.40	2.40	2.40	2.40	2.22	2.07	1.99	2.19	2.23	2.04
E	2.54	2.49	2.43	2.36	2.28	2.19	2.13	2.15	2.21	2.04
					France					
A	4.9	4.9	4.9	4.9	4.9	4.9	4.9	4.9	4.9	4.9
B	4.32	4.50	4.64	4.76	4.81	4.88	4.95	5.08	5.05	4.98
C	4.32	4.48	4.61	4.73	4.77	4.84	4.91	5.05	5.05	5.00
D	4.90	4.90	4.90	4.90	4.68	4.58	4.51	4.65	4.70	4.73
E	4.97	4.83	4.76	4.71	4.69	4.61	4.54	4.63	4.81	4.84
					Italy					
A	7.9	7.9	7.9	7.9	7.9	7.9	7.9	7.9	7.9	7.9
B	7.37	7.54	7.69	7.82	7.86	7.94	8.00	8.12	8.08	8.02
C	7.37	7.53	7.66	7.79	7.83	7.90	7.97	8.10	8.09	8.04
D	7.90	7.90	7.90	7.92	-5.29	-3.94	-2.25	4.26	6.69	6.94
E	6.53	5.20	4.05	3.09	2.38	1.89	1.76	3.84	6.32	6.81
					United Kingdom					
A	4.8	4.8	4.8	4.8	4.8	4.8	4.8	4.8	4.8	4.8
B	4.32	4.46	4.58	4.68	4.71	4.77	4.83	4.96	4.94	4.87
C	4.32	4.45	4.55	4.65	4.67	4.73	4.80	4.94	4.94	4.88
D	4.80	4.80	4.80	4.80	4.82	4.66	4.55	4.67	4.70	4.71
E	5.08	5.12	4.93	4.76	4.65	4.54	4.47	4.59	4.79	4.81

Key: A = baseline simulation; B = single expenditure cut; C = accumulating expenditure cuts; D = tax function with 60 percent debt-to-GDP target; E = tax function with "phased-in" 60 percent debt-to-GDP target.

several years (simulation E) or suddenly with full force in 1999 (simulation D); the deficit ratios fall either way. The one point to note is that a gradual introduction allows the effects to be phased in much more smoothly. As a result the Italian deficit is reduced by 6 percent over a seven-year period (1995 to 2001) in simulation E, as opposed to sudden reductions of 13 percent over a two-year period (an 8 percent deficit turns into a 5 percent surplus during 1998 to 1999) in simulation D. Evidently the choice between gradualism and shock therapy is important in extreme cases. But the cost of this, in tax terms, is severe.

These results lead to the conclusion that deficit reductions *without* tax increases are unlikely to be successful. By implication, revenue raising is the only realistic way of getting deficits down—and to do that you have to *grow* out of debt rather than contract out of it. But to grow out of debt requires two instruments for the two targets (debt or deficit reductions and output growth).[17] Fiscal contractions alone are not sufficient.

This last point leads to another important conclusion: It may be easy enough to engineer a deficit reduction, but it is much more difficult to sustain it. We can see that in all four simulations—particularly in the French expenditure cuts and in the debt targeting simulations of Italy (and Germany). In each case the deficit reductions are substantially lost after 5 years—the return to the baseline is not always complete, but the deficit ratios have gone most of the way back even when they had been successfully cut to below 3 percent.

Thus our fifth lesson: It appears all too easy for the weaker economies to "squeeze in under the door"; that is, to deflate their economies until they satisfy the Maastricht criteria, but then to lose control so that they fail on the same criteria and become a risk to EMU's fiscal discipline—despite having maintained their original fiscal restrictions throughout. Hence this is not even a question of relaxing, having once been accepted as a member.

The reasons why these deficit ratios drift up again are fairly complicated. First the original fiscal contractions cut GNP at the same time. If those contractions stop once the 3 percent limit is reached, and if the economies' natural dynamics are stable and positive, then the cumulative effects of those GNP reductions will continue to work through the system to reduce national income to a new lower level. The deficit and debt ratios will start to rise again. That is one possibility.

However it seems more likely that rising rates are the result of the difference between cutting the deficit (a flow) and cutting debt (a stock). To satisfy a limit for the former does *not* imply that any particular limit has been satisfied for the latter, even if the two limits are consistent (which cannot be guaranteed anyway, except at certain rates of interest and initial conditions). Indeed the two indicators may travel in opposite directions. And if they do, taxes will have to rise in order to control (reduce) the debt burden. Those new tax rises

will further reduce national income and cause the now stabilized deficit ratio
to start rising again.

The stock-flow distinction in debt and deficit reductions

To illustrate the difference between debt and deficit reductions, consider the
case of a country with a fiscal deficit of 6 percent of GNP. Suppose it decides
to impose expenditure cuts (or tax increases) worth 3 percent of GNP over a
period of time. If the fiscal multipliers are unity, the budget deficit would be
3 units in 97 or 3.1 percent of GNP at the end of the exercise. But if the
multipliers are 1.5, say, the deficit will finish at 3.2 percent of GNP, and so
on. The Maastricht target is missed, but by very little.

Now consider the debt reduction case. Suppose the same country has a debt
ratio of 70 percent and imposes fiscal cuts worth 3 percent of GNP. With
multipliers of unity, the debt ratio will become 67 units in 97 at the end of the
exercise: a ratio of 69 percent and a very slow reduction. If the multipliers are
1.5, the ratio will finish up at 70.2 percent—that is a rise in the ratio! The
reason that this happens is that the deficit reduction is accompanied by a fall
in GNP, with the result that the deficit ratio does not change much. And,
although the fiscal contraction means a subtraction from absolute debt level,
the smaller GNP is now dividing into something close to the *old* stock of debt.
In a high debt country that stock of old debt will be very large, and the increase in its ratio can easily outweigh the effect of the subtracted element that
gives the new ratio. In fact the new debt ratio can be written as

$$\frac{b_t}{y_t} = \frac{b_{t-1}}{y_{t-1} + \Delta y_t} + \frac{pd_t + rb_{t-1}}{y_{t-1} + \Delta y_t}, \tag{4.5}$$

where pd_t = the primary deficit, r = the interest rate, and $\Delta y_t < 0$ as a result
of the fiscal cuts. Hence $b_{t-1}/(y_{t-1} + \Delta y_t)$ can easily rise faster than the second
term on the right falls, if b_{t-1} is large enough, even when we have created an
overall surplus $(pd_t + rb_{t-1} < 0)$. And the new ratio will *certainly* rise if pd_t
> 0 or if $rb_{t-1} \geqslant -pd_t$. This just shows the difference between a debt stock
and a deficit flow, both expressed as ratios. Thus deficit and debt ratios may
move in opposite directions, and the satisfaction of one does *not* automatically
imply progress toward satisfying the other.

Notice also that a debt reduction, unlike a deficit reduction, involves running an *overall* budget surplus, not just a primary surplus or a reduced primary
deficit.[18] From this one can see the political temptation to ignore the debt
criteria. And here we have a real dilemma since if the policymakers decide
not to act on the debt ratio for political reasons, the market will assume that
either a monetary bailout or a default will have to follow. Interest rates will
then rise, either as an inflation risk or a default risk premium, and the deficit

will increase again. As this is an endogenous market reaction, there is little policymakers can do to offset it.

The debt reductions

Unsurprisingly, given the small size of the deficit reductions, there are few significant reductions in the German, French, or British debt ratios (see Table 4.8). However these small deficit reductions are sufficient to bring the debt figures down to the required 60 percent limit.

The Italian case is more interesting. Although there are no interest rate falls with a jump to EMU or because risk premia are removed, Italy still shows significant gains with the debt ratio being brought back down to the 60 percent limit. This is quite an achievement, although it takes eight to ten years of tax increases to do it and requires explicit debt targets as well as rapid deficit reductions. But these debt reductions are also achieved because faster growth in the Italian economy means that 20 percentage points are already being removed from the Italian debt ratio. Fiscal policy has therefore to eliminate only 30 percentage points, rather than 50. A second reason is that reductions in the debt level will reduce interest rates and hence create a "crowding in" effect, as well as reduce interest payments in future deficits. With all these changes, output will rise relative to other scenarios. And finally, since the deflations are larger in the Italian economy, price deflation will be stronger than elsewhere. That in turn implies higher real balances and a lower real exchange rate in Italy (there are no realignments here), which, with forward-looking consumers, switches demand away from the other economies and toward Italy. That gives output another boost. Hence relatively faster growth underpins this relatively rapid reduction in Italian debt ratios. But some of that growth had to be constructed outside the fiscal restructuring program.

Output losses

What output losses have to be accepted to achieve these fiscal deflations? In fact the losses are relatively small since the deficit reductions are relatively small, Italy excepted (see Table 4.9). Typically a 1 percent reduction in the deficit ratio causes a 1.25 to 1.5 percent initial reduction in output levels. If that is all that happens (simulation B), the output losses decline to 0.5 percent per year after ten years, and tail away after twenty or twenty-five years. A debt target strategy (whether phased or not, simulations D and E) is rather less expensive with losses of one-third of a percent for Germany, France, and the United Kingdom. Those losses are not inconsiderable, but they are not disastrous and they are not permanent.

The cumulative 1 percent deficit reduction case (simulation C) is more costly because, per unit, it causes output losses of 1 to 2 percent per year,

TABLE 4.8
Debt Ratios, Successful Simulations (percent GDP)

#	1995	1996	1997	1998	1999	2000	2001	2005	2010	2015
					Germany					
A	53.8	57.8	59.5	60.3	60.9	61.4	61.7	61.5	61.8	63.0
B	53.9	57.9	59.6	60.4	61.1	61.5	61.8	61.6	61.9	63.1
C	53.9	57.9	59.6	60.4	61.1	61.5	61.8	61.6	62.0	63.1
D	53.8	57.8	59.5	60.3	61.0	61.1	60.9	59.6	59.9	60.3
E	54.0	58.1	59.7	60.6	61.1	61.3	61.3	60.1	60.0	60.4
					France					
A	56.8	61.5	62.0	62.2	62.0	62.4	62.6	62.1	61.9	61.9
B	56.7	61.2	61.6	61.7	61.3	61.6	61.9	61.9	62.4	62.6
C	56.7	61.2	61.6	61.7	61.3	61.5	61.8	61.7	62.2	62.6
D	56.8	61.5	62.0	62.2	62.1	62.1	61.9	60.1	59.5	59.2
E	56.8	61.5	61.9	62.0	61.6	61.7	61.7	60.0	59.6	59.9
					Italy					
A	115.0	116.9	115.8	114.6	113.3	111.8	109.9	99.4	96.4	96.4
B	115.7	117.6	116.4	115.2	113.5	111.9	109.8	99.7	97.3	97.5
C	115.7	117.7	116.4	115.3	113.6	111.9	109.9	99.7	97.3	97.6
D	115.0	117.0	115.8	114.8	106.5	95.0	83.4	52.1	51.3	58.0
E	114.1	114.3	110.2	105.1	98.9	92.4	85.4	58.8	54.2	58.9
					United Kingdom					
A	47.8	52.6	57.6	60.1	60.9	61.5	61.8	61.2	60.8	60.8
B	47.9	52.4	57.4	59.7	60.3	60.8	61.1	61.0	61.2	61.4
C	47.9	52.4	57.4	59.8	60.2	60.7	61.0	60.8	61.1	61.4
D	47.8	52.6	57.7	60.1	61.1	61.6	61.6	60.1	59.7	59.5
E	48.1	53.1	58.3	61.7	61.4	61.8	61.8	59.9	59.6	59.9

Key: A = baseline simulation; B = single expenditure cut; C = accumulating expenditure cuts; D = tax function with 60 percent debt-to-GDP target; E = tax function with "phased-in" 60 percent debt-to-GDP target.

TABLE 4.9
Output Losses (percent deviation from baseline)

#	1995	1996	1997	1998	1999	2000	2001	2005	2010	2015
					Germany					
A	0	0	0	0	0	0	0	0	0	0
B	-0.13	-0.08	-0.08	-0.09	-0.12	-0.11	-0.11	-0.13	-0.12	-0.11
C	-0.13	-0.09	-0.08	-0.09	-0.12	-0.11	-0.12	-0.14	-0.15	-0.14
D	0	0	0	0	-0.38	-0.21	-0.08	-0.01	-0.06	-0.08
E	0.30	-0	-0.03	-0.06	-0.07	-0.08	-0.09	-0.02	-0.06	-0.08
					France					
A	0	0	0	0	0	0	0	0	0	0
B	-0.76	-0.78	-0.73	-0.66	-0.47	-0.40	-0.37	-0.32	-0.25	-0.19
C	-0.76	-0.79	-0.77	-0.72	-0.54	-0.48	-0.46	-0.44	-0.41	-0.39
D	0	0	0	0	-0.37	-0.20	-0.09	0.01	-0.04	-0.04
E	0.02	-0.03	-0.06	-0.07	-0.06	-0.07	-0.09	-0.01	-0.01	-0.03
					Italy					
A	0	0	0	0	0	0	0	0	0	0
B	-0.87	-0.90	-0.88	-0.84	-0.63	-0.54	-0.49	-0.43	-0.36	-0.29
C	-0.87	-0.92	-0.91	-0.89	-0.68	-0.61	-0.57	-0.55	-0.53	-0.52
D	0	0	0	-0.02	-4.3	-3.7	-2.7	0.29	-0.16	-0.95
E	-0.36	-0.83	-1.11	-1.25	-1.3	-1.3	-1.2	-0.47	-0.30	-0.91
					United Kingdom					
A	0	0	0	0	0	0	0	0	0	0
B	-0.94	-0.86	-0.75	-0.66	-0.45	-0.38	-0.36	-0.34	-0.26	-0.18
C	-0.94	-0.89	-0.81	-0.74	-0.51	-0.45	-0.44	-0.46	-0.43	-0.38
D	0	0	0	0	-0.31	-0.18	-0.06	0.01	-0.06	-0.08
E	0.07	0.07	-0.02	-0.09	-0.11	-0.12	-0.12	0.02	-0.03	-0.07

Key: A = baseline simulation; B = single expenditure cut; C = accumulating expenditure cuts; D = tax function with 60 percent debt-to-GDP target; E = tax function with "phased-in" 60 percent debt-to-GDP target.

which are still around two-thirds of a percent after twenty years. That represents substantial losses—a *permanent* recession on the scale of that in the 1991 to 1994 period. The lesson here is that it is the *repeated* deflations that are really costly.[19] Unfortunately this is the strategy that policymakers actually seem to have chosen.

Italy of course is a special case again. The output losses may need to be as much as 3 to 4 percent per year to achieve the deficit and debt reductions recorded in Tables 4.7 and 4.8.[20] That represents zero growth for about four years and a recession that is twice as bad as that from 1991 to 1994. Phasing the debt targets in over ten years reduces the output cost of the associated debt reductions (Table 4.9), but even then the output losses are only halved. It seems that output losses are the unavoidable price of achieving deficit and debt reductions.

Price deflation

Any package of deflation will reduce price inflation, and this is what we see throughout Table 4.10. That is the good news. Deficit and debt reduction policies will reduce price increases by up to 0.75 percent per year on average, and 2 to 4 percent in the case of Italy. This is on "steady state averages" of 3 to 4 percent, and 2 percent for Germany, so they are quite significant reductions. The strongest deflationary pressure comes from the schemes with explicit fiscal cuts (simulations B and C); debt targets do not have significant inflation reducing consequences in themselves.

To put the same point in another way, we can see now the cost of the overexpansionary fiscal policies in Europe. At times they have perhaps doubled the rate of inflation, which would otherwise have held, and have seriously complicated the process of monetary control and price stability—even in Germany. Closer coordination of fiscal as well as monetary policies would perhaps have been preferable.[21]

Instrument paths

In the case of monetary policy we see a consistently looser policy. This shows that changes in the policy mix lie at the heart of these deficit reductions, since each fiscal contraction generates a monetary counterreaction in order to maintain output. However this monetary loosening is very slight: For example, simulations B and C have around 0.1 percentage points cut from interest rates. But France, Italy, and the United Kingdom have rather little scope to cut interest rates within their exchange rate bands. Instead Germany has to bear the brunt of monetary relaxation for the whole ERM (see Tables 4.11 and 4.12).

Finally we see that average tax rates are decreased (simulations B and C) when government expenditure cuts are involved because debt is under target.

TABLE 4.10
Price Deflation (percent deviation from baseline)

#	1995	1996	1997	1998	1999	2000	2001	2005	2010	2015
					Germany					
A	0	0	0	0	0	0	0	0	0	0
B	0.03	-0.02	-0.06	-0.08	-0.19	-0.19	-0.17	-0.15	-0.16	-0.15
C	0.03	-0.02	-0.06	-0.08	-0.21	-0.22	-0.20	-0.18	-0.20	-0.21
D	0	0	0	-0.01	-0.01	-0.17	-0.25	-0.04	-0.07	-0.11
E	-0.01	0.01	-0.01	-0.01	-0.03	-0.05	-0.08	-0.10	-0.07	-0.11
					France					
A	0	0	0	0	0	0	0	0	0	0
B	-0.15	-0.40	-0.59	-0.70	-0.68	-0.62	-0.54	-0.43	-0.43	-0.41
C	-0.15	-0.40	-0.61	-0.73	-0.72	-0.62	-0.61	-0.54	-0.60	-0.64
D	0	0	0	0	-0.01	-0.19	-0.26	-0.06	-0.09	-0.15
E	0	0.01	0	-0.02	-0.04	-0.06	-0.10	-0.11	-0.06	-0.12
					Italy					
A	0	0	0	0	0	0	0	0	0	0
B	-0.15	-0.43	-0.65	-0.78	-0.81	-0.75	-0.67	-0.54	-0.53	-0.50
C	-0.15	-0.43	-0.66	-0.81	-0.84	-0.80	-0.73	-0.64	-0.70	-0.76
D	0	0	0	-0.08	-0.76	-2.61	-3.50	-1.00	0.13	-1.26
E	0.01	-0.21	-0.52	-0.81	-1.04	-1.18	-1.72	-1.17	-0.46	-1.24
					United Kingdom					
A	0	0	0	0	0	0	0	0	0	0
B	-0.13	-0.40	-0.58	-0.65	-0.63	-0.55	-0.47	-0.36	-0.35	-0.30
C	-0.13	-0.40	-0.59	-0.69	-0.68	-0.61	-0.53	-0.46	-0.49	-0.49
D	0	0	0	0	0.01	-0.16	-0.22	-0.08	-0.10	-0.17
E	0	0.04	0.04	0.01	-0.03	-0.07	-0.12	-0.09	-0.05	-0.15

Key: A = baseline simulation; B = single expenditure cut; C = accumulating expenditure cuts; D = tax function with 60 percent debt-to-GDP target; E = tax function with "phased-in" 60 percent debt-to-GDP target.

TABLE 4.11
The Change in Tax Rates (percent deviation from baseline)

#	1995	1996	1997	1998	1999	2000	2001	2005	2010	2015
					Germany					
A	0	0	0	0	0	0	0	0	0	0
B	0.03	0.05	0.05	0.05	0.05	0.03	0.02	0.02	0.04	0.03
C	0	0	0	0	0	0	0	0	0	0
D	0	0	0	0	1.26	1.64	1.72	0.51	0.51	1.20
E	-0.66	-0.39	-0.03	0.31	-0.67	1.01	1.27	0.85	0.61	
					France					
A	0	0	0	0	0	0	0	0	0	0
B	-0.94	-1.74	-2.41	-2.96	-3.42	-3.78	-4.01	-4.11	-3.44	-2.75
C	0	0	-0.01	-0.01	-0.01	-0.01	-0.01	-0.01	-0.01	-0.01
D	0	0	0	0	1.62	1.82	1.89	0.78	0.54	0.31
E	-0.37	0.39	0.73	0.98	1.02	1.37	1.66	0.91	-0.02	-0.11
					Italy					
A	0	0	0	0	0	0	0	0	0	0
B	-1.12	-2.11	-2.94	-3.6	-4.12	-4.50	-4.71	-4.65	-3.86	-3.07
C	0	0	-0.01	-0.01	-0.01	-0.01	-0.01	-0.01	-0.01	-0.01
D	0	0	0	0.01	78.3	65.9	52.6	10.2	-2.96	-1.41
E	7.74	15.24	20.85	24.89	27.14	28.40	28.21	14.95	0.03	-0.48
					United Kingdom					
A	0	0	0	0	0	0	0	0	0	0
B	-0.68	-1.32	-1.86	-2.28	-2.67	-2.98	-3.19	-3.36	-2.87	-2.33
C	0	0	0	-0.01	-0.01	-0.01	-0.01	-0.01	-0.01	-0.01
D	0	0	0	0	0.36	0.88	1.11	0.34	0.28	0.26
E	-1.21	-1.38	-0.41	0.46	0.90	1.31	1.60	0.69	-0.15	-0.10

Key: A = baseline simulation; B = single expenditure cut; C = accumulating expenditure cuts; D = tax function with 60 percent debt-to-GDP target; E = tax function with "phased-in" 60 percent debt-to-GDP target.

TABLE 4.12
Nominal Interest Rates (percent deviation from baseline)

#	1995	1996	1997	1998	1999	2000	2001	2005	2010	2015
					Germany					
A	0	0	0	0	0	0	0	0	0	0
B	0.01	0	-0.01	-0.01	-0.05	-0.06	-0.05	-0.02	-0.04	-0.04
C	0.01	0.01	-0.01	-0.01	-0.06	-0.07	-0.07	-0.04	-0.06	-0.07
D	0	0	0	0	0	-0.05	-0.10	0	-0.02	-0.07
E	-0	0	0.01	0	-0.01	-0.02	-0.03	-0.04	-0.01	-0.06
					France					
A	0	0	0	0	0	0	0	0	0	0
B	0	0	0	0	-0	-0	-0	-0	-0	-0
C	0	0	0	0	-0	-0	-0	-0.01	-0.01	-0.01
D	0	0	0	0	0	-0	-0.02	-0.03	-0.02	-0.03
E	0	0	0	0	-0	-0	-0	-0.01	-0.01	-0.01
					Italy					
A	0	0	0	0	0	0	0	0	0	0
B	0	0	0	0	-0	-0	-0	-0	-0	-0
C	0	0	0	0	-0	-0	-0	-0	-0	-0.01
D	0	0	0	0	0	-0	-0.01	-0.02	-0.01	-0.02
E	0	0	0	0	-0	-0	-0	-0	-0	-0.01
					United Kingdom					
A	0	0	0	0	0	0	0	0	0	0
B	0	0	0	0	-0	-0	-0	-0	-0	-0
C	0	0	0	0	-0	-0	-0	-0	-0	-0.01
D	0	0	0	0	0	-0	-0.01	-0.02	-0.01	-0.02
E	0	0	0	0	-0	-0	-0	-0	-0	-0.01

Key: A = baseline simulation; B = single expenditure cut; C = accumulating expenditure cuts; D = tax function with 60 percent debt-to-GDP target; E = tax function with "phased-in" 60 percent debt-to-GDP target.

But tax rates increase when debt targets alone are introduced (simulations D and E)—sometimes spectacularly so since the model predicts a 70 percent increase in average tax rates for Italy in the full force tax reaction function, simulation C. Phasing-in reduces those increases to something more sensible—a mere 30 percent increase. It is these figures, rather than output losses, that reflect the real costs of a successful deficit reduction.

Notice also that changes in policy mix are needed despite the clear evidence of non-Keynesian (expansionary) effects. Table 4.12 implies positive effects from "crowding in," falling risk premia, and increasing fiscal credibility as deficits or debt are reduced. Similarly consumption, being a function of wealth, will be smoothed and offset the contractions in the short term. Finally Table 4.11 shows evidence of Ricardian equivalence, expenditure cuts reduce tax rates, and simulation E has negative or lower tax rate hikes than simulation D, which has no Ricardian equivalence. Thus our fiscal cuts are not all contractionary. But, unfortunately, the usual negative expenditure effects still outweigh the positive "credibility" effects. That is why the changes in policy mix are needed.

Deficit Reductions in Practice: Can They Be Expansionary?

How well do these observations fit the experience of countries that have actually engaged in deficit reduction programs in recent years? Did those countries also discover that growth is necessary if fiscal consolidation is not to lead to rises in the deficit ratio? Or did they discover that the output losses were only small, implying that strong non-Keynesian effects offset the usual contractionary mechanism?

Experimental control versus historical experience

Recent European experience provides some insight on the historical costs of fiscal restructuring. Our task, should those costs turn out to be small or nonexistent, is to determine whether that is because fiscal contractions contain their own expansionary elements as many have claimed.[22] Or is something else happening at the same time?

The difficulty with relying on a historical analysis to identify the non-Keynesian expansionary effects is that such an analysis lacks the experimental control necessary to separate the consequences of any fiscal changes from the consequences of any other measure, or from what would have happened anyway. To get the necessary experimental control, one has to simulate a suitable "counterfactual," or to analyze the components of the fiscal policy multipliers taken from a model that contains the potential non-Keynesian as well as Keynesian effects. And if the model is nonlinear, this will show how the strength of the expansionary elements varies with the level of activity, and with the initial level of debt and interest rates, as compared to the contractionary elements.

Controlling for the sources of expansion

Table 4.13 gives a first look at the historical record. It is of interest to pick out the Danish experience in 1983 to 1986 and the Irish case of 1986 to 1989, since they are the cases highlighted in Giavazzi and Pagano's (1990, 1995) analysis.

If the expansionary components are roughly the same across countries per unit fiscal cut, then higher growth in these cases would be due to accompanying changes in the policy mix or to differences in initial conditions, but not from the fiscal restructuring itself. However that is still not proof since there might still be structural differences that leave the expansionary components larger in Denmark and Ireland than elsewhere. The problem with that argument is that the Irish contraction of 1982 to 1984 clearly does not have the expansionary properties that appeared in 1986–1989, and it is hard to imagine that the Irish fiscal structure could have changed so radically within four years. We can dismiss that case therefore; something else must have caused it.[23]

Similarly if we can find other explanations for the Danish growth, then it would be wrong to attribute their success to expansionary fiscal contractions. In fact both countries show growth rates that are double the average of all the contraction cases, and both are at the top of the distribution of growth rates for those contracting fiscally. So growth certainly is a key factor. Can we say where that growth came from? Anderson and Risager (1988) identify a number of sources, none of them fiscal. The largest is clearly the monetary relaxation that took place four months after the fiscal contraction started. At that point a new and much lower wage bargain was struck, reducing unit labor costs and improving the prospects for inflation, competitiveness, and hence the supply side. As a result interest rates fell 1.6 percent, extending a fall of 0.9 percent four months earlier when the government had refused to devalue, and a smaller fall a month later when the EMS currencies realigned (but Denmark did not). Thus, although this monetary easing may well have been part of a general restructuring exercise, none of it has a fiscal origin. (In fact, government expenditures did not actually fall!) Instead Anderson and Risager point out that the fiscal policy announcement effects were negligible; that output first declined for six months before rising strongly with monetary easing and improving competitiveness; and that there had been a one-off 25 percent increase in the M2 money supply after nine months. Hence a change in the policy mix (a monetary relaxation and supply-side improvements) can account for the entire episode.

Does this generalize to the rest of Table 4.13? There are several points to

TABLE 4.13 Budgetary Retrenchment Experiences, 1974 to 1994 (percent)

Country	Period	Total Change in Primary Structural Surplus*	Total Change in the Budget Balance*	Intensity* (I)	Annual Growth Effect (G)	Output Cost	Long-term Interest Rate Effect in Short Term	Long-term Interest Rate Effect	Short-term Real Effective Exchange Rate	Long-term Real Effective Exchange Rate	EU
				Past Retrenchments							
UK	1979-82	5.6	1.9	1.4	-0.8	0.5	-0.5	-1.8	31.7	43.8	4.0
Germany	1981-84	8.1	0.9	2.0	-0.7	0.3	0.5	-0.5	-10.1	-14.1	-4.0
Sweden	1981-87	8.5	8.3	1.2	1.2	-1.0	0.8	1.9	-5.0	-8.8	…
Ireland 1	1982-84	5.9	3.4	2.0	-1.4	0.7	-1.3	-0.5	10.4	10.0	3.0
Belgium	1982-87	10.6	5.5	1.8	-0.5	0.3	0.6	-1.4	-12.9	-4.5	-1.0
Denmark	1983-86	12.4	12.5	3.1	1.8	-0.6	-5.9	-8.5	2.8	6.8	-0.5
Ireland 2	1986-89	8.2	9.1	2.0	-0.7	0.4	-0.6	-3.7	-2.9	-5.5	-0.5
Netherlands	1991-93	4.5	1.8	1.5	0.4	-0.2	0.0	-0.4	-1.3	2.7	-1.0
Average	4.6 years	7.1	5.1	1.6	9.0	-0.1	-0.5	-1.4	-2.3	4.1	…
				Ongoing Retrenchments							
Greece	1990-94	11.0	2.3	2.2	-1.1	0.6	5.8	5.0	4.3	9.7	10.0
Italy	1991-94	4.7	1.9	1.2	-0.3	0.7	1.1	-1.1	-0.8	-16.1	1.5
Spain	1992-94	3.2	-1.7	1.1	-1.2	1.2	-0.6	-1.3	-8.5	-13.5	…
Average	na	6.3	0.8	1.5	-1.1	0.8	2.1	0.9	-1.7	-6.6	…

Notes: *percent GDP; I = average change in the primary surplus over the adjustment period; output cost = G/I.
Source: Pisani-Ferry and Cour (1995)

make. First, adjustment costs are always lower if they are calculated for the cyclically adjusted budget deficit (as here) rather than from the actual deficit. The cyclically adjusted deficit is necessarily smaller on average and therefore cheaper to eliminate. Unfortunately the Maastricht Treaty is defined in terms of actual deficits. Second, the difficulty with Table 4.13 lies in the way the impact of the fiscal contractions on growth is measured. If this is negative or small, then the fiscal cuts would appear to have strong expansionary elements. Yet the growth effect is defined as:

$$G = \frac{\sum_{t=1}^{T}(y_t - y^*_t) - (\hat{y} - \hat{y}^*)}{T} \tag{4.6}$$

where y_t is the country's growth rate during the cuts and y^*_t that of the EU over the same restructuring period; while $\hat{y}$ and $\hat{y}^*$ are the corresponding quantities over the whole period 1971 to 1994. Hence the cost of fiscal restructuring will always appear small if the short-run growth rate of a country, relative to that in the EU, is the same as its long-run growth trend as a proportion of that in the EU (whatever the absolute cost in terms of lost growth), or if the fiscal cuts bring a country's growth down to the EU average in a period when that country would otherwise have had growth above trend.

In other words, from Table 4.13 you cannot tell whether the low costs of fiscal adjustment are because fiscal contractions genuinely have few contractionary effects, or whether it is because the distribution of growth rates has moved down as a whole (for example, they all contract together); or because the country, which had started moving up the distribution, is temporarily made to move down again (for example, an expansionary country is brought back into line). In any of those cases, the actual costs of contraction could have been rather large. Hence this measure means very little if we cannot control for what would have happened otherwise (the counterfactual) or for other sources of growth (that is, what would have happened anyway).

The theoretical literature, however, goes some way to resolving the issue. Barry and Devereux (1995) construct a small two-sector model containing crowding in, consumption smoothing, expectations, Ricardian equivalence and varying degrees of wage flexibility. They find fiscal contractions cause consumption and investment to contract unless either the demand for labor in the nontradable sector is highly elastic and wages are flexible, or wages are inflexible and the contraction temporary. But in either case, the current account deteriorates and output contracts. Hence employment invariably falls. And that must be the key result since, if employment falls, unemployment payments will have to rise and the original fiscal deficit reduction will be wiped out. Economic theory therefore suggests that fiscal contractions will be *net* contractionary, and that the deficit reductions (in the absence of supporting measures) will be short-lived when unemployment starts to rise again.[24] Germany's experience in 1995 to 1996 appears to be a prime example of this series of effects.

Accompanying policy changes

What accompanying policies were used in these cases? Evidently there are monetary expansions here since *short-run* real exchange rates fall; with prices sticky, this is consistent with nominal depreciations and an initial fall in long-run interest rates. That implies an easing of monetary policy and an initial expansion of demand. In the longer term, interest rates fall further (monetary easing, default risk premia removed). But real exchange rates rise, so the nominal depreciations have ceased with the result that interest rates do not rise again. Crowding in continues, therefore, while the appreciating real exchange rate may lead to increases in capacity output. Finally, most of these fiscal contractions have taken place against a background of lower inflation in the adjusting countries than in the nonadjusters. Hence whatever the nominal money stocks may be doing, real money stocks are increasing compared to elsewhere. But unless all these additional policy changes were totally ineffective, the non-Keynesian side of fiscal policy cannot have been a significant force.

Extending the period of analysis

Table 4.14 contains another selection of deficit reduction exercises. Of the twelve cases reported, the average duration was 5.5 years; the average reduction in the actual deficit ratio was 4.4 percent. That implies an average reduction of just 0.8 percent per year, which is in line with the slow reductions in Table 4.7. Moreover just over half of these reductions were sustained in the sense that 50 percent of the original reduction survives as long as three years. A more stringent definition—that they should genuinely survive (that is, that the ratio should not rise again)—would have produced a much higher "failure" rate. That too is entirely consistent with Table 4.7.

Finally we have included data on output growth and rates of growth of the money supply in Table 4.14. Since the growth differential for each deflating country versus the EU-12 is positive on average, it appears that the deflating countries do tend to grow faster than those with no debt and deficit deflation problems. However that does not say that they grow fast in absolute terms. From the next column we see that some do, but most do not. The monetary growth figures, however, are significantly larger. This is prima facie evidence that the deflating countries have indeed tried to expand their money supplies by enough to retain a little growth. Moreover a clear majority of those who followed that strategy, that is, six out of the nine whose monetary expansions

TABLE 4.14 Large-Scale Budgetary Adjustments, 1974 to 1994 (percent)

Country	Period	Change in the Actual Fiscal Balance*	Change in the Cyclically Adjusted Primary Balance*	Mean Annual Change*	Nominal Exchange Rate (1)	Real Exchange Rate (2)	Risk Premium (3)	Growth Differential (4)	GDP Growth Rate	Growth in the Money Supply (M2)	Durable? (5)
Denmark	1983-86	12.5	12	3	1.6	4.3	-5.9	1.6	2.9	10.9	y
Belgium	1982-87	5.7	10.3	1.7	-8.3	-18.7	0.6	-0.8	1.2	6.2	y
Norway	1978-85	9.1	10	1.2	-12.3	-21.4	0.2	1.8	3.4	11.6	n
Ireland	1986-89	9.1	9.2	2.3	-3.9	-14.6	-0.6	0.7	3.0	7.2	y
Sweden	1981-87	8.2	8.8	1.2	-4.0	-6.5	0.8	0.2	2.0	6.3	n
Ireland	1982-84	3.5	6.9	2.3	-0.4	-0.6	-1.3	1.2	2.3	5.1	n
UK	1979-85	1.5	5.8	0.8	21.4	37.7	-0.5	-0.1	1.1	13.2	y
Germany	1980-85	1.4	5.6	0.9	-5.2	-9.8	2.5	-0.2	0.9	4.5	n
Spain	1983-87	2.1	5	1	-13.0	-8.5	1.5	0.64	3.0	10.1	n
Netherlands	1980-86	-0.1	4.9	0.7	-0.3	-14.6	0.2	-0.5	1.0	5.2	y
Finland	1988-91	0	4.7	1.2	6.7	11.2	-0.0	-1.9	...	4.7	y
Italy	1980-83	-0.5	3.8	1	-10.4	-2.8	3.8	0.9	0.3	10.1	y
Average	na	4.4	7.3	1.4	-2.3	-3.7	0.1	0.3	1.7	8.1	na

Notes: *percent GDP; (1) change in the nominal effective exchange rate relative to the EC 12 between the year before the launching of the program and the second year of its implementation; (2) change in the real effective exchange rate (unit labor costs in manufacturing) relative to the EC 12 between the year before the launching of the program and the second year of its implementation; (3) change in the long-term interest rate relative to Germany (for Germany, change in the interest rate) between the year before the program and the second year of its implementation; (4) average growth differential relative to the EC 12 over the period; (5) the adjustment is considered durable if at least 50 percent of the improvement in the primary balance persists after three years.

exceeded 5 percent, enjoyed durable deficit reductions. This is exactly what we should expect them to do, if they wished to get their deficit ratios down quickly.

Summary

In this chapter we have looked at Maastricht-type fiscal reductions to meet the criteria for monetary union. We found that deficit reductions need to be conditioned on the debt target. The two cannot be treated entirely independently. Given that, successful deficit reductions require additional policy measures *and* a detailed reform of the tax system if incomes are not to fall and the fiscal ratios to start rising again. Those additional measures might include a mild relaxation in monetary policy to accompany the fiscal contractions, or wider ERM bands, or wage restraint and price deflations. But the mix of tax and expenditure reforms needs to be carefully designed. The sensitivity of the outcomes shows it is very easy to unleash the kind of liquidity squeeze and financial instability that would undermine the whole enterprise.

From this strategy we also learn that tax revenues and growth are the key to deficit reductions; expenditure cutting alone will not do it. As a result, the Germans at least have become worried that some countries will "squeeze in under the EMU door" in 1999, and then threaten the whole enterprise by losing control of their deficits and debt thereafter. That has prompted the Germans to propose their "stability pact" of yet tighter deficit criteria. We show that to be the wrong approach since it will just make control of the fiscal ratios more difficult and a liquidity crisis more likely.

Finally these simulations have not been constructed to suggest that, without EMU, European governments would not undertake any fiscal restructuring and that life would be better if they did not. They probably would because their ability to steer their economies could be seriously damaged if they did not. These simulations simply show what can be expected to happen if they were to successfully unwind the deficits accumulated over the past ten to fifteen years.

Notes

1. Financial support from the ESRC's GEI initiative is most gratefully acknowledged.

2. Luxembourg is the only country with a deficit less than 3 percent of GNP. The German deficit is usually quoted at 2.4 percent of GNP for 1995. However that is the national accounts definition. The federal government's "statistical" accounts show a deficit of 4.1 percent, and the public sector's debt shows a jump from 51 percent to 58

percent for the same period. Moreover in late 1995, Germany admitted its deficit was 3.6 percent of GNP even on the lower (national accounts) definition and forecast a rise to 4.3 percent for 1996.

3. Kenen (1995a).

4. See, for example, Hughes Hallett and Ma (1996b) for an analysis of debt reductions and von Hagen and Lutz (1995) for a much more pessimistic view of the costs of deficit reductions.

5. Masson et al. (1990), Bartolini and Symanski (1993). The version used here has the "rest of the EMS" as a single integrated bloc, the national accounts of which cannot be broken down into individual countries except by arbitrarily dividing each variable in some fixed proportions (Masson et al., 1991). That tactic seemed too arbitrary to be worthwhile, even if it does mean that we are unable to say anything specific about the different experiences of interesting cases like Ireland and Belgium.

6. The fiscal expenditure variable used here covers government investment and consumption programs, but not social security or interest payments.

7. In the modeling of German unification, the IMF estimates the total cost will be DM 1,700 billion to the year 2001 (McDonald and Thumann, 1990). We suppose that half of that cost will be paid for by central and local government, spread as a declining balance over fifteen years to cover fiscal transfers, social security, infrastructure, and private investment support. Accordingly we add DM 850 billion to the exogenous government spending, spread as DM 56 billion, 160 billion, 120 billion, and 70 billion in 1990, 1991, 1992, and 1993, respectively; and then DM 37 billion each year until 2005. That corresponds to a fiscal shock of 7.9 percent of GDP at its peak, but of 1.5 percent or less after 1994. These figures run below current expenditures, estimated by the Bundesbank still to be running at DM 200 billion annually in 1995, but include the operating deficits of the Treuhand agency from 1991 and Treuhand's debt of DM 325 billion.

8. Germany, on our baseline, does not breach the 3 percent deficit target and does not engage in the nominal or accumulator expenditure cuts. It does engage in the simulations involving debt targets however. In reality Germany breached the 3 percent limit by the end of 1995, so these simulations will underestimate the costs of financial retrenchment.

9. Note that for operation reasons, tax rates adjust to eliminate the gap from the debt target of the last period, rather than the contemporaneous deficit ratio target, which cannot be known at the point at which tax rates had to be adjusted. To do this, we use the model's own parameter values of $\alpha_1 = 0.04$ and $\alpha_2 = 0.3$.

10. These two rules come from the NIGEM and MSG multicountry models, respectively, and are introduced as illustrations of typical alternative rules (see Church et al., 1996).

11. Since the model does not solve for the deficit-to-GNP ratio explicitly—but only for each part individually—we first calculate, using France as an example, what 4.9 percent of baseline nominal GNP is and subtract or add the difference between present deficit and required deficit depending on whether the baseline deficit in MULTIMOD is above or below the required level using a residual adjustment. That implies some autonomous changes in fiscal policies as well as some adjustment in taxation as a consequence.

12. By tax regime, we mean the rules that link tax rates and changes in tax rates to the underlying fiscal imbalances. Since the model does not distinguish between different types of taxes (direct, indirect, corporate, on wealth, etc.) we cannot say exactly what form the change of tax regime might take—only what the change in average impact has to be. There is some evidence that shifts toward indirect taxation and cuts in welfare payments may in fact be more effective than increases in direct taxation or other expenditure cuts (Bartolini et al., 1995; Alesina and Perotti, 1995). Whether that result survives in our case is a matter for further research.

13. Neutral taxes means $\alpha_1 = \alpha_2 = 0$ in equation (4.1). As an indication of the sensitivity of the fiscal criteria to the new tax regime, we had to search for those sustainable debt targets, and the Italian targets had to be reduced by degrees—prorated in equal steps down from 92 percent in 1999 to 76 percent in 2004—in order to prevent taxes from rising (and income falling) too fast.

14. Although much smaller in scale, this combination of output losses and liquidity squeeze is exactly the same mechanism that drove the financial and political instability in the 1930s.

15. Although the result is extra inflation and a reversal of the fall in interest rates as inflationary expectations take hold, both effects are fairly small.

16. This supply-side improvement and the fact that "all hell does not break loose" even after several years of adjustment are also key lessons from the Alesina and Perotti (1995) analysis.

17. Hughes Hallett and Ma (1996b) point out that a rapid debt or deficit reduction program will be easier and cheaper since to get the ratio down in a hurry will require measures to protect income levels. Slower debt reductions implies no such constraint since it then does not matter much if income falls, provided only that it falls more slowly than the absolute level of the debt or deficit. It is the need to get the fiscal restructuring done within a realistic period of time (or at a reasonable political cost) that makes a second instrument necessary.

18. Note that all EU countries would in fact have to run primary surpluses even to reduce their deficit ratios, let alone their debt ratios, since a debt burden of 60 percent costs 3 percent of GNP in service payments alone at interest rates of 5 percent. No EU country can claim lower figures (Luxembourg excepted) at present.

19. It is interesting to compare this result with the French experience of "competitive deflations" since 1985 (see Fitoussi et al., 1993).

20. Von Hagen and Lutz (1995) report much greater output costs: averaging 6 percent per annum over four years, with price falls of 30 percent, before Italy returns to its baseline.

21. Hughes Hallett and Ma (1995) examine this point in more detail.

22. Giavazzi and Pagano (1990, 1995), Bertola and Drazen (1993), Sutherland (1995), Pisani-Ferry and Cour (1995).

23. Nevertheless, for highly indebted countries it does seem likely that the expansionary components are larger than for "ordinarily" indebted countries (Giavazzi and Pagano, 1995). What we observe here is that, even then, those expansionary effects are not numerically large enough to offset the contractionary elements. Bradley et al. (1993) have shown this to be true even for the Irish case.

24. MULTIMOD does not compute unemployment rates explicitly, and government expenditures are only partly endogenized. So the link from unemployment back to the deficit is not properly modeled. It is therefore likely that the reversal of the fiscal reductions in our simulations have been underestimated.

5

Monetary Union with Variable Geometry

Jean Pisani-Ferry

The difficulties encountered by several European countries in meeting the conditions for membership in Economic and Monetary Union (EMU) spelled out by the Maastricht Treaty, and the existence of an opting out clause imply that European monetary union should be initiated by a subset of member states. Other countries are expected to join them at a later stage, but only if they meet the convergence criteria and, in fact, are willing to participate. The United Kingdom and Denmark remain formally uncommitted to participating in the single currency, and Sweden has indicated its intention not to join the single currency in 1999. Unlike the preceding stages of integration, EMU will thus have a distinctive, variable-geometry flavor.

This was not unintended, since it was anticipated from the outset that monetary union would not immediately comprise all EU member states. Neither is multispeed integration a new feature of European integration. But there is something new in the current developments. The possibility must be considered that some member states may decide—or be forced—to abstain from monetary union for a protracted period.

Since its creation, the European Community's basic philosophy has been that, over the medium term, all EU countries would eventually converge toward the same degree of integration and implement the same policies. Variable geometry was therefore limited to temporary derogations for new and catching-up member states, or to membership in agreements that were not formally part of the Community system. While they might be "temporarily unable" to do so, all member states were assumed to be willing to participate in all areas of integration. This philosophy is enshrined in the treaty, and it is made clear to new members on the occasion of their accession that they must accept the entire acquis communautaire.

It is becoming increasingly apparent that monetary union is different for

legal, economic, and political reasons. The Maastricht Treaty formally introduced variable geometry into Community law, through the opting-out clauses
negotiated by Britain and Denmark.[1] This right to abstain from participation
in monetary union was subsequently extended to all member states on an
informal basis and was eventually recognized at the European Council of Flor-
ence, in June 1996, as the leaders of the Community stated that membership
in the new Exchange Rate Mechanism (ERM)—which is considered among
the required criteria for entering Stage III of EMU—would be "facultative."
Any member state could therefore opt out from the single currency simply by
abstaining from becoming part of this new ERM. This amounts to an explicit
recognition of a political reality: Although several member states will no
doubt be "willing, yet temporarily unable" to join EMU, some others might
rather be "unwilling, although able."

The variable-geometry approach to monetary union can moreover be justified on economic grounds. Standard monetary theory provides fundamental
reasons why participating in the single currency may not be equally desirable
for all member states. It is well known that the costs and benefits of forming
a monetary union depend positively on the degree of economic integration
between the participating countries, and negatively on the extent of the structural and behavioral asymmetries among them.[2] Whether or not the benefits
exceed the costs is a purely empirical matter that cannot be decided a priori.

Finally, to require all member states to participate in monetary union would
involve significant political risks. Membership in the single currency will
imply renouncing policy autonomy in the monetary field and accepting tight
discipline in the fiscal field. A country unwilling to subscribe to such a commitment or unable to deliver on it would be better off abstaining from entering
the monetary union. Forced participation would be a recipe for policy conflicts
and political crises.

For all these reasons, the issue of differentiated monetary integration has
gained prominence in European policy debates. At its December 1995 summit
in Madrid, the European Council initiated discussions on the management of
monetary relations between the members of the Euro-core (the "ins") and the
other EU members (the "outs"). Following the German proposal for a "stability pact," parallel discussions were simultaneously launched on the organization of fiscal discipline among the members of the monetary core. Results
from these discussions were endorsed by the European Council at its meeting
in Dublin in time for implementation prior to the start of monetary union.
More generally, variable geometry was put forward by President Chirac and
Chancellor Kohl as they jointly proposed that the upcoming revision of the
treaty includes an explicit provision that would acknowledge the right for a
subset of member states to develop tighter cooperation in some policy areas,
while remaining within the Community framework.

The variable-geometry approach to monetary union however raises fundamental questions over the future of the European Union. Do some member states have solid reasons to retain exchange rate flexibility? Should the initial core of EMU participants be large or small? Will monetary union create a permanent divide between the monetary "elite" and the other members? Can most, if not all, member states be expected to join the single currency soon? Will temporary exclusion from the monetary core have lasting consequences for the outsiders? Will the cohabitation of the "ins" and the "outs" give rise to conflicts that might endanger the single market? Will it be necessary and possible to coordinate monetary policies between the "ins" and the "outs"? These questions are at the heart of the current policy discussions on membership and on the arrangements for the outsiders.

This chapter discusses the economics of differentiated monetary integration in Europe. The first section examines the case for variable geometry through looking at relevant criteria for deciding on the principle of and the timing for membership in monetary union. The second proposes a framework for analyzing relations between the "ins" and the "outs." The third discusses alternative schemes for organizing a monetary union with variable geometry in Europe. Conclusions are drawn in in the fourth section.

Criteria for Membership

The Maastricht criteria focus attention on specific performance indicators. This has the disadvantage of distracting attention from a more fundamental issue, namely, the benefit that member states themselves may derive from participating in monetary union (it should be remembered that the purpose of the Maastricht criteria has never been to determine what is the interest of the applicant countries, but rather to protect monetary union from the detrimental influences of members not fulfilling stability criteria). In what follows, I set aside the usual Maastricht criteria to examine the evidence on the economic benefits of membership in monetary union for the member states of the EU. The analysis starts with structural criteria derived from the optimum currency area literature. The role of policy priorities is discussed next.

Structural criteria

Since discussion on EMU began at the end of the 1980s, economic research has accumulated considerable evidence on the distribution of costs and benefits of membership in monetary union.[3] As noted by Tamim Bayoumi and Barry Eichengreen (1996a), most studies have followed an identical route, which can be described as "operationalizing the theory of optimum currency areas" through attempting quantitative evaluations of country-specific or asymmetric shocks within the EU. This route is not without drawbacks as it rests on the assumption that shocks do not depend on the exchange rate regime. There is evidence that this assumption may not be the case, and recent research suggests that the optimum currency area criteria might be endogenous rather than exogenous (Frankel and Rose, 1996). Furthermore, the relative situation of the member states is evolving, and measures based on performance observed during the past two or three decades may understate actual convergence (Boone, 1997). But it has the merit of providing an assessment of the relative situation of individual member states vis-à-vis monetary union. Thereafter, I examine whether this body of evidence leads to support variable geometry on purely economic grounds.

In the following tables, Germany is taken as the reference country, and Luxembourg, which is already in a monetary union with Belgium, is ignored.[4] This leaves thirteen countries to be considered. I envisage three different categories of criteria and two–to–three criteria for each category. The choice of the criteria was constrained by the availability of comparable data for all thirteen countries. This prevents using a wider range of indicators, but preserves homogeneity in the treatment of the countries. Here I briefly describe the criteria, for which precise definitions are given in Appendix 5.1.

- Stability. A first approach, which was used in the early literature on EMU (Vaubel, 1978), is to use actual exchange rate stability as an indicator of the past incidence of shocks. Rows one and two of Table 5.1 therefore report indicators of both nominal and real exchange rate stability vis-à-vis the DM.
- Shocks. A second approach is to attempt to measure directly the degree of asymmetry of shocks. There are several possible methods for this purpose. Bayoumi and Eichengreen (1992, 1996a) rely on bivariate VARs to disentangle shocks to GDP from responses, and to distinguish aggregate demand shocks (which have no permanent affect on output) from aggregate supply shocks (which do affect output in the long run). I report as shock indicators the correlation of aggregate demand and aggregate supply shocks between each country and Germany over the 1963 to 1990 period (thus, the period of German unification is excluded). An alternative route, which is conceptually similar, is taken by Mélitz (1996). It estimates pooled univariate GDP equations to extract the asymmetric and symmetric components of the innovations. Here, his ratio of asymmetric to symmetric disturbances is used as an indicator of the asymmetric character of shocks.
- Structures. In principle, asymmetric shocks—at least those that could endanger monetary union—originate in differences between economic structures.[5] Following Kenen (1969), industrial specialization is frequently mentioned as a potential source of asymmetries in Europe, as it is in the United States (Bini-Smaghi and Vori, 1993; Krugman, 1993;

Bayoumi and Eichengreen, 1996a). However, comparable and detailed production and employment data by industry are only available for all EU member states at highly aggregated classification levels. Therefore, I rely on export data instead, which are taken as providing indirect evidence of the structure of production, and I report both a Finger index of export similarity with Germany and the correlation of exports growth rates over the 1971 to 1990 period (also vis-à-vis German exports).[6] Finally, the difference between trade with the core ERM countries and total trade (both as a percentage of GDP) is also reported. Since benefits from monetary union should depend positively on the degree of economic integration within the union, this criterion is meant to represent the benefits side of participating in a core monetary union.

Table 5.1 summarizes the results from this exercise by giving the ranking of the thirteen countries for each of the eight criteria, as well as for their grouping in three broader categories, and the overall ranking obtained by giving equal weight to the three categories (this weighting is admittedly somewhat arbitrary; the rationale for it is to give equal importance to the stability, shocks, and structures criteria).[7] It also reports the ranking obtained by Daniel Gros (1996a), which uses a wide range of indicators.[8]

The indicators display a reasonably high degree of consistency. First, indicators within each category are positively correlated: The coefficient of correlation of ranks is 0.8 between the two measures of exchange rate stability; the correlation of ranks between the Mélitz measure of asymmetry and the Bayoumi-Eichengreen measure of asymmetry in supply shocks is 0.7 (and 0.5 for demand shocks); correlation between the ranking according to the Finger index of export structure similarity and the correlation of export growth rates is 0.8. This suggests a degree of robustness of the results with respect to variations in the choice of indicators or in estimation techniques. Second, the average rankings for the three categories of criteria are also positively correlated (Table 5.2). This indicates that there is a relation between symmetry of structures, symmetry of shocks, and actual exchange rate stability: Countries with similar structures tend to endure more symmetric shocks and to experience more exchange rate stability.[9] This suggests that shocks originate in structural differences, rather than in divergent policy choices.

The resulting overall ranking can therefore be considered fairly robust. It suggests that Austria, Belgium, France, the Netherlands, and possibly Denmark are natural candidates for the Euro-core. At the other extreme, Greece, Ireland, Portugal, and Spain seem to be characterized by higher historical real exchange rate volatility, a lower correlation of shocks, and less homogeneity in economic structures. For them, participation in a monetary union might therefore involve significant costs. Italy, the United Kingdom, Sweden, and Finland occupy a middle position. This categorization is broadly consistent

TABLE 5.1 Criteria for Membership in Monetary Union (Rank Orderings*)

Criteria	Austria	Belgium	Denmark	Spain	Finland	France	Greece	Ireland	Italy	Netherlands	Portugal	UK	Sweden
Stability (total)	*1*	*3*	*4*	*10*	*7*	*5*	*12*	*6*	*8*	*2*	*8*	*12*	*10*
-Nominal exchange rate stability	1	3	4	9	10	5	11	6	8	2	7	12	13
-Real exchange rate stability	1	3	4	11	6	5	13	8	9	2	10	12	7
Shocks (total)	*2*	*2*	*4*	*10*	*9*	*1*	*13*	*12*	*4*	*4*	*10*	*8*	*7*
-Demand shocks	1	5	4	13	1	3	10	12	2	8	6	9	6
-Supply shocks	5	2	2	10	6	1	13	12	7	4	1	8	8
-Asymmetry	3	2	10	6	9	1	13	1	7	4	12	8	5
Structures (total)	*1*	*2*	*7*	*10*	*1*	*3*	*12*	*13*	*4*	*6*	*8*	*4*	*9*
-Finger index for exports	2	5	8	12	9	1	12	1	3	7	10	3	6
-Trade with core	2	1	10	3	12	9	6	13	4	7	5	8	12
-Export correlation	1	3	4	1	7	2	13	12	9	5	10	5	8
Overall ranking	*1*	*2*	*5*	*10*	*9*	*3*	*13*	*12*	*6*	*4*	*10*	*7*	*8*
Ranking by Gros (1996)	4	1	11	3	12	2	13	8	6	5	10	6	9

Note: *Rankings exclude Luxembourg and Germany.
Source: European Commission and author's calculations.

TABLE 5.2
Correlation Ranks for Three Categories of Symmetry Criteria

Symmetry Criteria	Stability	Shocks	Structures
Stability	1.0	0.70	0.48
Shocks		1.0	0.88
Structures			1.0

with that of Gros (1996a), but with the significant exceptions of Spain (which Gros includes in the core) and Denmark (which he ranks among the likely outsiders).

It should be kept in mind, however, that this characterization relies on historical data, which frequently go back to the 1970s and even to the 1960s. For countries undergoing structural convergence, it may lead to overly pessimistic conclusions. This may especially apply to countries like Ireland and Spain. This intuition is confirmed by Boone (1997), who relies on time-varying estimation methods to test for convergence over time.

Policy priorities

The above criteria are based on structures and long-run behavior. There may also be reasons why a country could decide (or be forced) to delay its participation in monetary union. An obvious reason for this would be a failure to meet the Maastricht convergence criteria; but as the performance of the EU member states vis-à-vis the Maastricht convergence criteria is subject to close monitoring by observers and financial markets, there is no point in refining the forecasts for 1997. A more interesting approach is to examine on what grounds member states could themselves be led to postpone their entry.

Failure to achieve inflation convergence could obviously be a reason for delay as national inflation within monetary union would automatically translate into real exchange rate appreciation. However, this argument has lost a large part of its empirical relevance. Except for Greece, recent data and current OECD, IMF, or Commission forecasts for 1997 indicate a high degree of inflation convergence. There would therefore be little justification for a country to delay entry on inflation grounds. Budgetary and unemployment issues are clearly much more serious causes for concern.

The fiscal issue was given prominence by the Maastricht entry conditions. But those conditions tend to focus attention on a specific timetable and numerical criteria for the deficit and the public debt, whereas the key issue vis-à-vis membership in EMU is not whether and at what pace European countries should implement fiscal adjustment, but rather whether fiscal adjustment—

which is required anyway—should be carried out under fixed or flexible exchange rates.

The dilemma of macroeconomic policy can be highlighted by contrasting
two alternative strategies. The first one is to compensate the restrictive effects
of a fiscal retrenchment program through monetary expansion and/or exchange rate depreciation.[10] As this is basically what Italy did in 1992 to 1995
after withdrawing from the ERM, it can be termed the "Italian" strategy. The
opposite choice is to underline commitment to a fixed exchange rate vis-à-vis
a strong currency in order to bring down depreciation expectations and lower
the interest rate on public debt. The Belgian policy of pursuing a fixed exchange rate vis-à-vis the mark, can be termed the "Belgian" strategy.

Assume that the policymaker's objective is to minimize the output cost of
fiscal adjustment, that is to meet a specified target B^* for the government
balance, while minimizing the deviation of output Y from potential output Q.
The government's balance depends on tax revenues τY, the interest burden on
public debt iD (the debt is assumed to be constant) and expenditures G :

$$B = \tau Y - iD - G. \tag{5.1}$$

The interest rate on public debt i equals foreign interest rate i^* plus a risk
premium Φ:

$$i = i^* + \Phi. \tag{5.2}$$

Finally, deviations of output from potential output depend on demand factors,
that is the exchange rate E and public expenditures G (the tax rate τ is assumed
to be constant):

$$Y - Q = \theta G + \gamma E. \tag{5.3}$$

There are two exchange rate regimes: flexible exchange rates, in which the
authorities use the exchange rate as an instrument, but which implies a positive risk premium on public debt ($\Phi > 0$), and monetary union, which immediately results in a zero risk premium ($\Phi = 0$) but at the cost of sterilizing
the exchange rate instrument (hence, E is constant).[11] The country starts with
output at level Y_0 and inherits government balance B_0 and risk premium Φ_0. It
is also committed to meeting the B^* target at time 1. It can either seek participation in monetary union at time 0 ("Belgian" strategy), or delay it until time
1 ("Italian" strategy).

Rewriting the model in first differences and grouping equations (5.1) and
(5.2) gives:

$$b = \tau \gamma e - (1 - \tau \theta)g - D\Phi \qquad \text{and} \tag{5.4}$$
$$y = \theta g + \gamma e. \tag{5.5}$$

From (5.4), it is obvious that if $b = B^* - B_0 < D\Phi_0$, the "Belgian" strategy is optimal. Entering monetary union at time 0 does not involve any cost, since the entire deficit reduction results from the drop in the risk premium. When $B^* - B_0 < D\Phi_0$, however, deficit reduction requires bringing down public expenditures, that is $g > 0$. The preferable strategy may be to offset the restrictive effects of this policy through exchange rate depreciation, that is to set $e = (\theta/\gamma)(b + D\varphi)$ where φ is the possible increase in the risk premium resulting from the depreciation of the currency ("Italian" strategy). The desirable timing of entry in monetary union therefore depends on the factors underlying the deficit. Countries whose primary balance is already at a satisfactory level should seek early entry, while countries with an excessive primary deficit should rather delay it.

Practical implementation requires setting a target level for the primary surplus. The standard approach is to derive it from a debt stabilization condition:

$$PRIMS = \left[\frac{(1 + i)}{(1 + \hat{y})(1 + \hat{p})}\right] * d \qquad (5.6)$$

where d is the debt-to-GDP ratio, $\hat{y}$ is trend output growth and $\hat{p}$ is trend inflation. However, stabilizing the debt ratio does not correspond to the objectives set out in the Maastricht Treaty for countries whose debt exceeds 60 percent of GDP. Therefore, condition (5.6) has to be tightened in order to ensure convergence toward the 60 percent level for countries starting from a higher debt level. The primary surplus required in order to eliminate each year α percent of the gap between the current debt ratio $\tilde{d}$ and the target level 60 percent is:

$$PRIMC = \left(\left[\frac{(1 + i)}{(1 + \hat{y})(1 + \hat{p})} - (1 - \alpha)\right] * d - \alpha\tilde{d}, PRIMS\right). \qquad (5.7)$$

With $\alpha = 5$ percent, this corresponds to the criterion proposed by Gros (1996a) for deciding the entry of member states starting from an excessive debt level.[12]

The comparison between PRIMC and the actual primary surplus gives a criterion for evaluating which countries would benefit from pursuing fiscal adjustment in a flexible exchange rate environment, and which would benefit from renouncing monetary autonomy (Table 5.3). As PRIMC depends on the interest rate and the inflation rate, it can alternatively be calculated in a "Belgian" (PRIMCb) or an "Italian" (PRIMCi) environment. The same applies to the required budgetary effort, defined as the difference between the target primary surplus and the actual, 1996 primary surplus. Results turn out to be quite similar in both cases, with a slight advantage for the "Belgian" scenario. This is because countries with higher inflation tend to have higher, ex-post real interest rates.

TABLE 5.3
Required Changes in the Primary Budget Balance (percent GDP, 1996)

Country	Debt ratio	Primary Surplus	PRIMCb	Effort	Effort (difference with Germany)
Germany	61.3	-0.9	1.5	2.4	0
Austria	71.8	-0.5	2.3	2.8	0.4
Belgium	129.9	5.1	5.9	0.8	-1.6
Denmark	71.9	2.0	2.1	0.1	-2.3
Spain	68.0	0.3	1.4	1.1	-1.3
Finland	60.1	-1.5	1.2	2.7	0.3
France	55.1	-0.8	1.0	1.8	-0.6
Greece	108.5	3.6	4.1	0.5	-1.9
Ireland	80.2	2.3	2.4	0.1	-2.3
Italy	124.4	2.8	6.0	3.2	0.8
Netherlands	78.0	2.1	2.9	0.8	-1.6
Portugal	70.3	1.1	1.5	0.4	-1.9
Sweden	78.7	-0.8	2.8	3.6	1.2
United Kingdom	56.1	-1.8	1.2	3.0	0.6
Average	79.6	0.9	2.6	1.6	-0.7

Notes: PRIMCb is required primary surplus with German inflation and interest rates; "effort" is PRIMCb minus actual primary surplus.
Source: OECD data and author's calculations.

On the basis of these calculations, all EU members would need to undertake additional budgetary efforts (this is partly because budgetary data are not corrected for cyclical factors). However, adopting the "Italian strategy" would only be justified for countries in which above-average adjustment efforts are required. Countries facing the same adjustment could rather participate in monetary union and implement the same policy mix (in the terms of the pre-ceding model, they could jointly depreciate their exchange rate vis-à-vis the rest of the world). In other words, from the applicant's standpoint, the relevant criterion for determining the date of entry in the monetary union should not be the absolute size of the required budgetary effort, but rather its relative magnitude vis-à-vis the other members of the monetary core. Column five therefore displays for each country the difference between its required effort under a "Belgian" strategy and that of Germany.

Taking a 1 percent threshold, the only country that might have grounds for delaying entry because it would need to implement a tighter fiscal policy than Germany is Sweden. Eight countries could implement a less restrictive fiscal policy than Germany, and for Denmark and Ireland, one could even wonder whether they would gain from appreciating their currency vis-à-vis the mark. This result indicates that for the vast majority of member states, there is no major contradiction between fiscal adjustment and the adoption of fixed exchange rates.[13] This is an indication of the high degree of fiscal convergence that has been achieved in the Community. Actual budget deficits tend to understate this convergence because interest costs on the public debt depend on the country's probability of entering EMU.

Should high unemployment deter entering monetary union?

Unemployment has repeatedly been mentioned in policy discussions, either as an obstacle to monetary union, for example, by the governor of the Bank of England (George, 1995), or as a possible additional criterion; but the argument is rarely stated in a precise way. Advocates of monetary union generally claim that, as the largest part of European unemployment is structural, it should be addressed through labor market policies and that no connection should be made with monetary unification (for an argument along these lines see Gros, 1996a, and Chapter 2 of this volume).

The distinction between the cyclical and equilibrium (or structural) components of unemployment is conceptually useful for discussing its interrelations with monetary union. Differences among member states in the size of cyclical unemployment are indicators of different positions in the business cycle, which may affect the timing of entry. As the objective of price stability requires monetary policy to be tightened as the economy approaches equilibrium employment, a country might suffer from entering monetary union with above- or below-average cyclical unemployment. Desynchronized cyclical positions were among the factors behind the crisis in the ERM in 1992, especially in the case of the United Kingdom, and it would certainly not be advisable to start monetary union in a situation where participating economies would have diverging short-term needs.

Differences in the equilibrium component of unemployment should not be a cause for concern if they can be considered permanent. These differences could result from a variety of factors, including the structure of the labor force, labor market institutions, unemployment insurance, government regulations, regional imbalances, and so forth (see Chapter 2). They could be considered to be the result of divergent trade-offs between unemployment and other policy objectives (wage inequality, job security, and so forth), or of different political-economy equilibria, for example as a result of the weight of "insiders" in wage bargaining.[14] Whatever the reasons, stable differences in the equilibrium unemployment rate would in principle not affect the choice of participating in monetary union, as they would only imply that national unemployment rates would fluctuate around different means.[15]

Let us now assume, however, that the government of a country participating in EMU successfully reduces equilibrium unemployment through structural reform. As this government would not coordinate its policy with the other EMU members, there would be no reason for the common monetary policy to respond to such a move. Without an expansionary macroeconomic policy, lowering the NAIRU would risk transforming structural unemployment into cyclical unemployment.[16] Higher cyclical unemployment would in turn translate into lower wage increases and, therefore, both employment gains and a depreciation of the real exchange rate. Eventually, unemployment would converge toward the new, lower NAIRU. However, this would be a lengthy process, as the reduction in actual unemployment could only result from a price adjustment. Both model simulations (Alexander, 1994) and lessons from the French experience of "competitive disinflation" (Blanchard and Muet, 1993) indicate that the payoff of a structural labor market policy would be significantly delayed (under EMU).

National equilibrium unemployment rates therefore cannot be considered irrelevant for deciding upon a country's participation in EMU. A government considering labor market reforms would better implement such reforms before fixing its exchange rate, unless similar reforms are going to be implemented by the other participants in the monetary union. The rationale for retaining exchange rate flexibility is the same as in the case of fiscal adjustment: Large policy moves undertaken in isolation create asymmetric shocks that call for autonomous monetary policy responses.

Table 5.4 displays data for assessing the position of the member states vis-à-vis the unemployment criterion. Column 1 gives the 1996 unemployment rate. Columns 2 and 3 display two alternative measures of cyclical unemployment. The first one is simply the increase in unemployment since its latest cyclical trough. The second one is derived from OECD measures of the "non-accelerating wages rate of unemployment" (NAWRU). Finally, Columns 4 and 5 give two alternative measures of equilibrium unemployment: the level of unemployment at its last cyclical trough (assuming that at that time all unemployment was structural), and the OECD's 1996 NAWRU.[17] Table 5.4 uses the same metric as the previous tables, namely Germany is taken as a benchmark and data for all other member states (except Luxembourg, which is omitted) are differences with corresponding German figures.

German unification obviously complicates comparisons over time. The data in Table 5.4 underestimate structural unemployment in Germany, as it is implicitly assumed that East German structural unemployment equals that of West Germany. Assuming, on the contrary, that all East German unemployment is structural, German structural unemployment would rise by roughly 2 percentage points, that is, the figures in Column 2 would be increased by a

TABLE 5.4
Unemployment Indicators: Differences between EU 13 and Germany

Country	(1) Unemployment 1996	(2) Change since Last Trough	(3) Cyclical Component 1996	(4) Last Unemployment Trough	(5) NAWRU 1996
Austria	-4.6	-3.5	0.1	-1.1	-4.2
Belgium	0.8	-1.6	1.6	2.4	1.0
Denmark	-3.0	-4.2	-0.8	1.2	-0.6
Finland	6.7	7.5	0.3	-0.8	5.8
France	3.4	-1.4	2.0	4.8	0.1
Greece	0.8	-1.4	1.4	2.2	-1.6
Ireland	3.3	-5.9	-1.5	9.2	3.2
Italy	3.0	-1.1	0.9	4.1	1.1
Netherlands	-2.7	-4.1	-0.4	1.4	-3.3
Portugal	-1.7	-1.5	0.7	-0.2	-3.8
Spain	13.2	1.2	1.1	12.0	11.3
Sweden	1.0	3.6	0.5	-2.6	-2.9
UK	-0.8	-3.6	-0.1	2.8	-2.6

Notes: (1) National unemployment rates, Eurostat definition; (2) change in unemployment since last trough; (3) current unemployment rate less NAWRU, IECD definition; (4) Eurostat definition; (5) NAWRU, OECD definition.
Source: OECD and author's calculations.

corresponding amount, and the figures in Column 4 would be reduced accordingly. However, to the extent that labor markets in West and East Germany are still segmented, it is West German unemployment that matters for assessing the inflationary pressures.[18]

Spain and Ireland exhibit unemployment rates significantly above the German level. This also applies, but to a lesser extent, to France, Ireland, and Italy, while unemployment is clearly below the German level in Austria, Denmark, and the Netherlands. For Spain and Ireland, as well as to a lesser extent for France and Italy, this gap can mostly be ascribed to structural factors. In Finland, however, at least part of the increase in the relative unemployment rate can be considered of a cyclical nature. Finally, the Netherland's relative performance can be ascribed to structural policies, while the evidence seems less clear for Austria and Denmark.

These data suggest that high cyclical unemployment could be a handicap to Finland's early EMU entry, and that Austria and Denmark might experience inflationary pressures before the other monetary union members because of their lower cyclical unemployment. Medium-term difficulties could arise for countries with high structural unemployment like Spain and possibly also Ireland, France, and Italy.

Summing up, this investigation confirms the variety of national situations as regard the potential costs and benefits of participation in the monetary union. It suggests that Belgium and the Netherlands would hardly have economic grounds for not participating in EMU from the outset; that some consideration might be warranted for Austria, Denmark, and France, but that on the whole these countries should have little reservations toward participating in EMU; Italy, the United Kingdom, Finland, Sweden, and Portugal might question whether their economic structures guarantee that they would benefit from monetary union, and some of these countries (especially Finland, Sweden, and Italy) might find grounds in their macroeconomic situation for delaying entry. The obstacles for Ireland and Spain are mainly structural. They lie in their below-average degree of structural convergence (which may have improved in recent years) and in the level of structural unemployment. Finally, Greece should remain out both for structural and macroeconomic reasons.

The Dynamics of Variable Geometry

Events illustrate the complex dynamics of variable geometry. In 1995, it was conventional wisdom that Italy, Portugal, and Spain would not be members of the core EMU. But during the course of 1996, as it became increasingly likely that monetary union would start in 1999 with a subset of member states, Italy, Portugal, and Spain accelerated their convergence efforts in order to avoid being left out. This gave rise to a debate on the relative merits of a narrow or a broad EMU core. Although that debate is likely to have been decided by the time this volume comes into publication, the broad-versus-narrow discussion of EMU membership provides an important illustration of the dynamics of variable geometry—and one that will remain relevant as the European Union continues to deepen and widen.

Policy discussions on the topic are generally confused because different people rely on different implicit models of how differentiated integration would work. A widespread view among the potential "outs" is that the "ins" could attempt to form an exclusive club; but among the potential "ins," it is frequently feared that the "outs" will benefit from not being subject to tight monetary discipline, and that they could run beggar-thy-neighbor exchange rate policies. In a similar way, some people argue that being temporarily excluded will lead the "outs" to accelerate their convergence efforts, while others maintain that they are likely to diverge from the core union, and that EMU will create a permanent divide within the EU. Whether the forces that will be set in motion by the formation of a Euro-core are centripetal or centrifugal will have profound implications for the future of European integration. It also has more immediate consequences for the design of the new EMS and the implementation of the Maastricht convergence criteria.

In recent years, research has begun to explore these issues. However, different researchers apparently come up with different conclusions. Some of them (Martin, 1994, 1995, 1996) emphasize the risk of inadvertently rendering temporary exclusions permanent, because prohibition from participating in integration from the outset could lead countries to decide to abstain from it permanently. Other researchers however hold a different view, such as Gros (1995, 1996a) who emphasizes the benefits of monetary union for highly indebted countries. Laskar (1995) shows that both cases could arise. Alesina and Grilli (1993) and Laskar (1996b) also stress that temporary exclusion could turn out to be lasting, but only because the insiders would prefer to bar entry to new members. Mélitz (1995) looks at the balance between the benefits of enlarging monetary union and the cost of further reducing exchange rate flexibility. Frankel and Rose (1996) claim that optimum currency area criteria are in fact endogenous, and that symmetry among countries participating in the core will increase, thereby rendering the core more homogenous with respect to the outsiders.

Disagreements on the issue can generally be traced back to different assumptions regarding the underlying preferences of the participating countries, the externalities involved, or the decision rules for membership in monetary union. It is therefore necessary to analyze the different cases in a coherent way. The aim here is not to work out precise results from a specific model, but rather to provide a framework for analyzing the effects at work and for comparing the results from existing models.

A framework for analysis

As shown by Laskar (1996a), exploring all the possibilities in a variable-geometry setting is an exhausting task. But the analysis can be made simpler by limiting it to the cases that are relevant in a European perspective. Let us consider the case of monetary union in a three-country setting. Assume that there are three countries of which two, France and Germany, have an identical preference for monetary union over the status quo. The third country may either share their will to participate in the union but be temporarily unable to join it (call it Italy) or have a preference for the status quo (call it the United Kingdom). At time 0, France and Germany may form a core union, or they may decide to wait for country three. At time *1*, Italy or Britain may participate in the formation of the union (if France and Germany chose to wait) or join the existing union (if they formed a core union at time *0*).[19] There are therefore four cases to consider (Table 5.5).

Let U_i ($i = S, D, C$ or T) represent the welfare of France and Germany in

TABLE 5.5
Alternative Union Scenarios

		Italy or United Kingdom	
		Participates	*Does not participate*
France and Germany	*Wait*	Delayed Union (*D*)	Status Quo (*S*)
	Do not wait	Two-speed Union (*T*)	Core Union (*C*)

the four cases, and V_i ($i = S, D, C$ or T) that of country three. The following assumptions can be made without losing generality.

- France and Germany (identical utility U) have a preference for union and for not waiting:

$$U_T, U_D, U_C > U_S \quad \text{and} \quad U_T > U_D \tag{5.8}$$

These assumptions are rather straightforward and correspond to the stated policy preferences of both countries.

- The United Kingdom (utility V) has a preference for the status quo when compared to whatever union:

$$V_S > V_D, V_T, V_C. \tag{5.9}$$

This assumption does not require justification at length.

- Italy (utility V), which has a preference for participating in the union, favors delaying it until being able to join it. But it prefers a two-speed union rather than the status quo:

$$V_D > V_T > V_S \tag{5.10}$$

This is also a very natural assumption, which is in accordance with the stated preferences of many members of the EU that are not ready to participate in monetary union from its outset. However, it is sometimes argued that Italy might prefer a two-speed strategy, because the formation of an initially narrow union would provide information on the actual working of the union, hence that $V_T > V_D$ (Artus, 1995). This will be discussed in the following section. Note also that no assumption is made as regards V_C.

Decision rules

The above hypotheses are straightforward. They imply that in the absence of a variable-geometry option, France, Germany, and Italy would choose to form a union (with some delay), while France, Germany, and Britain would not. The question to be answered is in what respect the option of variable geometry changes the outcome. Let us now consider how the decision to form a monetary union will be made.

The drafters of the Maastricht Treaty devoted considerable energy to the definition of precise entry rules. However, speculation on who would be admitted started before the treaty was ratified and has been going on ever since. The basic reason for uncertainty is that the treaty blends criteria and discretion, which blurs the decision rules. In what follows, three alternative rules are therefore considered.

- Unanimity. For regional or global unions to be formed, they must be Pareto-superior to the status quo. At time *0*, the three countries thus decide by unanimity on formation of union at time *0*, and membership at times *0* and *1*.[20]
- Variable geometry with opting out and opting in. France and Germany may form a restricted union if they wish, the third country may choose to opt in or to opt out. Therefore, at time *0* France and Germany decide on the formation of a two-country union. Country three decides on entry at time *1*.
- Variable geometry with a club rule for the admission of new members. This is the same as variable geometry with opting out and opting in, except that opting in at time *1* is subject to the approval of France and Germany. Members of the core therefore have a veto on the admission of new members.

The unanimity rule is the usual Community rule for treaty revisions, and to the extent that all countries will vote on membership in monetary union in 1999, the "outs" could be able to block the formation of a core union if some countries do not strictly meet the convergence criteria. But as argued before, the right to opt out from monetary union was extended in practice to all member states. Reality therefore seems to be getting closer to variable geometry with opting out and opting in.[21]

There is, however, no real opting in for countries not strictly fulfilling the public finance criteria (that is for the vast majority of member states), because participation of individual member states in the monetary union will be subject to a qualified majority vote according to Article 109J. This will be a purely formal procedure for member states narrowly fulfilling the criteria, but not for those exceeding the Maastricht ceilings for the fiscal deficit and or the public debt. As observed by Paul de Grauwe, it will only require a coalition among a subset of the likely "outs" to block a decision to soften the criteria to the exclusive benefit of the "ins."[22] Failure by the would-be members of the core to meet the public finance targets might thus result in reintroducing near unanimity in the decision rules. Unanimity has therefore not lost relevance.

The club rule is not formally part of Community law, but the fear exists among would-be outsiders that the entry conditions for monetary union will be tighter for new applicants than for the initial members. There are two reasons why entry criteria could be tightened in practice: The first is that the differential criteria could automatically become tighter after the formation of the monetary union; this will at least be the case for the interest rate criterion, due to the elimination of currency risk premia for the members of the core. A tightening might also apply to the exchange rate and interest rate criteria, due to the inferior credibility of the "outs." A second reason is that the members of the core will have at least a blocking minority in the council that decides on the admission of new members and they might use this voting power to impose a stricter interpretation of the criteria than for initial membership.[23] It is therefore also interesting to consider variable geometry with a club rule for the admission of new members.

Unanimity

Let us start with unanimity. Under this rule, decisions on membership at times *0* and *1* are taken simultaneously by unanimity at time *0*. Table 5.6 gives the outcome of the decisions by the two players (where *T* stands for two-speed, and so forth). The third country has a veto on the formation of the union, which implies that Britain will block the formation of whatever union.

A more interesting case is that of Italy, which shares with the other two countries a preference for monetary union but may force them to delay its formation until time *1*. As Italy has to decide irrevocably on participating in the union before it is created, it cannot gain information from letting France and Germany start without it. Hence, it might block attempts at a two-speed union. This leaves a core union as the remaining variable-geometry option, and Italy may only accept this if it is better off remaining outside that union, rather than participating in a delayed union, that is if $V_C > V_D$. For this core

TABLE 5.6
Voting on Monetary Union with Unanimity Rule

		Italy	
		Accepts F-G union	*Rejects*
France and Germany	*Accept Italy at time 1*	T	D
	Refuse Italy	C	D

union to be formed, however, it has to be preferred by Germany and France also, that is $U_C > U_D$. In all other cases, the equilibrium solution is D (Table 5.7).

The result is straightforward: With the unanimity rule the only possible variable-geometry outcome is a permanent core union (two-speed union is not a possible outcome if country three prefers a delayed union). But for this solution to be adopted it has to be preferred by all three countries. This rules out any outcome in which country three would embark on beggar-thy-neighbor policies, for example, competitive devaluations and so forth; otherwise Germany and France would rather wait for Italy. Why would all countries share an interest in creating a permanent core union? Two possibilities are that all recognize the existence of cross-country differences in the distribution of the costs and benefits of EMU, or that monetary union involves positive externalities for the outsiders that the insiders are willing to accept. In other words, core EMU members could be willing to pay an economic price for the formation of a core union, while the other countries would decide on economic grounds to remain outside that union (and possibly pay a political price for it). The formation of a core union would in such a case result from differences across the EU in the distribution of economic and political benefits of monetary union. Peaceful divorce, rather than forced convergence, would in this sense be a Pareto-superior solution.

For a two-speed union to be decided upon, side payments would have to be introduced. They could take the form of a commitment by the members of the core to accept country three at a given time and under certain (preferential) conditions.

Opting in and opting out

From the point of view of the likely insiders, unanimity has the disadvantage of giving a veto to the outsiders. This is a reason for introducing an opting-in rule. With this rule, the game becomes sequential. Decision at time *0* belongs to France and Germany, who may either go or wait. Decision at time *1* belongs to country three, who may either enter or stay out. The corresponding game tree is depicted in Figure 5.1.

TABLE 5.7
Decision on Monetary Union with Unanimity Rule

		Italy	
		$V_C > V_D$	$V_C < V_D$
France and Germany	$U_C > U_D$	C	D
	$U_C < U_D$	D	D

144

Figure 5.1
Decision Tree for Monetary Union with Opting In/Out

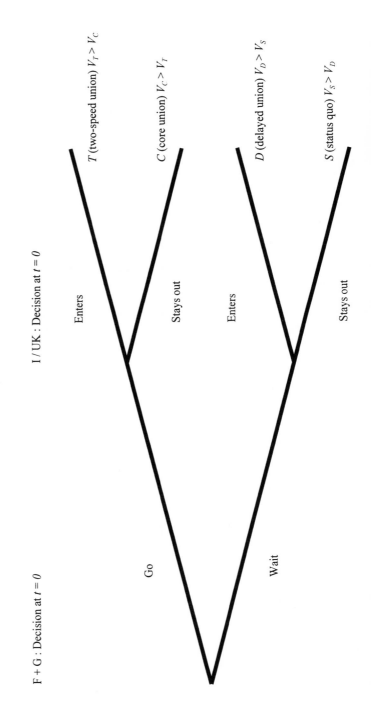

F + G : Decision at *t = 0*

I / UK : Decision at *t = 0*

Go

Wait

Enters

Stays out

Enters

Stays out

T (two-speed union) $V_T > V_C$

C (core union) $V_C > V_T$

D (delayed union) $V_D > V_S$

S (status quo) $V_S > V_D$

Introducing the option of variable geometry obviously deprives the United Kingdom of its veto power. There is no incentive for France and Germany to wait because it would perpetuate the status quo. The United Kingdom's decision then only depends on the comparison between V_T (participating in a two-speed union) and V_C (remaining outside the core French-German union): whether or not it has a preference for the status quo becomes irrelevant. The same applies to Italy: after the French-German union has started, its preference for a delay becomes irrelevant.

Let us therefore assume that Germany and France do not wait (I shall come back to their decision later) and analyze the behavior of country three at time *1*. The case where $V_T > V_C$ can be taken as representing "forced convergence": the French-German move leads Britain or Italy to participate, irrespective of their underlying preferences for or against monetary union. There can be several rationales for it. First, the benefits of monetary union can be restricted to its members, while part of the costs fall on the outsiders. This is the case in a formal model of optimum currency areas like that of Bayoumi (1994), because monetary union involves exclusive microeconomic benefits (for example savings on transaction costs, better access to Euro-denominated financial business) as well as a loss of macroeconomic stabilization that impacts on neighboring countries. Therefore, monetary union imposes a negative externality on the outsiders ($V_C < V_S$), which may lead them to seek entry even if they would prefer the status quo (that is $V_C < V_T < V_S$). As illustrated by the 1996 discussions on the operation of the TARGET payment system, the exclusive character of some of the microeconomic benefits of monetary union could be a matter for decision rather than being exogenous: A decision by the members of the core to grant to their own financial institutions competitive advantage for doing financial business within the monetary core would logically lead British financial institutions to lobby for the United Kingdom's membership in EMU.[24]

A second reason for "forced convergence" involves credibility, as discussed by Gros (1995): Whatever their underlying preference for monetary union, renouncing participation in it could jeopardize the credibility of monetary policy in high-debt countries like Italy or Belgium, because it would be interpreted as giving preference to a monetization option. De Grauwe (1997) provides a model that illustrates the potential for speculative attacks against the currencies of high-debt countries. Similar cases can also be found in different settings. With the last EU enlargement in mind, Baldwin (1995) examines the attraction of regional trade integration in a political economy model in which integration within the core is detrimental to the profits of non-member firms, and concludes that it is likely to give rise to a "domino effect." In the context of enlargement, Martin and Ottaviano (1995) find that delaying the Central and East European countries' accession may be counter-productive if integration within the core attracts capital and entrepreneurs at the expense of peripheral countries. All of these models have in common the fact that integration within the core imposes negative externalities on the outsiders, therefore giving rise to centripetal forces.

The opposite case, $V_C > V_T$, can be labeled as free-riding. In this case, country three remains outside the union not because it has a preference for the status quo, but because it prefers to remain outside a two-country monetary union rather than to join it. There could be several reasons for such behavior: One possibility is that the formation of a narrow monetary union could increase the inflation differential between the "ins" and the "outs" (and therefore the short-run cost of inflation convergence for the "outs") because the "outs" would lack the inflation discipline provided by participation in a monetary union (Martin, 1996). Another is that an initially high-inflation country may eventually gain more by deciding to free-ride on a monetary union rather than to participate in it, if the low-inflation countries deny it the credibility benefits of an early admission (Martin, 1995). Finally, a country excluded from early admission could lose some of the benefits it expects from monetary union, for example because it would not be able to participate in the appointment of the members of the European Central Bank's (ECB) board and in the definition of the common monetary objectives and procedures, which would result in procedures being biased against its preferences.[25]

The choice of not entering the union at time *1* might also result from the third country's imperfect information on the working of monetary union (Artus, 1995). Whatever its a priori preferences, keeping open the option of entry until after having observed the behavior of the French-German monetary union could help determine the entry decision.

The conclusion from this discussion is that whether introducing a variable-geometry option will give rise to "forced convergence" or to "free-riding" cannot be decided a priori. As there are valid arguments on both sides, the issue is essentially an empirical one for each country. This is in striking contrast with the verdict of the literature on trade regionalism (see, for example, Winters, 1996), which concludes that the formation of a regional trade agreement is detrimental to outsiders (or at best neutral) and leads outside countries to join existing trading blocs unless the insiders deny them entry (which may happen).

Let us now examine the behavior of France and Germany. There is no reason for them to wait for Britain, but they may choose to wait for Italy. As Table 5.8 shows, if France and Germany prefer a delayed union to a core union—because they know that if they wait, Italy will join—they will choose to wait and the outcome will be a delayed union. The reason is that if France and Germany do not wait, Italy may choose to remain outside, leaving France and Germany in a core union.[26]

It is important to emphasize that Italian "free-riding" could result from the sequential nature of the integration game rather than from any genuine prefer-

TABLE 5.8
Decision on Monetary Union with Opting Out/Opting In Rule
Italy

		$V_C > V_T$ *"Free-riding"*	$V_C < V_T$ *"Convergence"*
France and Germany	$U_C > U_D$	(go) C	(go) T
	$U_C < U_D$	(wait) D	(go) T

ence for such a behavior. In other words, we could have $V_D > V_C > V_T > V_S$, in which case a temporary exclusion would turn into permanent abstention in spite of an underlying preference for monetary union. For the members of the core, the obvious policy response to such a risk would then be (1) to try to lead Italy to commit irrevocably to membership at a given time, and therefore to commit themselves to letting it in if certain precise conditions are fulfilled, and (2) to attempt to reduce V_C through supporting Italian convergence and through involving Italy in preparations for monetary union. The concrete implications of such a strategy could involve the creation of an associate membership status, a renewed ERM, and so forth.

Summing up, with an opting in/opting out rule there is never an incentive for France and Germany to wait for a country like Britain, which has expressed reservations toward monetary union. On the contrary, their decision to go ahead could subsequently lead Britain to join, in the same way most of the European Free Trade Association (EFTA) members eventually chose to become full members of the EU. There could be however an incentive to wait for countries like Italy, which have expressed preference for participating in the single currency but whose convergence is deemed insufficient, or alternatively to make preparations to enhance Italy's convergence.

Monetary union as a club

Introducing an opting in clause creates difficulties because it may lead countries to make a choice that does not square with their a priori preferences. Can it be corrected through giving the insiders a veto on the admission of new members? Introduction of a club rule allows France and Germany to deny any third country accession to the union at time *1*. The game tree remains the same as in Figure 5.1, but after a narrow union has started, a third country can only join if $U_T > U_C$. This represents a gain for France and Germany, but these two countries may still have to wait for Italy if they prefer a delayed union to a permanent core union: Although they can prevent Italy from opting in, they cannot prevent it from opting out. Table 5.9 gives the result of the

TABLE 5.9
Decision on Monetary Union with Club Rule
Italy

		$V_C > V_T$ *"Free-riding"*	$V_C < V_T$ *"Convergence"*
France and Germany	$U_C > U_D$	(go) C	(go) C if $U_C > U_T$ (go) T if $U_C < U_T$
	$U_C < U_D$	(wait) D	(go) T

game. It is apparent that the decision by France and Germany to go or to wait for Italy does not change. However, the outcome changes, as they can bar entry of new members if they prefer the core union. This happens when there is both a French and a German preference for a narrow union and Italian "convergence." This is the case analyzed by Alesina and Grilli (1993), where the members of the core choose to deny admission to new members although they would have accepted forming a union with them. Hence their decision depends only on the comparison between C and T, not on their preference for monetary union when compared to the status quo.

Introducing variable geometry therefore has the clear advantage of making monetary union possible for a subset of member states, but involves two significant costs. The first is that the creation of a narrow union could lead to the participation of countries that do not share the other members' preference for monetary union. Over time, this could give rise to instability, as a significant number of the union's members could in fact have a preference for a flexible exchange rate regime. This would represent a significant risk for EMU but one that can—in principle—be addressed, first, through the enforcement of the convergence criteria, and second, because the members of the core will have a say (if not the decision) on the admission of new members.[27]

The second cost is that the creation of a narrow monetary union prevents the outsiders from seeking entry. In theory, this effect could lead countries that are willing to participate in monetary union to abstain from joining it after it has been created. Whether or not this risk will materialize is a matter for speculation. But what is clear is that no provision in the Maastricht treaty aims at addressing this risk. In other words, the drafters of the Maastricht Treaty seem to have been obsessed with the risk of "forced convergence" and to have completely overlooked the risk of "free-riding." A priority in the discussions on the relationship between the "ins" and the "outs" should be an attempt at minimizing this risk.

"Ins" and "Outs": Monetary Cohabitation after 1999

Since 1995, organizing monetary cohabitation between the future participants in monetary union (the "ins") and the outsiders (the "outs") has been an urgent practical exercise in variable geometry. The issue was put on the agenda of the Ecofin by the European council of Madrid, and a number of proposals have already been made (Thygesen, 1995, 1996; CEPR, 1995; Gros, 1996a; Nayman and Pisani-Ferry, 1996; Spaventa, 1996; Wyplosz, 1996). Two views emerge from this debate.

The first view, which was clearly expressed by Thygesen (1996), is that the Maastricht framework remains essentially adequate. According to this view, the vast majority of member states will ultimately join the single currency. Furthermore, several of the outsiders may choose to mimic participation in EMU through irrevocably pegging their currency to the euro (the new European currency) on a unilateral basis. In other words, the "one market, one money" logic remains valid, and monetary union will become part of the acquis communautaire within a few years. Flexibility may however be necessary in the short run, and monetary relations between the "ins" and the "outs" should be organized within the framework of a renewed Exchange Rate Mechanism, the rationale for which is presented by Spaventa (1996) and Wyplosz (1996). This is the option chosen by the officials after the informal Ecofin meetings of Verona (June 1996) and Dublin (September 1996).

The opposite view was put forward in a CEPR (1995) report by a group of academics. They claim that monetary union should not be considered as being part of the core European integration policies (as, for example, the single market), but should rather be considered as an optional "open partnership." They suggest that the monetary policies of the "ins" and the "outs" could be coordinated through the adoption of national inflation targets, as proposed by Persson and Tabellini (1996a). There are indications that the British and Swedish governments sympathize with this view.

Any assessment of the possible institutional mechanisms has to be based on a clear definition of the objectives. Two possible objectives should be clearly distinguished. One is to guarantee the degree of exchange rate stability that is necessary for ensuring the viability of the European single market. Another is to offer support to the countries that wish to join EMU but will not be able to participate in it from the outset, in order to facilitate convergence toward membership in the single currency. Both are valid objectives, but they are of different natures.

One market, many monies?

It was argued previously that there are economic grounds for considering variable geometry as a possibly durable configuration among the current fifteen member states. This is obviously even more true in the perspective of enlargement to the East. Central and Eastern European economies are undergoing profound and rapid changes in their production structures and in their trade patterns, which imply that considerable uncertainty remains as regards the equilibrium level of the real exchange rate. Their degree of integration in the European economy is still far lower than those of current member states, which could result in asymmetric shocks. Moreover, price stability cannot be considered as firmly established, which should prevent them from irrevocably renouncing the option of devaluation. This does not mean that countries in transition cannot gain from adopting a fixed exchange rate strategy (in fact some of these countries have adopted such strategies), but rather that it would be premature to consider monetary union as a component of the acquis communautaire and to require the associated countries to commit irrevocably to it on the occasion of their accession. In short, enlargement can only reinforce the case for variable geometry in European monetary integration.

A different argument rests on political considerations. It is becoming increasingly evident that significant sectors of public opinion in several member states express strong reservations toward membership in monetary union.[28] As participation in EMU would deprive governments of monetary policy autonomy and significantly constrain fiscal policy, it may require a higher degree of enduring political commitment than what some member states can deliver.

Against this background, the EU should explicitly recognize the right for any member state not to participate in EMU, make clear to the accessing countries that monetary union is not part of the acquis communautaire, and offer alternative options. If only a subset of member states participate in monetary union, however, the close correspondence between real and monetary unification illustrated by the "one market, one money" slogan that was at the heart of the EMU project will be broken. This raises the issue of the degree of exchange rate variability that can be considered compatible with the operation of the single market.

Barry Eichengreen (1996) argues that economic integration does not require monetary integration for economic reasons, but on political-economy grounds. This view does not dispute that only monetary union would ensure that the full benefits of economic integration would be reaped (through the elimination of transaction costs, and much more important, through the removal of exchange rate uncertainty), but only that monetary union would be indispensable to the operation of the single market on purely economic grounds. In other words, if monetary union yields additional microeconomic benefits over and above those provided by economic integration, there is no reason to require all member states to participate in it. On the contrary, the variable-geometry option would be preferable, and as developed above it would presumably lead most EU countries to join the monetary core.

However, there are strong political-economy reasons to consider that excessive exchange rate variability would endanger the single market. The basic reason for it is that economic integration within the single market completely deprives national governments of conditional trade protection instruments like temporary quantitative restrictions and antidumping procedures and binds them with tight disciplines in fields such as government subsidies, merger control, or public procurement. Neither trade policy nor (at least in principle) industrial policy can therefore be relied upon by a member state to counter competition from within the EU that would be deemed "unfair." When facing sectoral interest groups that call for protection and/or subsidies, governments are (or should be) impotent.[29]

For these rules to be observed strictly, it is essential that interest groups do not coalesce along national lines. Although the EU Commission is entrusted with the task of enforcing the common competition policy, its political legitimacy is hardly sufficient to impose discipline upon governments prone to yield to the pressure of powerful interest groups. It would probably be insufficient to impose discipline upon the government of a large member state in the case of a political crisis. This is why large real exchange rate fluctuations are dangerous: They tend to unite the usually disparate interests of the various industries within the tradable goods sector. In the early 1990s, this potential for political mobilization in response to exchange rate volatility was exemplified by German and especially French reactions to the depreciation of the lira and other European currencies.[30] Although the Commission claimed that there was little evidence of major effects of exchange rate fluctuations (EU Commission, 1995), governments in strong-currency countries, especially France, were quick to call for sanctions against depreciating countries and for increased leeway in the distribution of subsidies to sensitive industries. In the absence of exchange rate discipline, there are reasons to fear that European competition policy would be in great danger of being held hostage in disputes between strong- and weak-currency countries. This would destroy the credibility of the common competition policy, impair the mutual trust that is the very basis of the single market, and ultimately lead to its de facto fragmentation.

The viability of the single market therefore does not require a single currency nor fixed exchange rates. It does require, however, that countries not participating in EMU subscribe to minimum discipline in order to prevent exchange rate misalignments among EU member states.[31]

The second objective, which is of a completely different nature, is to ensure that the formation of a core EMU will not impair the convergence efforts of the "outs." It is admittedly rather speculative to try to figure out how countries will behave after they are barred early membership in monetary union. The preceding discussion on externalities indicates that both centripetal and centrifugal forces can be expected to be set in motion. Whether the monetary core will attract the "outs" or repel them will depend on a number of factors that cannot be anticipated with any certainty. What is clear, however, is that only the first alternative was envisaged at the time of the preparation of the Maastricht Treaty. The purpose of the convergence criteria was to exclude member states that would not be fit for EMU, assuming that all of them would try to enter monetary union as soon as possible—except Britain perhaps, and there only on political grounds. The alternative scenario—that countries would *choose* to stay out of EMU—was simply not envisaged. Consequently, the Maastricht convergence mechanism is full of sticks, but has no carrots.

The issue can best be represented in a multiple equilibria framework. If exclusion from monetary union risks driving the "outs" toward a high-interest-rate, high-deficit, high-inflation equilibrium, what is needed is a mechanism that would increase the probability of convergence toward the "good" low-interest-rate, low-deficit, low-inflation equilibrium. In other words, the purpose of institutional arrangements between the "ins" and the "outs" should be to correct the undesirable spillover effects of the formation of a core union.

Assuming monetary union starts in 1999, three categories of "outs" will probably emerge: Some countries may choose to opt out from participating in a renewed ERM, either because they do not wish to participate in EMU, or because they prefer to retain exchange rate flexibility during their convergence. This could be the case of the United Kingdom, Sweden, and some of the Central and Eastern European countries when they join the EU. It does not matter very much whether countries would make this choice because they are "unwilling" or "unable" to participate in a monetary agreement. What is important is that if (present or future) member states express a preference for floating, the "ins" would de facto be constrained to accept it.

A second category of member states would probably be willing to enter into monetary arrangements, either temporarily or as a more permanent feature, but would wish to retain the option of realignment. This would especially be the case of countries with insufficient inflation performance, for example Greece, and of some future member states from Central and Eastern Europe.

A final group of countries would presumably be willing to mimic a full participation in monetary union, even if they are prevented entering EMU because of still excessive deficits or public debts. Such a strategy would have the advantage of enhancing the credibility of convergence efforts and thereby of reducing the interest burden on public debt; this would probably have been the case of Italy if it had failed to be admitted in 1999.

To summarize, the various situations of the future "outs" should be taken into account. However, only the "outs" can decide to which category they belong. Therefore, what the Union should offer is a clear menu of options.

A common law for the floaters

For countries not participating in the single currency, the legal basis for a surveillance of exchange rate policies with a view to avoiding misalignments is found in Article 109m of the Maastricht Treaty, which states that exchange rate policies are "a matter of common interest." The precise meaning of this provision is obviously open to interpretation, but a reasonable reading is that exchange rate misalignments should be avoided.

How should this objective be achieved? In CEPR (1995), Dewatripont et al. propose to coordinate monetary policies through the mandatory adoption by all EU members of inflation targets. Their proposal builds upon the British and Swedish experiences and is based upon the research by Persson and Tabellini (1996a, 1996b). The member states and the ECB would announce precise quantitative targets for inflation (though not necessarily the same targets). Member state performance would be monitored by the European System of Central Banks (ESCB), and penalties (blame, dismissal of the governor) would be imposed on the central banks of countries missing their targets. Persson and Tabellini (1996b) claim that such an arrangement would "[remove] the incentive to engage systematically and deliberately in competitive devaluations," and "[force] monetary policy to respond to shocks in a way that stabilizes the exchange rate." They add that its advantage is that "exchange rates would remain a matter of common interest," but that "exchange rate stability ought to be the result of successful monetary policies, not the explicit target for these policies."

The rationale for adopting an inflation target is straightforward. Fixing a nominal variable (the price level) for each country would in principle prevent the central banks from embarking on noncooperative policies in response to symmetric shocks. Thus, the Nash noncooperative equilibrium would be eliminated from the game's solutions.

There are, however, a number of objections: To begin with, coordination through inflation targets would obviously require this monetary policy framework to be adopted by all participants, including the ECB, and to be implemented in a similar way. This would put a significant constraint on the monetary strategy of the central banks, as it would, for example, require them to inflate in response to a common deflationary shock in order to reach the former target. Some central banks, and the ECB, might be reluctant to commit to this specific monetary policy technique.

Another objection is that inflation targets do not ensure exchange rate stability. The Italian experience of 1993 to 1995, when inflation remained roughly stable while the DM exchange rate dropped by 35 percent, illustrates that meeting preannounced inflation targets does not ensure exchange rate stability if other countries do not follow the same rule. Furthermore, as noted by Thygesen (1996), international experience tends to show that neglecting exchange rate objectives in favor of domestic objectives generally results in higher exchange rate instability.

Finally, the EU could only penalize countries exceeding their inflation target in the case of negative spillover effects on other member states. In the absence of such effects, it would have no justification to impose sanctions on a high-inflation country. Thus, the sanctions envisaged in the CEPR report would in reality penalize exchange rate misalignments, and discussions on inflation targets would inevitably derive from assessing the deviation of real exchange rates from their equilibrium level. What would then be the advantage of coordinating inflation targets instead of the real exchange rate?

Given these objections, it would be preferable to recognize the right of member states not to embark on monetary coordination and to interpret Article 109m as requiring that they avoid misalignments. This requirement could then be implemented in two alternative ways.

A first possibility would be to entrust the EU Commission with the task of monitoring the evolution of the real exchange rates of the countries not participating in ERM2 and of reporting misalignments to the Council. The Council would examine the case, and if economic policy in the country is considered responsible for the misalignment, it would issue recommendations under Article 103, which states that "where it is established . . . that the economic policies of a Member State . . . risk jeopardizing the proper functioning of economic and monetary union, the Council may . . . make the necessary recommendations to the Member State concerned . . . [and] . . . decide to make its recommendations public." A further step (for which there is however no clear legal basis) would be for the Council to take sanctions in the case of noncompliance, as envisaged under the excessive deficit procedure. This common law approach would only be applicable to countries not participating in a contractual arrangement with the ECB. This would make clear that member states retain the right not to participate in monetary arrangements, but that they will then be held responsible for their exchange rate, and face the risk of sanctions if autonomy is a pretext for conducting beggar-thy-neighbor policies.

A second option would be for the ECB and the countries not participating in ERM2 to cooperate in order to limit real exchange rate variability within the EU. This could involve a variety of arrangements: currency band systems like those adopted by Chile and Israel might suit some of the CEECs; a more ambitious goal would be to implement a target zone system along the lines suggested by Bergsten and Williamson (1994) and Volcker (1995): Such an arrangement could be less demanding than participation in ERM2 because it could rely on "soft" bands rather than on publicly announced central rates and bands, but it would at least require some degree of commitment toward defending the exchange rate against market pressures through sterilized interventions and monetary policy changes.

The first option would have the advantage of preserving flexibility and national autonomy as long as it does not lead to threatening the functioning of the single market. It would have two shortcomings: It could leave room to excessive discretion in the assessment of misalignments, and the actual strength of the exchange rate discipline might be in doubt. The second option would be more cooperative in character, but support for target zones has much weakened since the late 1980s. Furthermore, the burden of adjustment would inevitably fall upon the "outs," which could limit the attractiveness of this option.

Issues in the design of ERM2

For countries that are on a convergence path toward membership in monetary union, participation in ERM2 should enhance the prospects of convergence and reduce exchange rate uncertainty. There are however significant differences between the potential pre-"ins" regarding the degree of commitment toward exchange rate stability that is appropriate. Countries that are structurally fit for entering EMU have completed their convergence toward price stability, and for which remaining adjustments in the primary budgetary surplus are of the same order of magnitude as for the members of the monetary core, could benefit from committing to a fully fixed exchange rate vis-à-vis the euro. Other countries could make use of wide margins and avoid forsaking the possibility of realignments.

Gros (1996a) proposes that countries "that are very close to qualifying for full membership" could be granted a form of associate status in EMU. These member states would irrevocably bind their currencies to the euro without participating in the decision of the European Central Bank. This would technically be equivalent to adopting a currency board. This could prove to be an attractive option for a few smaller countries, fully committed to participating in EMU but handicapped by their fiscal situation, that could in this way reduce the interest burden on their debt.

Such a status might not be suitable for larger countries, if only for political reasons. Therefore, ERM2 should offer different options for member states that would be willing to commit to monetary discipline, but not to relinquish monetary autonomy in anticipation of EMU. This could take the form of bilateral contracts between the EU and individual member states, through which the ECB would commit to supporting exchange rate stabilization and the country would commit to pursuing policies that are conducive to convergence.

A key issue is under what conditions the ECB would conduct interventions in favor of a partner currency. Although the disproportion in size between the monetary core and individual pre-ins will make the risk of jeopardizing price stability a relatively minor one, the ECB will certainly not commit to unconditional and unlimited intervention (this commitment anyway lost its credibility in the ERM crisis). Intervention could only be conditional upon the preservation of price stability in the monetary core, and upon the fulfillment of certain convergence targets by the pre-ins. This raises the question of the relative responsibilities of the Council and the ECB. The decision to suspend an intervention that threatens to jeopardize price stability can only be taken by the ECB alone. But the decision to suspend an intervention guarantee should not be left to the discretion of the ECB alone, whose mandate does not include macroeconomic surveillance of the pre-ins. This would turn the ECB into some kind of IMF, which is certainly not part of its mandate. Rather, the monitoring of convergence and any decision to withdraw or to modify intervention guarantees should involve the Council.

Conclusions

The aims of this chapter were threefold: first, to determine whether there is an economic case for variable geometry in the monetary integration of Europe; second, to examine the difficulties that may arise if the option of differentiated integration is explicitly introduced; and third, to discuss the organization of monetary relations between the "ins" and the "outs" of monetary union.

The case for variable geometry rests on the existence of structural asymmetries between member states. It is well known that countries whose industrial structure or trade patterns differ markedly from those of the monetary union as a whole could be subject to idiosyncratic shocks and therefore suffer from losing monetary and exchange rate autonomy. Examination of a variety of indicators suggests that this might be the case for Greece, Ireland, Portugal, and Spain. On the contrary, Austria, Belgium, France, the Netherlands, and possibly Denmark are natural candidates for the Euro-core.

A different motive for integration to proceed at an uneven pace rests on medium-term policy priorities. As inflation convergence is now nearly complete, the two main reasons why policies may differ are the fiscal situation and unemployment. Countries for which disproportionate adjustments in the primary balance are still needed may adopt an "Italian" strategy of fiscal adjustment cum currency depreciation, while countries that need to reduce the interest burden on public debt may choose a "Belgian" fixed exchange rate strategy. On this basis, calculations indicate that only Sweden could gain significantly from delaying participation in EMU. Fiscal convergence has been proceeding at a rapid pace, and on purely budgetary grounds, there would be little justification for delays. Turning to unemployment, motives for delaying entry could be a comparatively high or a comparatively low cyclical unemployment, and a comparatively high NAIRU that the government seriously intends to reduce through structural reforms. On this basis, Finland would appear to be in a situation where delay could be advocated on cyclical grounds; Spain and to a much lesser extent Ireland, France, and Italy could also consider delaying entry if there is an intention to introduce structural labor market reforms (which is not necessarily the case).

This analysis suggests that although the overall degree of convergence is high, some countries could have economic reasons for not participating in monetary union in 1999, and maybe not in 2002 either. Although decisions will not be based on economic criteria alone, this suggests that variable geometry might emerge as a durable configuration. This is even more true if the perspective of enlargement is taken into account.

The formation of a core EMU will impact the behavior of the outsiders. After such a union is formed by a subset of member states, what matters for the "outs" is no longer whether they would prefer the status quo, but whether they prefer to become part of monetary union or to remain outside. Since monetary union is likely to have spillover effects on the outsiders, this is a different choice.

How the "outs" will behave depends on the decision rules for the formation of monetary union and the admission of new members, and on the kind of spillover effects that will predominate. Although the rules are spelled out in the Maastricht Treaty, the fact that decisions will be taken through a vote and involve interpretation of the criteria tends to blur the decision rules. More precisely, the "outs" may have a say on the admission of the would-be "ins" in 1999, and the "ins" may have some form of blocking power in the later enlargement of the core.

It is not possible to determine a priori whether variable geometry will give rise to centripetal or to centrifugal forces. What can be said is that it involves two significant hazards. The first is that the creation of a narrow union could lead to the participation of countries that do not share the other member's preference for monetary union. Over time, this could give rise to instability, as a significant number of the union's members could in fact have a preference for a flexible exchange rate regime. However, this risk can be addressed, first, through the enforcement of the convergence criteria, and second, because the members of the core will have a say (if not the decision) on the admission of new members.

The second risk is that the creation of a narrow monetary union could prevent the outsiders from seeking entry. This effect could in theory lead countries that are willing to participate in monetary union to abstain from joining it after it has been created. Whether or not this risk will materialize is a matter of speculation. But what is clear is that no provision in the Maastricht Treaty aims at addressing this risk. A priority in the discussions on the relationship between the "ins" and the "outs" should be an attempt at minimizing this risk.

Discussions on the organization of relations between the "ins" and the "outs" involve both the objective of ensuring real exchange rate stability within the single market and that of facilitating the process of convergence of the "outs." If variable geometry turns out to become a durable feature of European integration, both objectives should be distinguished. The EU should recognize the right of member states not to participate in monetary union and take measures to ensure a sufficient degree of exchange rate stability within the single market. At the same time, it should facilitate convergence for countries wishing to join monetary union.

Exchange rate stability within the single market does not need to be complete. What is required is that misalignments are avoided, because they would endanger the observance of the basic rules of the single market. For that purpose, coordination through inflation targets would hardly be an appropriate device. Rather, the EU could either organize a surveillance of monetary and exchange rate policies with the explicit aim of avoiding misalignments, or set up cooperative exchange rate arrangements.

A renewed ERM may help to foster convergence and to limit long-term interest rate spreads between the "ins" and the "outs." It should accommodate differences among the "outs," which could be done through bilateral contracts. A key issue is under what conditions the ECB would conduct interventions. Unlimited and unconditional interventions, like in the old ERM, are no longer on the agenda, but it is important that the ECB is not given discretion in exercising policy conditionality vis-à-vis the "outs."

Appendix 5.1
Criteria for the Measurement of
Asymmetries within the EU

1. Stability

- Standard deviation of first differences in the log of the nominal DM exchange rate, January 1979 to December 1995 (Bundesbank data).
- Standard deviation of first differences in the log of the real DM exchange rate (measured with consumer price indexes), February 1970 to December 1995 (Bundesbank data).

2. Shocks

- Correlation of demand shocks between country x and Germany, 1963 to 1990, from Bayoumi and Eichengreen (1996a).
- Correlation of supply shocks between country x and Germany, 1963 to 1990, from Bayoumi and Eichengreen (1996a).
- Ratio of the variance of asymmetric to symmetric shocks to GDP, pooled regression estimates for eighteen European countries, 1962 to 1989, from Mélitz (1996).

3. Structures

- Finger index of the similarity between the product composition of exports of country x and that of Germany, seventy products, 1993. Source: author's calculations with CEPII-CHELEM data.
- Trade (average of exports and imports) with core ERM countries (Ger-

many, France, Benelux, Austria) less trade with the rest of the world (ROW), percent of GDP, 1994. Source: CHELEM-CEPII databank.

• Correlation of export growth rates between country x and Germany, 1971 to 1990, annual OECD data.

Notes

1. As well as through the social protocol agreed upon by eleven member states, with the exception of the United Kingdom.

2. See the literature on optimal currency areas and CEC (1990).

3. Pisani-Ferry (1994), Bayoumi and Eichengreen (1996a), and Mélitz (1996) provide critical surveys of this research.

4. An alternative choice could be to take the likely core members as a collective reference. This would have the advantage of avoiding making German idiosyncrasies a reference for other member states. However, it would require using a clustering procedure. For an analysis along these lines, see Jacquemin and Sapir (1995).

5. Shocks can also arise from national economic policies or idiosyncratic behavior. To the extent that monetary union amounts to a change in the policy regime, these shocks should in principle not be considered invariant.

6. A drawback of this method is that services are ignored.

7. Bayoumi and Eichengreen (1996b) derive an aggregate OCA index from a cross-sectional estimate of the determinants of bilateral nominal exchange rate variability. They use the estimated coefficients of the righthand side variables as weights for the construction of the index. The drawback of this method is that it rests on the assumption that the countries' actual past monetary policy behavior was in some sense optimal.

8. Additional criteria may include measures of the ability of various countries to adjust to shocks (labor market flexibility, and so forth). Comparable data of this kind are missing.

9. The significant exception is the trade indicator, which favors smaller countries doing most of their trade with the core ERM countries.

10. I assume here that fiscal retrenchment involves a (short-term, at least) output loss.

11. This ignores the problems arising from the maturity of public debt.

12. With the usual approximations, the corresponding budget balance to GDP ratio is: $b = -\alpha \bar{d} + (\alpha - \hat{p} - \hat{y})d$, with $\alpha = 5$ percent, $\bar{d} = 60$ percent, and $\alpha \bar{d} = 3$ percent. Hence, although this criterion is conceptually distinct from the 3 percent ceiling mentioned in the treaty, it is numerically identical if nominal GDP growth (meaning $\hat{p} - \hat{y}$) is α percent per annum.

13. Aglietta and Uctum (1996) reach similar conclusions.

14. This is, for example, the conclusion of the comparison between Spanish and Portuguese unemployment carried out by Blanchard and Jimeno (1995). For a discussion of European unemployment along these lines see CEPR (1994).

15. However, to the extent that equilibrium unemployment would actually result from national choice, differences in equilibrium unemployment would signal underly-

ing differences in the acceptance of unemployment, which could impact short-term policy preferences.

16. The precise effect of a lower NAIRU would depend on the factors behind its reduction. Some structural policies could result in reducing unemployment in the short run, for example, in the case of tax-based reductions in the cost of low-skill labor in a classical unemployment situation, which would increase labor demand and aggregate supply, while lowering the NAIRU.

17. Columns 2 and 4 add up to Column 1, but Columns 3 and 5 do not give an exact decomposition of the 1995 unemployment rate, since they refer to the 1994 unemployment rate. Furthermore, the OECD and Eurostat data differ.

18. The argument should apply to other countries also, for example, Italy.

19. It is assumed that the third country is able to qualify at time *1*.

20. Membership could be conditional on objective criteria; however, it is assumed that the third country is able to fulfill them.

21. As already mentioned, any country can opt out from entering monetary union simply by abstaining from becoming part of the new European monetary system.

22. See Paul de Grauwe, "Failures of the euro exam," *Financial Times*, 5 July 1996.

23. It is also sometimes advocated that such a rule should be introduced (von Hagen and Frattiani, 1995).

24. See, for example, *The Economist*, 3 August 1996. A joint report by the Banque de France and French banks has expressed opposition to giving to the outsiders' banks access to intra-day liquidity provided by the European System of Central Banks through the TARGET system. See "Passage à la monnaie unique," report of a working party set up by the Banque de France and the banking community, July 1996.

25. This could be a significant loss for countries like Britain whose views on the conduct of monetary policy differ markedly from those of Germany (see the debates in the European Monetary Institute on inflation targeting, the use of reserve requirements, and so forth). Being absent when the final decision on the rules is made implies a loss of influence on some permanent features of the common monetary regime. However, the relevance of this argument does not seem to be great for Italy.

26. Hence, when France and Germany have a preference for remaining in a core union, they do not wait for Italy. When they prefer a delayed union, their best strategy depends on the outcome of the subgame determined by Italy's preferences. Thus, France and Germany only wait for Italy if $U_D > U_C$ and $V_C > V_T$, which is to say, when they prefer to have Italy in, while Italy prefers to free-ride. Note that the relative utility of a two-speed union for Germany and France does not intervene in the decision, because there is no way to force Italy to commit itself to participate at time *1*.

27. In fact, a merit of the convergence criteria could be that through imposing a tax upon EMU applicants, it could correct the (negative) externality arising from the formation of the core.

28. See Pisani-Ferry, Hefecker, and Hughes Hallett (1997).

29. There are obviously exceptions, as illustrated, for example, by the public subsidies granted to ailing banks or airline companies. However, repeated recourse to such subsidies would precisely threaten the operation of the single market.

30. See Pisani-Ferry, Hefeker, and Hughes Hallett (1997). In 1995, the French gov-

ernment was given the right to modify the distribution of Community aid in favor of sectors affected by the devaluation of the lira.

31. This is widely acknowledged, including by the governor of the Bank of England who recently declared that "if our exchange rate did gyrate as a result of deliberate, persistent policy, [the "ins"] would feel justified taking actions against us to protect the Single market," *Financial Times*, 16 September 1996.

6

The Political Economy of European Monetary Union: A Conceptual Overview

Jeffry Frieden and Erik Jones

Europe's on-again, off-again relationship with Economic and Monetary Union (EMU) reaches back to the late 1960s. The relationship was "on" with the 1968 Werner Plan, "off" with the economic turmoil of the mid-1970s, "on" with the creation of the European Monetary System (EMS), "off" with the recession of the early 1980s, "on" with the 1988 Delors Plan, and "off" with the exchange rate crises of the early-to-mid 1990s. Much like a Mexican soap opera, the "on" periods in the relationship have been accompanied by inflated rhetoric about Europe's glorious future, while the "off" periods have been greeted with exaggerated cries of disaster. As Europe's leaders prepare to cycle through another round of great expectations and (perhaps) equally great disappointments, two questions spring to mind: What is so important about monetary union, and why has it been so difficult to accomplish?

The answers to these questions lie in the general area that we refer to as the "political economy" of monetary union—*where* politicians and the public perceive their interests in supporting or opposing monetary union as a policy objective; *how* monetary union as a policy process must compete with other programs for public attention and resources; and *what* monetary union entails as a public symbol. Clearly this is a lot of ground to cover, and much of it is shrouded in a dense undergrowth of vague concepts and ideas. Nevertheless, as Dyson (1994) suggests, it is impossible to understand the historical development (and therefore the future prospects) of EMU without taking the whole range of factors into account.

The purpose of this chapter is not to provide a definitive interpretation of EMU. Rather it is to outline a framework within which such an interpretation would be possible, or at least conceivable. We argue that the political economy

163

of EMU is best understood at the intersection of three different levels of analysis—in terms of Europe as a whole, the member states separately, and the socioeconomic groups or regions within member states. Therefore, the three sections that follow introduce each of these levels in turn. In the concluding section, we begin the work of tying the three levels together in a single framework for analyzing EMU from the top down (and from the bottom up). At the same time, we begin to synthesize the conclusions drawn from the other chapters in the volume to underscore what the "new" political economy of EMU is all about.

A Matter of State

The Maastricht Plan for EMU is alternately celebrated as a major step toward a united Europe (Padoa-Schioppa, 1994), vilified as a subversive plot to impose Franco-German domination (Connolly, 1995), lauded as a sophisticated formula for economic cooperation (Gros and Thygesen, 1992), and dismissed as a misguided attempt to circumvent the functioning of the market (Fratianni, von Hagen, and Waller, 1992).[1] Whether in support or opposition, however, the consensus of opinion is that EMU is a matter of tremendous importance, a great affair of state. EMU will change the language and symbolism of world commerce, it will facilitate travel and trade for hundreds of millions of people, and it will influence interest rates and fiscal policies, meaning all forms of investment and all activities of government.

Because of its importance, EMU attracts both politicians and other policies. For example, the political leaders of many member states appear to support EMU, not because of any deeply felt desire for fixed exchange rates or a single currency, but because they fear that exclusion from the monetary projects of the European Union (EU) would relegate them to second-class status (Eichengreen and Frieden, 1994a). This effect is perhaps strongest in the United Kingdom, where John Major's Conservative government pledged itself to a wait-and-see approach to EMU in order to "maintain bargaining leverage in Europe," and where Tony Blair's Labour government quickly adopted much the same approach for much the same reason (Sowemimo, 1996; Hughes Hallett, 1997). Moreover, such high-profile ambivalence extends beyond the Anglo-Saxon world. The attraction of EMU as a great affair of state is also felt in France, where both the Gaullist president Jacques Chirac and his Socialist prime minister Lionel Jospin were elected on platforms to give priority to the fight against domestic unemployment but soon proclaimed their dedication to the pursuit of European monetary unification (McCarthy, 1996; Jones, forthcoming). It is also evident, though perhaps less visible, in Scandinavia, where neither Danish nor Swedish politicians are willing to rule out EMU altogether, and where politicians from both countries tacitly admit that they will join

EMU if the United Kingdom does as well (Moses, 1998; Iversen and Thygesen, 1998).

The pull of EMU on other policies derives both from the European Union as a forum for intergovernmental bargaining and, more recently, from the symbolism of Europe as a grand ideal. EMU attracts other policy issues in intergovernmental bargaining as some member states attempt to trade off support for monetary union in exchange for reciprocal support in other areas from those member states most interested in achieving monetary union. In this way, issues become linked tactically if not intellectually. To give a text book example (Dinan, 1994: 74): German chancellor Willy Brandt supported monetary union in the late 1960s in part as a means of securing French president Georges Pompidou's acceptance of Ostpolitik.

This type of tactical linkage among policy issues is a long-standing feature of European integration and of international negotiations generally (Wallace, 1990). In a multilateral and multifaceted arrangement such as the European Union, it is common for countries to trade across policy dimensions. The more important a particular policy is, the more dimensions it affects, and the more opportunities for linkage to other issues it affords. This explains why monetary union has become "central" to so many EU negotiations.[2] It also explains why any attempt to avoid discussing EMU is virtually doomed to failure: During preparations for the 1996 Intergovernmental Conference (IGC), European statesmen were hopeful that EMU was the one part of the Maastricht Treaty that did not need fixing, and therefore should not appear on the agenda (CEC, 1995; Hennes, 1996). When the IGC concluded at the June 1997 summit in Amsterdam, EMU dominated the discussion and the heads of state and government accomplished few of the institutional reforms that had made the IGC necessary in the first place.

Some issue linkages are more emotional than tactical or intellectual and derive from political symbolism rather than machination. For example, the negotiation of EMU alongside the institutional reforms embedded in the Maastricht Treaty created a symbolic linkage between monetary integration and the "democratization" of the European Union. Therefore, when the Danes rejected the Maastricht Treaty during the June 1992 referendum, EMU was tarnished as somehow "undemocratic" (Sandholtz, 1993a). A similar linkage exists between monetary union and unemployment: Although few economists believe monetary union will increase employment dramatically, politicians acknowledge that monetary union as a "great policy development" must somehow address unemployment as a "great problem of the day" (Jones, forthcoming).

The pull of monetary integration on politicians and other policies is difficult to demonstrate systematically or to measure. At some times, Europe's leaders focus their attention on staying on the bandwagon. At others, they are more deeply engaged in tactical maneuvering through detailed negotiations. And finally, sometimes Europe's leaders are held captive to the great symbols of the day. Nevertheless, EMU's pull is a real force in European affairs. In order to illustrate this point, we draw attention to three fundamental linkages created during the recent history of European monetary integration: The first is between the European Monetary System (EMS) and the disinflation of the 1980s; the second is between EMU and Maastricht convergence during the 1990s; and the third is between monetary union and political union.

The EMS and austerity

The origins of the European Monetary System lay in German chancellor Helmut Schmidt's desire to insulate the German economy and German foreign policy from the influence of the Carter administration. French president Valéry Giscard d'Estaing added to this ambition his own desire to build Europe into a regional force in the global economy. For much of the negotiation of the EMS, the other member states of Europe simply latched on to one or both of these "grand designs" for monetary cooperation. Only the United Kingdom remained aloof, largely because of concerns that such a system would strengthen political ties to the continent at the expense of national sovereignty and trans-Atlantic relations (Ludlow, 1982).

Once the EMS was established, however, the role of monetary integration in further uniting Europe became less important than the need for disinflation, fiscal consolidation, and export competitiveness. The landmarks of the early EMS period are found in exchange rate crises, currency realignments, and budget proposals. European finance ministers adjusted the parities of the exchange rate mechanism seven times in its first four years of operation— reducing the value of the French franc by almost 40 percent against the deutsche mark (Gros and Thygesen, 1992).

The transition from the crisis period of the early 1980s to the more stable middle years of the decade is defined by French president François Mitterrand's April 1983 decision to strengthen disinflation and austerity measures despite rising domestic unemployment. While this decision was rooted in a larger program for relaunching European integration via the Franco-German relationship, the link between participation in the EMS, disinflation, and austerity emerged as paramount. Mitterrand accepted the need to strengthen austerity measures and to shore up French participation in the EMS because a failure to do so threatened to diminish the role of France in Europe (McCarthy, 1990).

After 1983, the EMS became the principal vehicle for promoting monetary stability and fiscal consolidation in Europe. For countries with traditions of high inflation and fiscal laxity, such as France and Italy, the EMS offered to "bind" the hands of national politicians and to shunt the blame for disinflation or austerity onto vaguely defined market forces and faceless Brussels bureau-

crats (Giavazzi and Pagano, 1988). For countries with traditions of low inflation and fiscal rectitude, such as Germany, the EMS promised to prevent
competitive devaluations and to "broaden the zone of monetary stability"
(McNamara and Jones, 1996). Currency realignments became less frequent
and so, too, did political controversy over the functioning of the ERM.

The second turning point in the history of the European Monetary System
came with the hardening of the EMS in 1987 simultaneous to international
recognition of the excessive weakness of the U.S. dollar vis-à-vis the rest of
the world. Shortly after the Group of Seven leading industrialized nations
exacted a statement from the United States that it would defend the dollar and
take efforts to curb its budget deficit, Europe's finance ministers met to balance the instruments used in defending the ERM (Helleiner, 1994: 184; Gros
and Thygesen, 1992: 94–5). Participation in the exchange rate mechanism of
the EMS changed from being a bulwark of disinflation and austerity to an
indicator of monetary and fiscal stability. Here again, participation in the EMS
was an important symbol of being a healthy part of a robust Europe. As a
result the minor parity adjustments between currencies in the ERM made in
January 1987 held until the early 1990s. Meanwhile, new entrants to the European Community began the process of adapting to the rigor of ERM membership, while older members such as Italy and the United Kingdom changed
their attitudes to move closer to Europe's monetary core.

The Maastricht Treaty and convergence

The direction of the linkage between the European monetary system and
disinflation or austerity changed during the negotiation of the Maastricht
Treaty. Where the EMS served to foster stable money and sound finances,
would-be participants in EMU were required to demonstrate such stability
from the outset. To qualify for EMU, the Maastricht Treaty stipulated that a
member state must participate in the EMS, have a consumer price inflation
rate within 1.5 percent and long-term interest rates within 2 percent of Europe's top three inflation performers, have a fiscal deficit at or below 3 percent
of GDP, and an outstanding public debt at, below, or declining toward 60
percent of GDP.

The linkage between monetary integration and economic policymaking
changed for the member states because the role of monetary integration recy-
cled from a broadening of the zone of monetary stability back to the consolidation of Europe (Hughes Hallett and Ma, 1995). Put another way, the
Maastricht convergence criteria had a political, not an economic, justification.
Germany supported EMU as a demonstration of its Western commitments and
in order to soften concerns about its increasing dominance on the continent,
while France accepted a German-style European monetary constitution in exchange for the prospect of obtaining greater influence over European mone-

tary policy, and therefore European interest rates (Sandholtz, 1993a). Within this context, the convergence criteria served as a demonstration of "commitment" on the part of the rest of Europe not to abuse the German-style institutions of EMU for non-German economic policy objectives (McNamara and Jones, 1996).

With the changeover in the relationship between monetary integration and fiscal policy from benefit to obligation, the scope for linking monetary integration to other policy dimensions increased. In larger terms this meant that a reform of the political institutions of the Community would be held parallel to the reform of its economic structures. In more specific terms, it meant that the economically weaker countries could lever off of the convergence requirements for EMU to extract "cohesion" funds for use in their own development (Italianer, 1993; Sandholtz, 1993b; Dyson, 1994). Meanwhile, financial markets began to center on the convergence criteria as convenient indicators for sound economic management and commitment to exchange rate stability. Although there was little economic rationale to the criteria, it soon became clear that a failure to make progress toward meeting them would have immediate economic effects (Eichengreen and Wyploz, 1993).

Monetary union and political union

The larger objective of using EMU to cement ties within Europe also created space for more emotional linkages, most notably between monetary union and "political union." Discussion of this linkage took place throughout the Maastricht negotiations and with increasing fervor after the Danish veto of the treaty (Padoa-Schioppa, 1994: 185–191). Nevertheless, the precise meaning of political union remains unclear, and use of the term appears to differ from case to case.

For example, one interpretation of the linkage between monetary union and political union is the development of more substantial institutions of governance at the European level (Eichengreen and Frieden, 1998). In this view, monetary union will necessitate common financial market regulation, tax guidelines, and labor market institutions. These cannot be provided without appropriate EU representative political bodies to oversee them, just as in national political systems. Nor can they be implemented without some mechanism for coordinating economic policy objectives and for reconciling differences in economic outcomes (Eichengreen, 1994: 101–111). Political union, therefore, holds many of the attributes of an economic superstate, a federal Europe. This view is put forward most strongly by opponents of monetary union such as found in the United Kingdom, who argue that EMU will lead inexorably to the demise of the national state (Padoa-Schioppa, 1994: 185).

At the opposite extreme, is the view that EMU will only work if it unites countries with similar economic and therefore political aspirations. So long as all member states agree implicitly on the monetary constitution of the union, and on the importance of holding that monetary constitution outside the arena for political debate, that is all the political union EMU requires. This view is held by countries such as Germany, which seek in a best-case scenario to restrict the number of participants to a homogenous subset of the EU member states (Tietmeyer, 1994). A second-best solution would allow for a broader group of countries on the condition that the political influence of dissenters from the economic and political consensus is marginal.

Most countries place the link between monetary union and political union somewhere between superstate federalism and forced consensus. France, for example, supports national control over fiscal resources and labor markets, but argues that there should be some political institution capable of providing the broad guidelines for the direction of European macroeconomic policy. The problem, however, is that such compromise positions feed the concerns of EMU's opponents in the United Kingdom while diminishing the ardor of EMU's supporters in Germany. Having attempted to use EMU as a means to foster European unification more generally, Europe's leaders have inadvertently linked debates over the merits of EMU to larger discussions about the appropriate form for Europe.

All through 1997, EMU was the central issue of debate. Italy worried about being excluded, France about the arbitrariness of the convergence criteria, the United Kingdom about the specter of a European superstate, and Germany about the erosion of Europe's consensus over the appropriate constitution for monetary affairs. In each case, however, the concern was more about issues linked to EMU than about the merits of a monetary union *per se*. Thus while it is difficult to measure the extent of these linkages, it is clear they are a force to be reckoned with.

A Question of National Welfare

Up to this point, we have ignored any motivations for participating in EMU based on considerations of economic self-interest. This is not because we believe European politics to be devoid of such material interest, or because we think EMU will have no economic impact on Europe as a whole or on the member states in particular. On the contrary, domestic considerations have predominated in the formulation of national policy toward EMU, and economic issues tend to predominate among domestic considerations. Certainly, negotiations at the EU level, developments in the European political economy more generally, and broader global trends have all been important. But in every EU member state, domestic economics and politics, including complex national particularities, have exerted powerful influences on policy in even the smaller and more open European countries.

The three questions at the heart of national debates over EMU are about what countries are suited to join a particular type of monetary union, what type of monetary union is most suited for particular countries, and how both the member states separately and the union as a whole will be judged in global financial markets. Put another way, these debates pivot on the structure of national political economies, the composition of the monetary union, and its stability in the world economy.

Optimal currency area considerations

Questions of economic structure derive from the general theory of optimum currency areas (Tavlas, 1993). This theory suggests that an optimum currency area has highly integrated labor and capital markets (Mundell, 1961), trades a relatively small percentage of its domestic product with the outside world (McKinnon, 1963), and has either a homogenous industrial structure across regions or some means to compensate for the possibility of region-specific shocks to economic performance (Kenen, 1969). A currency area is too large if it encompasses segregated labor and capital markets, too small if it trades a substantial percentage of its GDP with the outside world, and unstable if it encompasses diverse economic structures and makes no provision for compensating for region-specific economic shocks.

The theory of optimum currency areas describes the attributes of the monetary union as a whole but also sheds light on suitable structures for would-be member states. The ideal candidate has integrated factor markets with the rest of the union, trades more with countries in the monetary union than with those outside, and has similar industrial structures to the rest of the union. From this basis, constructing a set of numerical indicators of "suitability" should be straightforward, obviating the need for debate (see, for example, Gros and Vandille, 1995).

The problem is that the theory of optimum currency areas provides no clear cause-effect relationship between the structural attributes of a country and its participation in a monetary union.[3] In other words, the theory of what constitutes an optimum currency area does not answer questions about how monetary integration will affect factor markets, trade patterns, or the location of economic activity. This is problematic because any cause-effect relationship between monetary integration and the domestic structures of member states has implications both for the member state and for the union—implications that may not coincide in a useful manner either across countries or across levels of analysis.

If monetary union increases factor mobility, that would benefit the union as a whole, but it might cause problems for the recipients of labor migration

(Germany, Scandinavia) as well as for those countries that find themselves losing skilled workers (Portugul, Spain, or even Italy). If it diverts trade toward other member states in the union, this might be helpful for those countries striving to diversify their trading patterns (Ireland, Finland), but it would hinder the efforts of other countries to maintain traditional relationships (Britain and the Commonwealth, France and West Africa). Finally, if monetary integration promotes (or changes) the geographic concentration of production, the costs and benefits could be distributed arbitrarily and to the net detriment of the union as a whole (Krugman, 1991; Krugman and Venables, 1993).

Domestic debates over monetary union necessarily consider not only whether the country is suited for EMU but also whether participation will remain advantageous once the monetary union is formed. In this way, the range of structures to be taken into account extends beyond those suggested by the theory of optimum currency areas and therefore beyond a simple statistical aggregation of indicators for or against. What started as a concise general analysis devolves into a case-by-case examination.

Variable geometry

Structural considerations become even more complicated when they allow for a change in the composition of the monetary union. Consider, for example, the plight of a small country with two larger neighbors. The smaller country conducts much of its trade with these larger neighbors, shares industrial facilities and infrastructure, and enjoys relatively close cultural relations (which facilitates labor mobility). If both of the large countries join the monetary union, then the smaller country would have few problems joining as well. If one of the larger neighbors joins while the other stays out, the smaller country will be caught in the middle. In structural terms, it is as suited to join in the monetary union as it would be to form a separate union with the country that stays outside.

This smaller country example is not fiction: For Belgium caught between France and Germany during the late 1970s and early 1980s, Austria between Italy and Germany in the early 1990s, and the Scandinavian countries between Germany and the United Kingdom for much of the postwar period, this smaller country example is a bitter reality (Jones, Frieden, and Torres, 1998). Moreover, the logic of the argument applies to larger countries as well. France trades a great deal with Italy and Spain, and competes with Italian and Spanish products in EU markets. Thus it is hardly surprising that France would support these countries in their bid to join the monetary union: by joining the union, Italy and Spain will actually improve the structural position of France.

In this tug of war between structure and composition, what is good for the goose is not always good for the gander. While the participation of Spain and Italy might make a monetary union more attractive to France, it could have the opposite effect on Germany—which trades with the two Mediterranean countries but which does not compete with them in EU markets. Finding a compromise solution requires some mechanism for protecting French manufacturing competitiveness without diminishing the level of integration or the degree of industrial homogeneity of the monetary union—particularly as seen from Germany. The complexity of this challenge is discussed in some detail by Jean Pisani-Ferry in Chapter 5. For our purposes, the point to stress is a relatively simple one: National economic interest in joining a monetary union may depend as much on relations between third countries as on the structural suitability of a particular member state.

Market credibility

A final point about the welfare implications of EMU is that national interest in monetary union depends as much on perceptions as on reality—on whether actors in global financial markets believe that monetary union is a good thing in general or for a particular country, as much as on whether EMU or EMU membership is a good thing in fact. This is "true" not as a philosophical assertion about the appropriate ontology for evaluating economic welfare (see, for example, Searle, 1995) but rather because markets are driven by perceptions. And market outcomes will determine to a large extent the welfare effects of monetary integration.

Concern for perceptions forges the link between EMU as a great affair of state and EMU as a question of national welfare. Heads of state and government are attracted to EMU because they worry about perceptions— particularly those drawing on metaphors such as center and periphery, core Europe, concentric circles, and so forth. As with the example of John Major mentioned earlier, many countries in Europe fear they will lose leverage in international negotiations if they do not take part in EMU: In this case, opting out of EMU entails the perception of opting out of Europe—leaving the core for the periphery. The result is a loss of influence generally, as well as the potential loss of bargaining concessions or inward investment specifically. The perception that a country is not a part of core Europe carries a real cost in terms of national economic welfare.

The role of perceptions extends beyond international negotiations and into the more volatile arena of global capital markets. And, perceptions in those markets carry immediate implications, particularly in regard to monetary policy instruments such as interest rates and exchange rates. Market perceptions about governments and their policies translate immediately into the prices of financial assets both foreign and domestic. Stable perceptions reveal themselves through interest and exchange rate premia (or discounts), while changes in perceptions emerge as volatility and speculative attacks (Frenkel, 1983).

From this perspective, the objective for a country's leaders is to make perceptions work in their favor. If politicians and central bankers can convince markets that inflation will remain stable, then interest rates and exchange rates should remain stable as well. And if they can convince markets that inflation rates are convergent, the premiums (and discounts) will diminish. Of course changes in the nonfinancial (real) economy must eventually work their way through the financial system. However, so long as politicians succeed in creating the impression that everything is under control, markets will not react in an arbitrary or speculative manner.[4] In this sense, EMU is part of a confidence game—an attempt to convince the major players in global financial markets not to speculate against intra-European exchange rates or against the government policies behind them. The currency of this confidence game is credibility.

Credibility has three separate dimensions with respect to exchange rate matters generally, and EMU more specifically: reputation, commitment, and (for lack of a better term) coherence. Reputation is easily explained: If a country has a history of following certain patterns of behavior, then it should be expected to do so in the future. Germany is the obvious example of this type of credibility. As Bundesbank presidents never tire of pointing out—usually during a conflict with the government over fiscal outlays—the secret to that country's success in maintaining price stability is that it has always done so (Kennedy, 1991; Marsh, 1992). A failure to support stable prices in the present—to take a recent example, through an irregular revaluation of gold reserves—would reduce German monetary credibility in the future.

Commitment is a somewhat more complicated aspect of credibility and relates more to changes in behavior than to consistency. Heads of state or government commit to a course of action by raising the cost of deviation to unacceptable levels or by removing future decisions from their own control. Membership in the EMS is an example of raising the costs of deviation. Without the EMS, Mitterrand would never have confronted the choice between austerity and "Europe." Central bank independence is an example of removing future decisions from political control. The Bundesbank not only holds the moral high ground as guarantor of Germany's reputation for price stability, it also has the power to resist federal government interference in monetary matters.

Of course neither form of "commitment" is wholly credible in and of itself. EMS membership "tied the hands" of politicians only until market speculators judged that the costs of nondeviation were sufficient to warrant a change of policy. And once commitment through the ERM was found wanting, speculation continued as a result of self-fulfilling prophecy—the market speculators believed policy could be changed, and so they changed it (Eichengreen and Wyploz, 1993). Similarly, commitment through delegation is only as credible as the relative cost of reversing the act of delegation, and as the general reputation for trustworthiness. When the Dutch government refused to heed its central bank's advice for a strong revaluation in line with Germany in the March 1983 ERM realignment, the "quasi-independent" status of the Dutch central bank was violated and premiums on Dutch interest rates increased (Brakman et al., 1991).

Coherence is the most nebulous of the three aspects of credibility. In broad terms, it relates to how well the monetary arrangement coincides with other aspects of macroeconomic policy and with the performance of the macroeconomy—fiscal policy as well as unemployment and trade competitiveness. So long as financial market actors believe the macroeconomic policy mix to be a coherent response to the economic situation, they will have little reason not to believe in the government's commitment to price and exchange rate stability. Once market actors suspect that the macroeconomic policy mix is inappropriate to the situation at hand, they will begin to anticipate policy changes. The credibility of the monetary arrangement in this context will depend upon the extent to which the government cannot change other aspects of the policy mix in response to the economic situation. Returning to the 1992 and 1993 ERM crises, at least part of the explanation for these events lies in the widespread perception among currency traders that unemployment in Europe had reached unacceptable levels, and that commitment to exchange rate targets was therefore likely to waver.

The Maastricht plan for EMU builds on all three facets of credibility. The central role of Germany in EMU taps into that country's reputation for currency stability and extends it with the implicit promise that the euro will be at least as stable as the deutsche mark. The European System of Central Banks and its headquarters, the European Central Bank, are technically independent of the member states, the Council of Ministers, and the European Council, removing the direction of monetary policy from the discretion of Europe's politicians. Finally, the treaty is replete with references to the need for macroeconomic coordination, either implicit and in the common interest, or explicit through the multilateral surveillance procedure. The purpose of such coordination is to ensure that all aspects of European macroeconomic policy cohere around the notion of currency stability in a credible manner.

Despite this effort to address all facets of financial market credibility, the Maastricht Plan for EMU suffers a serious shortcoming: The notion of credibility has theoretical and empirical limitations. Theoretically, although some ingenious explanations have been forwarded, it is not really clear why a government's commitment to monetary integration should be more "credible" than its commitment to an exchange rate, monetary, or inflation rate target. Empirically, many of the attempts to purchase credibility by way of a fixed exchange rate have collapsed, along with the credibility of the government "purchaser." After all, if credibility could be easily obtained, more governments would have recourse to this source. The Maastricht Treaty makes a considerable effort. However, the quality of the attempt is no guarantee of success.

Optimum currency areas, variable geometry, and market credibility all help to explain how monetary integration is perceived as an attempt to pursue the most economically desirable policies. However, such considerations ignore or downplay the fact that policymakers' incentives are not always to pursue policies that enhance national welfare. Even policymakers who would like to implement socially optimal policies often face contrasting pressures. Where monetary integration is the best possible national policy there may be countervailing and concentrated demands that conflict with this goal—such as calls for a depreciation to reduce import competition. Governments must weigh general against specific concerns, and there is no reason to believe that the general will always win out.

From Welfare to Distribution

The contrast between the general and the specific applies to domestic attitudes as well as to government action. Bluntly, public opinion about monetary union is largely unrelated to analysis of optimum currency areas, variable geometry, or credibility. For example, there is no statistical correlation between national support for monetary union and a country's relative structural "suitability" for membership in EMU (holding the composition of the monetary union constant). Figure 6.1 plots the percentage of national respondents supporting monetary union in a December 1995 survey against each country's average ranking within the European Union in terms of a number of optimum currency area indicators. Obvious core countries such as Austria and Germany show very weak support for EMU. Less obvious candidates for early membership such as Italy, Ireland, and Greece have much more favorable popular attitudes.

This disjuncture between popular attitudes and structural suitability is difficult to explain in precise terms. Therefore we focus on the broad differences between countries and country performance, the role of interest groups in defining the national interest, and the structure of political institutions. Along the way, we accede to the notion that politics is more often about the distribution of burdens than the creation of benefits (Thurow, 1980). And in the context of this struggle, the focus of attention must shift away from what EMU has to offer, to "for whom" and "under what conditions."

Political culture and the macroeconomy

Broad-brush explanations for differences in attitudes across countries build on assumptions about "political culture" and about the influence of changes in the business cycle. The political culture part of the explanation is more

J. Frieden & E. Jones

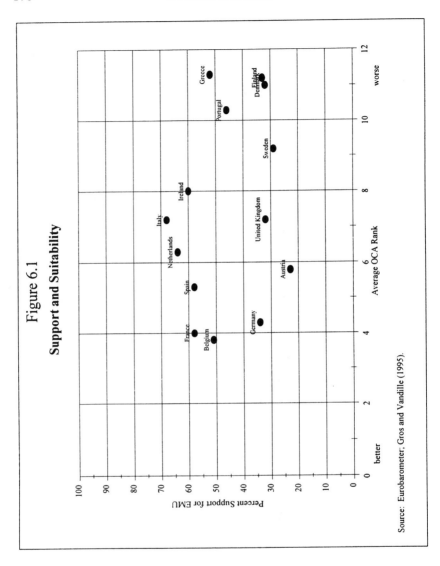

Figure 6.1

Support and Suitability

Source: Eurobarometer; Gros and Vandille (1995).

impressionistic than directly observable. For example, the citizens of many countries appear to have some attachment to their national currency, although the intensity of this attachment seems to differ from case to case. Irish nationalism seems not to have been offended by the one-to-one, no-margins parity with the pound sterling before 1979, few Italians express great attachment to the lira, and Luxembourg's surrender of currency autonomy to Belgium has only rarely been a significant issue in the seventy years the Belgium-Luxembourg union has been in place. By contrast, journalistic reports and some surveys indicate—albeit, again, at best impressionistically—that the Germans, French, and British are more reluctant to surrender national currencies.

A similar observation applies to price inflation. The population in some countries, such as Italy, seems less averse to inflation while in other countries, such as Germany, the public is very intolerant of rising prices. Explanations for why this is so are persuasive if somewhat less than rigorous. We can accept that German hyperinflation during the 1920s and after the Second World War translated into a powerful popular aversion to price increases without explaining why hyperinflation in other countries failed to have the same effect.

Taken together, these assertions about national political culture can explain why attitudes toward monetary union differ from one place to the next. The Germans are loathe to join EMU because doing so would mean sacrificing the deutsche mark as a national symbol and may also run the risk of inflation. Meanwhile, the Italians are less reticent to join because they are indifferent to the symbolism of their national currency and less haunted by the threat of rising prices. Indeed, European idealism may endow the euro with even greater symbolic importance than the lira whereas German participation in EMU ensures greater price stability than that offered by Rome. From this standpoint, the difference between German and Italian popular opinions regarding EMU is hardly surprising.

What such arguments about political culture cannot explain is why national attitudes—and the differences between them—should vary over time.[5] One means of correcting for this limitation would be to introduce macroeconomic performance as a second explanatory variable. The assumption here is that public opinion will be more supportive of monetary union when the economy is doing well, and less supportive when it is doing poorly. In other words, public opinion about EMU varies over time in response to changes in the business cycle. Therefore, in general terms, we expect to see a decline in support for a single currency over the course of the 1991 to 1994 recession. In more specific terms, we expect to see more dramatic changes in attitudes toward monetary union in those countries where macroeconomic conditions have changed more dramatically. Spanish opinion has arguably gone through a phase of extreme optimism between 1990 and 1992 to one of great pessimism after the 1992 to 1993 crisis, back to more guarded optimism.

However, neither aspect of this general analysis is wholly satisfactory. To begin with, the political culture argument posits a value set and yet provides no mechanism for value change.[6] It is one thing to assert that the Germans dread the memory of hyperinflation but another to predict when their fear will dissipate. A second concern is that the argument offers no clear relationship between macroeconomic developments and popular attitudes. As a result, recent findings by Eichenberg and Dalton (1993) that past changes in popular attitudes toward European integration correlate with changes in price inflation but not with changes in unemployment are hard to explain. Finally, the combination of political culture and the business cycle offers no insight into how popular attitudes translate into domestic politics.

Interest groups and regions

Forging the link between attitudes and politics requires making assumptions about motivation and collective action. And the assumption we make is that the most motivated groups will be those economically most affected by monetary integration. Monetary integration has a differential impact on groups in society. This is true both with regard to the ultimate goal—whether this be the ERM, a hard core, or full-currency union—and as concerns the transition. On both dimensions, distributional considerations are likely to play a role.

Monetary union itself can give rise to costs and benefits that vary among socioeconomic actors (Frieden, 1994; Hefeker, 1997a; Henning, 1994). Those heavily involved in cross-border economic activity presumably are most favorably inclined toward monetary union. Especially to the extent that they have EU-wide economic interests, whatever sacrifices monetary union may imply for national monetary independence are of little consequence for such regionally (or globally) oriented firms and groups. On the other hand, economic actors with interests solely in one national economy—especially producers of nontradable goods and services—gain little by stabilizing exchange rates and see governments forced to surrender monetary autonomy that they may value. All else equal, then, domestically oriented economic actors are unlikely to be so enthusiastic about monetary union as those that are globally or regionally oriented, although some may merely be indifferent rather than actively opposed. At the more sociological level, in many countries upper-middle-income groups have become quite pan-European in their professional and personal outlooks, and their views may be disproportionately represented among "opinion leaders" and others in positions of influence.

While longer-term considerations—whether monetary union is desirable or not—may be significant, in many cases it is not so much the ultimate goal but the *transition* to a fixed rate, the EMS, or full-fledged monetary union that gives rise to political conflict. National policies necessary to stabilize currency values often include unpopular monetary and fiscal austerity. At times, fixing exchange rates can lead to a real appreciation as national inflation rates converge only slowly to those of the anchor country. The effects of these real appreciations, especially in increasing import competition and reducing export competitiveness, can cause substantial domestic economic and political pressures for a devaluation. Such pressures are most likely to come from tradables producers hit by the transitional real appreciation. Because agriculture is cushioned from such relative price movements by the Common Agricultural

Policy (CAP), the principal sources of such concerns are likely to be nationally based manufacturers, especially of standardized products where competition on price is extremely important, and primary producers outside agriculture.

Even where, say, manufacturers might otherwise support monetary union, the immediate costs of a substantial real appreciation can drive them to demand a devaluation that jeopardizes progress toward monetary integration. During the 1992 to 1993 currency crises, it was common for industrialists in such countries as Italy, Spain, and Ireland to proclaim simultaneous support for monetary union and for devaluations to help restore their own competitiveness. In the aftermath of the crisis, similar rumblings about the level of the exchange rate sounded among manufacturers in Austria, Belgium, and the Netherlands—three countries universally regarded as being part of Europe's monetary core (Hochreiter and Jones, 1997).

Although the literature is not unanimous, we can attempt a tentative summary of interest-group divisions. Those with cross-border economic interests—such as internationally oriented banks and corporations—will tend to support monetary union, while domestically oriented firms will be indifferent or hostile. In the not unlikely event of a transitional real appreciation during the movement toward monetary integration, those hardest hit by ensuing price pressure—especially basic manufacturers and primary producers—will tend to push for relaxing the monetary link in order to allow a competitive devaluation.

There is certainly some empirical foundation to these arguments. In most EU members, regionally or globally active firms and banks have been strongly supportive of monetary integration; this is true even in Germany, where the big international banks might be expected to share some of the Bundesbank's skepticism (Hefeker, 1997b). By the same token, complaints from manufacturers and primary producers have certainly been important in those countries and instances in which a transitional real appreciation has threatened the national commitment to monetary integration—the cases of the Finnish and Swedish timber and wood products sectors are illustrative (Moses, 1998).

However, evidence about the impact of these distributional factors is controversial. Some believe that they play little or no role in monetary policymaking; others regard them as more important (Gowa, 1988). One clear problem is that it is extremely difficult to know how such interest-group concerns affect policy: We may be able to observe interest-group complaints or demands but rarely their direct or indirect impact on policymaking. It is likely that distributional effects are of more importance in some countries than in others, and more influential at some times than at others, but a precise sense of their operation is hard to establish. This illustrates the general principle that in the making of such an aggregate issue as macroeconomic policy, it can be difficult to identify clearly the group interests in play.

Like groups, regions within countries may differ in the degree to which they would benefit from monetary union or might be harmed by policies to achieve it. To some extent, regional considerations are simply a subset of the factors mentioned above. Some regions may be less fully integrated with potential monetary partners than others, or have other characteristics that raise (or lower) the efficiency costs of monetary union. Regions are often specialized in economic activities that may be affected by monetary union and transitional policies differently than the rest of the country. Regional public opinions can differ widely from those of the country as a whole. For all these reasons and more, there may be substantial differences in the attitudes of subnational regions to monetary union.

This is especially true in such countries as Spain, Belgium, and Italy where there are large socioeconomic and political differences among regions. In some cases, regional differences are correlated with industrial structure: As manufacturing regions, the Basque country and Catalonia differ substantially from the more agricultural Andalucia, and from Madrid's role as an administrative and financial center. In other cases, regional differences are related to sociopolitical or cultural characteristics that affect attitudes toward European integration more generally, as in the instance of Catalan and Scottish nationalists who see the EU as a potential counterbalance to Spanish and English influence.

Another difficult problem arises when plans for monetary union appear to threaten regional economic policy prerogatives that may be jealously guarded. This factor makes a distinction between regions and interest groups in all but the most corporatist countries: Regions often have specific political competencies related to the formation of monetary policy or macroeconomic policy more generally. To the extent that monetary integration threatens these competencies, regions may oppose monetary union *tout court*. In Germany, for example, the Länder are directly represented on the Bundesbank council; they would almost certainly not be represented in any potential European Central Bank. Some may resist the delegation of monetary policy for these sorts of institutional reasons.

Regional issues can thus be expected to surface in two situations. One is where there are large enough differences among regions in their economic and political character to give rise to disagreements over the inherent value of monetary union. The other is where aspects of monetary integration threaten existing prerogatives of regional authorities. Of course, the relevance of both sets of circumstances varies from country to country.

Institutions

Whatever underlying social and economic conditions prevail in EU member states, their impact on the future of monetary union is filtered through existing political institutions. Such institutions can have a substantial effect on policy outcomes generally, and in the monetary sphere.

Political parties are principal building blocks of public policy. Their structure, ideology, and influence vary tremendously among countries, and even within the same country. Some parties are inclusive and encompassing, while others are compact and homogenous; some are highly ideological while others are pragmatic; some have clear class constituencies while others rely on religious, philosophical, or regional appeals. A nuanced view of the impact of parties on monetary union requires detailed knowledge of each nation's party structure, and of each of its parties, but a few generalizations can be made (Alesina, 1989; Grilli, Masciandaro, and Tabellini, 1991).

Some believe that, with many exceptions, centrist and rightist parties tend to be more inflation averse than leftist. By the same token, leftist parties appear to many observers more inclined to pursue devaluations than centrist and rightist groups. The former may be because the austerity measures required to reduce inflation are particularly harmful to constituencies of the Left, especially workers. The latter may be because of the concentration of organized workers in traded-goods industries, or of a generally greater business enthusiasm for monetary integration. Whatever the reasons, the pattern seems common although not universal. This leads to an expectation that, all else equal, commitment to "hard money" in the context of monetary union may be more likely to be stronger in the Center and on the Right than on the Left. It should be noted, however, that in some countries where the Right and extreme Right are highly nationalistic, they too oppose monetary union.

Many of the partisan differences among countries are due to variations in electoral systems, which can affect the policy process. Most generally, it is widely believed that representatives of larger constituencies are more likely to attend to broad social concerns, while those from smaller constituencies are more prone to reflect particular interests. Some argue, for example, that systems of proportional representation are less likely to lead to polarized politics and erratic policies than are other systems. (It should be pointed out that other scholars believe quite the opposite.) Similarly, where the executive is elected separately from the legislature, it may face different electoral concerns than parliamentarians—typically more focused on broad national pressures than narrower local or sectoral ones (Rogowski, 1987; Eichengreen, 1992; Lohmann and O'Halloran, 1994).

The timing of elections can affect policymaking, especially to the extent that incumbents adjust macroeconomic policies to produce favorable conditions at election time. This is true even where election timing is determined by the incumbent government, both because of time limits on intervals between elections and because even where the party in power can determine the date of the election, it still has an incentive to manipulate the macroeconomy to political advantage. The incentive to pursue expansionary monetary policies is probably greater the weaker the government's electoral position; it may also be greater in minority and coalition governments than in single-party majority governments.

The institutional character of economic (and especially monetary) policymaking can also have an impact on outcomes. Perhaps the most common observation along these lines is that greater central bank independence tends to be associated with lower inflation, which implies greater ease of committing to a fixed exchange rate and perhaps also to monetary union (Cukierman, 1992). The causal status of this observation is controversial—it is hard to know whether central bank independence has an independent explanatory effect—but there is likely to be some relationship. It is probably not coincidental that Italy and, until recently, the United Kingdom have had central banks with little autonomy. However, during the 1980s Belgium and France had two of the least independent central banks in Europe, and yet were able to sustain their ERM commitments with great success. Nonetheless, inasmuch as independent central banks—which now, at least nominally, include all central banks in Europe including the Bank of England—promote monetary stability, they can also smooth the path to monetary union.

In a similar way, although it has been less closely studied, the relationship among bureaucracies with responsibility for policies related to monetary union can color national attitudes. Where, for example, the treasury or finance ministry has responsibility for the exchange rate but an independent central bank is charged with monetary policy, there is room for conflict over desirable and compatible policies. To the extent that the central bank is less subject to political influence than the executive, policy toward monetary union will be affected by their relative authority over relevant economic policy. While again the case is susceptible to challenge, it is likely that countries in which an independent central bank has authority over both monetary and currency policy will be most inclined to pursue policies driven by national economic considerations; as the central bank diminishes in independence and in authority over the exchange rate, monetary policies are more likely to reflect distributionally, geographically, or temporally narrower concerns.[7]

Similarly, national bureaucracies can have independent preferences over monetary integration. Some national authorities may regard delegating monetary policy to a European central bank as an undesirable loss of influence over policy and its perquisites. In this case, opposition to monetary union may come from national monetary authorities themselves who wish to maintain their influence over relevant policies. The example of the Bundesbank is only the most prominent example of a central bank for which monetary union is a threat rather than an opportunity.

For monetary policy and politics, some of the most important characteristics of any country are its labor market institutions. There is substantial evidence, in fact, that coordinated and centralized wage bargaining institutions have contributed to national efforts to reduce inflation and keep it under control (Calmfors and Driffill, 1988). Where wage patterns are established by encompassing labor unions and employers' peak organizations, workers and employers may internalize more of the positive and negative externalities created by their wage-setting behavior. This is relevant to the politics of monetary union: When labor and management can credibly commit to restraint, sustaining a fixed exchange rate and moving to a single currency is likely to be easier. When, on the other hand, labor relations are conflictive and decentralized, the transition to monetary union might be derailed by an unrestrained race by workers and employers to secure advantages before exchange rates are locked in place.

For example, the ability of Austria, Belgium, and the Netherlands to maintain their deutsche mark links were all expedited by the relatively centralized nature of their labor unions and wage-setting systems (Hochreiter and Jones, 1997). By the same token, British and Italian difficulties may have been exacerbated by the fragmentation of their wage bargaining institutions. Of course, this is only one of several considerations: Sweden has long had one of the more centralized wage-setting systems in Europe (although it has been disintegrating), yet this seems not to have helped the country avoid several rounds of inflation and currency depreciation (Moses, 1998). Nonetheless, there does appear to be considerable evidence that more encompassing and orderly labor market institutions, especially those involved in national wage bargaining, can smooth the path to monetary integration.

Institutional considerations are extraordinarily complex. Subtle differences can have powerful effects, and the relevant factors are often more informal than formal. Close attention to national institutional characteristics is important. Within this, some generalizations are possible (if not uncontroversial). The Left has typically been more ambivalent about monetary union than parties of the Center or Right. Parties in power, of whatever ideology, may be especially susceptible to pressures for expansionary monetary policies in the run up to elections, and when their position is precarious. Independent central banks are associated with "harder" monetary policies and seem especially effective when their authority extends to the exchange rate. Nations with cohesive and inclusive wage bargaining systems find it easier to achieve the monetary stability crucial to monetary union.

Political culture, macroeconomic performance, collective interest, geographic organization, and institutional structure all have roles to play in shaping attitudes toward monetary union and the policies intended to pursue (or ignore) it. The range of factors is daunting. And while it is possible to make some rough generalizations about what may be important, clearly there is substantial empirical work to be done.

Putting It All Together

EMU is an important policy development in Europe and perhaps even the
most important of the 1990s. Europe's economic and monetary union will
change the functioning of international commerce; it will directly affect the
lives of millions of people; it may even provoke deeper forms of European
integration. It is a symbol of belonging, a signal of sound economic governance, and a litmus test for French and German leadership.

EMU is also a complex issue, encompassing far more than the technical
term "economic and monetary union" would seem to imply. This complexity
resides at both ends of the policy—in EMU itself, and also in the member
states, groups, and regions that will be affected. The impact of monetary union
changes with exposure to world markets and according to the constraints of
domestic institutions. Moreover, political expression of attitudes toward EMU
varies with the level of organization and the opportunities for participation.

EMU has been difficult to accomplish perhaps *because* it is so important
and yet so complex. Writing in 1975, a high-level Reflection Group on "Economic and Monetary Union 1980" (CEC, 1975: 80–81) attributed Europe's
failure to implement EMU to three factors: an unwillingness to work collectively, an inability to foresee the economic turmoil of the 1970s, and an insufficient understanding of the institutional and political requirements for
monetary integration. By the 1990s, the first of these factors appears to have
been remedied. The European member states have passed through the turmoil
of the early part of this decade still committed to EMU. The second factor, an
inability to foresee the future, remains. However, the experiences of the 1970s
and early 1980s have lowered expectations about the stability of the world
economy while at the same time forcing policymakers to design more robust
institutions. Put another way, in comparison with the late 1960s and early
1970s, Europe's policymakers are now more strongly committed to constructing a monetary union, and their plans for that construction are more resilient
to the powerful influences of the global economy.

It is the third factor—an insufficient understanding of EMU—that continues
to pose problems both for Europe and for the member states. Principally,
the distributional consequences of monetary integration have proven to be
unpredictable. While it is possible to sketch out those factors responsible for
determining costs and benefits, they are too numerous and too closely interre-
lated to allow for the easy construction of coalitions in support of EMU either
within or across member states. Therefore, a defining feature of the new political economy of EMU is idiosyncrasy.

Nevertheless, there are many things we can claim to know about Europe's
future monetary union. To begin with, EMU is unlikely to contribute to Europe's unemployment problem (although continuing high levels of unemployment are sure to detract from EMU). Whether or not EMU takes place,

Europe's member states must tackle the rigidities in domestic labor markets responsible for translating short-term job losses into long-term (and long) unemployment rolls. Simply, as Viñals and Jimeno point out in Chapter 2, the high level of unemployment is symptomatic of structural problems that must be dealt with in any event.

The reality of Europe's unemployment problem seems to have gotten lost in the debates about the costs of EMU and particularly about the importance of asymmetric shocks. To be sure, the process of monetary integration does impose costs. However, as Gros argues in Chapter 3, these are relatively minor by comparison with other shocks to the economy whether through investment or through exchange rate volatility (directly, and not via its impact on trade flows). Seen this way, the benefits of monetary integration in the form of lower interest rate premiums and greater exchange rate stability should outweigh the costs—at least in aggregate terms. Whether the beneficiaries of EMU are strong enough or convincing enough to persuade others to side with them is a different matter.

Moreover, as Hughes Hallett and McAdam demonstrate in Chapter 4, the means for forming a monetary union will affect the balance of costs and benefits. Thus it is not enough to examine support for the goal of monetary integration. The process must be examined as well. And, it is important to note that the process will continue long after EMU begins—both in terms of the requirements for staying in EMU (such as the stability pact), and in terms of the requirements of joining at some future date. To understand the political economy of EMU, therefore, it is necessary to consider the distribution of costs and benefits within and between member states—and whether or not they participate in EMU from the outset.

Two questions are important to answer. The first is how will the member states interact in response to such costs and benefits? This is the problem of variable geometry as analyzed by Pisani-Ferry in Chapter 5. And, it is a problem that the designers of the Maastricht Treaty did not anticipate fully. The project was constructed as a win-win situation, with the principal concern being to limit membership to those who could best contribute to and benefit from the monetary union. With hindsight, it is obvious that not all countries prefer to join at the same time and on the same terms. By the same token, the costs of excluding countries are not uniform from one member state to the next. Different member states have different preferences, and so the dynamics of variable geometry are variable as well.

Therefore, the second question to answer is how national (and therefore also sub-national) preferences are formed. And consideration of preference formation brings this discussion full circle by focusing attention on perceptions of the costs and benefits of monetary integration, both economic and political. What we have provided is a framework within which such consideration may take place—an indication of where to look and what to look for.

What remains to be seen is whether the understanding of preferences will be sufficient to underwrite the commitment to construct a monetary union in Europe and, therefore, to prevent the great expectations for EMU from being met with equally great disappointment.

Notes

1. Here we perhaps overstate the distinction between Gros and Thygesen (1992), on the one hand, and Fratianni, von Hagen, and Waller (1992), on the other.

2. This concept of "centrality" is similar to what Keohane (1983) describes as a "nested" regime. The difference is that we focus more on what EMU has done to Europe than on what Europe has provided as a "nest" for EMU.

3. Obviously this is not the only problem with the theory of optimum currency areas. For example, both Gros (Chapter 3) and Bofinger (1994) emphasize the unrealistic assumptions of the theory about exchange rates and adjustment.

4. The belief in credibility as a panacea may be wishful thinking. As Buiter, Corsetti, and Pesenti (1996: 57–58) rightly point out: "There are plenty of financial shocks beyond the control of a national policy maker that may hamper convergence; careless political statements by influential foreigners are a good example. Through their impact on interest rates, speculative pressures generated by a throwaway comment or an infelicitously timed opinion in Frankfurt can rapidly reduce the effectiveness of domestic policy measures in Rome."

5. The failure to explain variations in the differences between national attitudes on EMU is a significant limitation of the political culture argument. The fact that some differences exist and remain consistent is sufficient to illustrate that national political cultures are important. If national differences became wholly erratic or, worse, convergent, the political cultures argument would lose explanatory power. See, for example, Inglehart (1990).

6. Of course this is the distinction between general arguments about national attitudes toward price and exchange rate stability and Inglehart's more careful analysis of value change.

7. Von Hagen (1992), von Hagen and Harden (1994), and De Haan and Sturm (1994) all make similar points with respect to fiscal policy.

A Note on Data Sources

In order to provide up-to-date, comparable data for each of the chapters, we have relied on four principal data sources. The Eurostat CD (Eurostat), the AMECO database of the European Commission (European Commission), the historical statistics of the OECD Economic Outlook (OECD), and the International Finance Statistics CD of the International Monetary Fund (IMF). In addition, we have asked our contributors to supplement these data sets with national sources where necessary. In each case, we have chosen to cite only the institution responsible for the raw data.

References

Aglietta, M., and M. Uctum (1996). "La consolidation budgétaire en Europe." *Economie internationale* 65:1, pp. 37–62.

Alesina, A. (1989). "Politics and Business Cycles in Industrial Democracies." *Economic Policy* 8 (April) pp. 55–98.

Alesina, A., and V. Grilli (1993). "On the Feasibility of a One-Speed or Multi-Speed European Monetary Union." *Economics and Politics* 5:2 (July) pp. 145–165.

Alesina, A., and R. Perotti (1995). "Fiscal Adjustment: Fiscal Expansions and Adjustments in OECD Countries." *Economic Policy* 21 (October) pp. 207–240.

Alexander, L. (1994). "Monetary Policy Constraints and the Impact of the Elimination of Structural Problems in European Labor Markets." Manuscript (March).

Alogoskoufis, G., C. Bean, G. Bertola, D. Cohen, J. J. Dolado, and G. Saint-Paul (1995). "Unemployment: Choices for Europe." *Monitoring European Integration, No. 5*. London: Centre for Economic Policy Research.

Anderson, T., and O. Risager (1988). "Stabilization Policies, Credibility and Interest Rate Determination in a Small Open Economy." *European Economic Review* 32, pp. 669–679.

Andrés, J., and I. Hernando (1995). "Inflación y crecimiento a largo plazo: Evidencia internacional." *Boletín Económico*. Madrid: Banco D'España (September) pp. 53–63.

Argimón, I., J. M. González Páramo, and J. M. Roldán (1995). "Does Public Spending Crowd Out Private Investment? Evidence from a Panel of 14 OECD Countries." *Working Document No. 9523*. Madrid: Banco D'España.

Artus, P. (1995). "L'union monétaire sera-t-elle attrayante pour les pays périphériques européens?" *Document de travail No. 1995-12*. Paris: Caisse des dépôts et consignations (July).

Baldwin, R. (1995). "A Domino Theory of Regionalism," in R. Baldwin, P. Haaparanta, and J. Kiander, eds., *Expanding Membership in the European Union*. Cambridge: Cambridge University Press.

Barran, F., V. Coudert, and B. Mojon (1996). "The Transmission of Monetary Policy in the European Countries." *Document de travail No. 96-03*. Paris: CEPII (February).

Barrel, R., J. Morgan, and N. Pain (1995). "The Employment Effects of the Maastricht Fiscal Criteria." *Discussion Paper No. 81*. London: National Institute for Economic and Social Research.

Barro, R. J., and D. B. Gordon (1983). "Rules, Discretion and Reputation in a Model of Monetary Policy." *Journal of Monetary Economics* 12 (July) pp. 101–121.

Barry, F., and M. Devereux (1995). "The Expansionary Fiscal Contraction Hypothesis: A Neo-Keynesian Analysis." *Oxford Economic Papers* 47:2 (April) pp. 249–264.

Bartolini, L., A. Razin, and S. Symanski (1995). "G-7 Fiscal Restructuring in the 1990s: Macroeconomic Effects." *Economic Policy* 20 (April) pp. 111–146.

Bartolini, L., and S. Symanski (1993). "Unemployment and Wage Dynamics in MULTIMOD." Staff Studies for the World Economic Outlook. Washington, D.C.: IMF (December).

Baxter, M., and A. C. Stockman (1989). "Business Cycles and the Exchange Rate Regime: Some International Evidence." *Journal of Monetary Economics* 23 (May) pp. 377–401.

Bayoumi, T. (1994). "A Formal Model of Optimum Currency Areas." *IMF Staff Papers* 41:4 (December) pp. 537–554.

Bayoumi, T., and B. Eichengreen (1992). "Is There a Conflict Between EC Enlargement and European Monetary Unification?" *Discussion Paper No. 636.* London: Centre for Economic Policy Research.

Bayoumi, T., and B. Eichengreen (1993). "Shocking Aspects of European Monetary Integration," in Torres and Giavazzi (1993) pp. 193–240.

Bayoumi, T., and B. Eichengreen (1996a). "Operationalizing the Theory of Optimum Currency Areas." Paper presented at the CEPR conference on Regional Integration, La Coruna, Portugal (April).

Bayoumi, T., and B. Eichengreen (1996b). "Ever Closer to Heaven; an Optimum-Currency-Area Index for European Countries." Paper presented at the 1996 EEA Congress, Istanbul, Turkey.

Bayoumi, T., and E. Prasad (1995). "Currency Unions, Economic Fluctuations and Adjustment: Some Empirical Evidence." *CEPR Discussion Paper No. 1172.* London: Centre for Economic Policy Research (May).

Bean, C. R. (1992). "Economic and Monetary Union in Europe." *Journal of Economic Perspectives* 6:4 (Fall) pp. 31–53.

Bean, C. R. (1994). "European Unemployment: A Survey." *Journal of Economic Literature* 32:2 (June) pp. 573–620.

Belke, A., and D. Gros (1997a). "Estimating the Costs and Benefits of EMU: The Impact of External Shocks on Labour Markets." *Center Discussion Paper No. 9795.* Tilburg: Tilburg University.

Belke, A., and D. Gros (1997b). "Evidence on the Costs of Intra-European Exchange Rate Variability." Paper presented at the 1997 International Seminar on Macroeconomics, Gerzensee, Switzerland.

Bentolila, S., and G. Bertola (1990). "Firing Costs and Labor Demand: How Bad Is Eurosclerosis?" *Review of Economic Studies* 57:3 (July) pp. 381–402.

Bentolila, S., and J. J. Dolado (1994). "Labor Flexibility and Wages: Lessons from Spain." *Economic Policy* 18 (April) pp. 53–99.

Bentolila, S., and G. Saint-Paul (1994). "A Model of Labor Demand with Linear Adjustment Costs." *Labour Economics* 1:3/4 (September) pp. 303–326.

Bergsten, C. F., and J. Williamson (1994). "Is the Time Ripe for Target Zones or the Blueprint?" in *Bretton Woods: Looking to the Future.* Washington, D.C.: Bretton Woods Commission (July).

Bertola, G., and A. Drazen (1993). "Trigger Points and Budget Cuts: Explaining the Effects of Fiscal Austerity." *American Economic Review* 83:1 (March) pp. 11–26.

Bini-Smaghi, L., and S. Vori (1993). "Rating the EC as an Optimum Currency Area." *Discussion Paper No. 187.* Rome: Banca d'Italia (January).

Blanchard, O. J. (1990). "Unemployment: Getting the Questions Right and Some of the Answers," in J. Drèze and C. R. Bean, eds., *Europe's Unemployment Problem.* Cambridge: MIT Press, pp. 66–89.

Blanchard, O. J., and P. Diamond (1992). "The Flow Approach to the Labor Market." *American Economic Review* 82:2 (May) pp. 354–359.

Blanchard, O. J., and J. F. Jimeno (1995). "Structural Unemployment: Spain versus Portugal." *American Economic Review* 85:2 (May) pp. 212–218.

Blanchard, O. J., J. F. Jimeno, et al. (1995). "Spanish Unemployment: Is there a Solution?" Manuscript. London: Centre for Economic Policy Research.

Blanchard, O. J., and L. F. Katz (1992). "Regional Evolutions." *Brooking Papers on Economic Activity I.* Washington D.C.: The Brookings Institution, pp. 1–75.

Blanchard, O., and P. A. Muet (1993). "Competitiveness through Disinflation: An Assessment of the French Macroeconomic Strategy." *Economic Policy* 16 (April) pp. 11–56.

Blanchard, O. J., and L. Summers (1986). "Hysteresis and the European Unemployment Problem." *NBER Macroeconomics Annual, Volume 1.* Cambridge: MIT Press, pp. 15–91.

Bofinger, P. (1994). "Is Europe an Optimum Currency Area?" *CEPR Discussion Paper No. 915.* London: Centre for Economic Policy Research (February).

Boltho, A. (1994). "A Comparison of Regional Differentials in the European Community and the United States," in J. Mortensen, ed., *Improving Economic and Social Cohesion in the European Community.* New York: St. Martin's Press.

Boone, L. (1997). "Symmetry and Asymmetry of Supply and Demand Shocks in the European Union: A Dynamic Analysis." *Working Paper No. 97-03.* Paris: CEPII (February).

Bover, O., M. Arellano, and S. Betolila (1996). "Unemployment Duration, Benefit Duration, and the Business Cycle." Manuscript. Madrid: Banco D'España.

Bradley, J., K. Whelan, and J. Wright (1993). *Stabilization and Growth in the EC Periphery.* Avebury: Aldershot.

Brakman, S., J. de Haan, and C. J. Jepma (1991). "Is de gulden hard genog?" *Economische Statistisch Berichten* (2 June) pp. 16–20.

Brenton, P., and P. Sinclair (1996). "Explaining Recent British Export Performance." Manuscript. Birmingham: Department of Economics, University of Birmingham.

Bryant, R. C., P. Hooper, and C. Mann (1993). *Evaluating Policy Regimes: New Research in Empirical Macroeconomics.* Washington, D.C.: Brookings Institution.

Buiter, W., G. Corsetti, and P. Pesenti (1996). "Interpreting the ERM Crisis: Country-specific and Systemic Issues." Manuscript (March).

Calmfors, L. (1994). "Centralization of Wage Bargaining and Macroeconomic Performance: A Survey." *OECD Economic Studies* 21 (Winter) pp. 159–191.

Calmfors, L., and J. Driffill (1988). "Centralization of Wage Bargaining: Bargaining Structure, Corporatism, and Macroeconomic Performance." *Economic Policy* 6 (April) pp. 13–61.

Canzoneri, M., and D. Henderson (1991). *Monetary Policy in Interdependent Economies*. Cambridge: MIT Press.

Canzoneri, M., J. Vallés, and J. Viñals (1996). "Do Exchange Rates Move to Address International Macroeconomic Imbalances?" Manuscript. Madrid: Banco D'España.

Centre for Economic Policy Research (CEPR, 1994). "Unemployment: Choices for Europe." *Monitoring European Integration No. 5*. London: Centre for Economic Policy Research.

Centre for Economic Policy Research (CEPR, 1995). "Flexible Integration." *Monitoring European Integration No. 6*. London: Centre for Economic Policy Research.

Centre for European Policy Studies (CEPS, 1995). "Proceedings of the CEPS International Advisory Council on Preparing for 1996 and a Larger European Union, Palais d'Egmont, 17–18 November 1994." Brussels: Centre for European Policy Studies.

Church, K. B., P. Mitchell, J. Sault, and K. F. Wallis (1996). "The Sensitivity of Global Model Simulations to Fiscal Closure Rules." Warwick: University of Warwick, Macroeconomic Modeling Bureau, mimeo.

Commission of the European Communities (CEC, 1975). "Rapport du groupe de reflexion 'Union économique et monétaire 1980.'" Brussels: Commission of the European Communities (March).

Commission of the European Communities (CEC, 1990). "One Market, One Money." *European Economy, No. 44*. Brussels: Commission of the European Communities.

Commission of the European Communities (CEC, 1993). *Growth, Competitiveness, Employment: The Challenges and Ways Forward into the 21st Century*. Luxembourg: Office for Official Publications of the European Communities.

Commission of the European Communities (CEC, 1995). "Progress Report from the Chairman of the Reflection Group on the 1996 Intergovernmental Conference." Brussels: Commission of the European Communities, SN 50/1/95 (REFLEX 10) REV1.

Connolly, B. (1995). *The Rotten Heart of Europe: The Dirty War for Europe's Money*. London: Faber and Faber.

Coor, P., E. Dubois, S. Mahfouz, and J. Pisani-Ferry (1996). "The Cost of Fiscal Retrenchment Revisited: How Strong Is the Evidence?" *Working Document No. 96-16*. Paris: CEPII (December).

Courchene, T. , et al. (1993). "Stable Money—Sound Finances: Report to the European Commission." *European Economy No. 53*. Brussels: Commission of the European Communities.

Cukierman, A. (1992). *Central Bank Strategy, Credibility, and Independence: Theory and Evidence*. Cambridge: MIT Press.

Danthine, J. P., and J. Hunt (1994). "Wage Bargaining Structure, Employment and Economic Integration." *Economic Journal* 104:424 (May) pp. 528–542.

De Boissieu, C., and J. Pisani-Ferry (1995). "The Political Economy of French Economic Policy and the Transition to EMU." *Working Paper No. 95-10*. Paris: CEPII.

Decressin, J., and A. Fatás (1994). "Regional Labor Market Dynamics in Europe." *CEPR Discussion Paper No. 1085*. London: Centre for Economic Policy Research.

Decressin, J., and A. Fatás (1995). "Regional Labor Market Dynamics in Europe and Implications for EMU." *European Economic Review* 39:9 (December) pp. 1627–1655.

De Grauwe, P. (1992). *The Economics of Monetary Integration.* Oxford: Oxford University Press.

De Grauwe, P. (1996). "The Economics of Convergence towards Monetary Union in Europe," in F. Torres, ed., *Monetary Reform in Europe.* Lisbon: Universidade Catolica Editora, pp. 121–148.

De Grauwe, P. (1997). "Exchange Rate Arrangements between the Ins and the Outs." Paper presented at the IMF-Foundation Camille Gutt Conference on EMU and the International Monetary System, Washington, D.C. (March).

De Grauwe, P., and W. Vanhaverbeke (1993). "Is Europe an Optimum Currency Area? Evidence from Regional Data," in Masson and Taylor (1993).

De Haan, J., and J. E. Sturm (1994). "Political and Institutional Determinants of Fiscal Policy in the European Community." *Public Choice* 80:1–2 (July) pp. 157–172.

De la Dehesa, G., A. Giovannini, M. Guitán, and R. Portes, eds. (1993). *The Monetary Future of Europe.* London: CEPR.

De Nardis, S., A. Goglio, and M. Malgarini (1994). "Regional Specialization and Shocks in Europe." Manuscript. Rome: Centro Studi Confindustria (September).

Dinan, D. (1994). *Ever Closer Union? An Introduction to the European Community.* London: Macmillan.

Drèze, J., and E. Malinvaud (1994). "Growth and Employment: The Scope of a European Initiative." *European Economic Review* 38:3/4 (April) pp. 489–505.

Dyson, K. (1994). *Elusive Union: The Process of Economic and Monetary Union in Europe.* London: Longman.

Eichenberg, R. C., and R. J. Dalton (1993). "Europeans and the European Community: The Dynamics of Public Support for European Integration." *International Organization* 47:4 (Autumn) pp. 507–534.

Eichengreen, B. (1992). *Golden Fetters: The Gold Standard and the Great Depression, 1919–1939.* New York: Oxford University Press.

Eichengreen, B. (1993). "Labor Markets and European Monetary Unification," in Masson and Taylor (1993).

Eichengreen, B. (1994). *International Monetary Arrangements in the 21st Century.* Washington, D.C.: The Brookings Institution.

Eichengreen, B. (1996). "A More Perfect Union? The Logic of Economic Integration." *Princeton Essays in International Finance No. 198.* Princeton: Princeton University (June).

Eichengreen, B., and J. Frieden, eds. (1994). *The Political Economy of European Monetary Unification.* Boulder: Westview.

Eichengreen, B., and J. Frieden (1994a). "The Political Economy of European Monetary Unification: An Analytical Introduction," in Eichengreen and Frieden (1994) pp. 1–23.

Eichengreen, B., and J. Frieden, eds. (1998). *Forging an Integrated Europe.* Ann Arbor: University of Michigan Press.

Eichengreen, B., and F. Ghironi (1995). "European Monetary Unification: The Challenges Ahead." *CEPR Discussion Paper No. 1217.* London: Centre for Economic Policy Research (July).

Eichengreen, B., and C. Wyploz (1993). "The Unstable EMS." *Brookings Papers on Economic Activity* 1, pp. 51–124.

Elmeskov, J., and M. McFarlan (1994). "Unemployment Persistence." *OECD Economic Studies* 21 (Winter) pp. 57–86.

European Monetary Institute (1996). *Annual Report*. Frankfurt: European Monetary Institute (April).

Faini, R. (1994). "Trade Unions, Fiscal Policy and Regional Development." *The Location of Economic Activity: New Theories and Evidence*. London: Centre for Economic Policy Research (December) pp. 179–202.

Fitoussi, J. P., et al. (1993). *Competitive Disinflations*. Oxford: Oxford University Press.

Flood, A., and A. Rose (1995). "Fixing Exchange Rates: A Virtual Quest for Fundamentals." *Journal of Monetary Economics* 36 (December) pp. 3–37.

Frankel, J., and A. Rose (1996). "Is EMU More Desirable Ex Post than Ex Ante?" Paper presented at the 1996 EEA Congress, Istanbul, Turkey.

Fratianni, M., J. von Hagen, and C. Waller (1991). "The Maastricht Way to EMU." *Essays in International Finance, No. 187*. Princeton: Department of Economics, Princeton University (June).

Frenkel, J. A. (1983). "Flexible Exchange Rates, Prices, and the Role of 'News': Lessons from the 1970s," in J. S. Bhandari and B. H. Putnam, eds., *Economic Interdependence and Flexible Exchange Rates*. Cambridge: MIT Press, pp. 3–41.

Frieden, J. (1994). "Exchange Rate Politics: Contemporary Lessons from American History." *Review of International Political Economy* 1:1 (Spring) pp. 81–104.

George, E. (1995). "The Economics of EMU." *Bank of England Quarterly Bulletin* 35:2 (May).

Giavazzi, F., and M. Pagano (1988). "The Advantage of Tying One's Hands: EMS Discipline and Central Bank Credibility." *European Economic Review* 32, pp. 1055–1082.

Giavazzi, F., and M. Pagano (1990). "Can Severe Fiscal Contractions Be Expansionary? Tales of Two Small European Economies." *NBER Macroeconomics Annual* 5, pp. 75–116.

Giavazzi, F., and M. Pagano (1995). "Non-Keynesian Effects of Fiscal Policy Changes: International Evidence and the Swedish Experience." *Working Paper No. 5332*. Cambridge: National Bureau for Economic Research.

Giovannini, A. (1993). "Economic and Monetary Union: What Happened? Exploring the Political Dimension of Optimum Currency Areas," in De la Dehesa, et al. (1993).

Goodhart, C. (1993). "The Political Economy of Monetary Union." London: London School of Economics and Political Science.

Gowa, J. (1988). "Public Goods and Political Institutions: Trade and Monetary Policy Processes in the United States." *International Organization* 42, pp. 15–32.

Gowan, P., and P. Anderson, eds. (1997). *The Question of Europe*. London: Verso.

Greenwood, M. J. (1975). "Research on Internal Migration in the United States: A Survey." *Journal of Economic Literature* 13:2 (June) pp. 397–434.

Greenwood, M. J. (1985). "Human Migration: Theory, Models and Empirical Studies." *Journal of Regional Science* 25, pp. 521–544.

Grilli, V., D. Masciandaro, and G. Tabellini (1991). "Political and Monetary Institutions and Public Financial Policies in the Industrial Countries." *Economic Policy* 13 (October) pp. 342–392.

Gros, D. (1995). "Self-Fulfilling Public Debt Crises." Manuscript. Brussels: Centre for European Policy Studies.

Gros, D. (1996a). "Towards Economic and Monetary Union: Problems and Prospects." *CEPS Paper No. 65*. Brussels: Centre for European Policy Studies (January).

Gros, D. (1996b). "Germany's Stake in Exchange Rate Stability." Manuscript. Brussels: Centre for European Policy Studies (May).

Gros, D., and E. Jones (1995). "External Shocks and Employment: Revisiting the 'Mundellian' Story." Manuscript. Brussels: Centre for European Policy Studies (February).

Gros, D., and T. Lane (1994). "Symmetry versus Asymmetry in a Fixed Exchange Rate System." *Kredit und Kapital*, 1, pp. 43–66.

Gros, D., and N. Thygesen (1992). *European Monetary Integration: From the European Monetary System to the European Monetary Union*. London: Longman.

Gros, D., and G. Vandille (1995). "European Trade Structures." Manuscript. Brussels: Centre for European Policy Studies (February).

Hefeker, C. (1997a). *Interest Groups and Monetary Integration*. Boulder: Westview.

Hefeker, C. (1997b). "Between Efficiency and Stability: Germany and European Monetary Union" in Pisani-Ferry, et al. (1997) pp. 39–71.

Helleiner, E. (1994). *States and the Reemergence of Global Finance: From Bretton Woods to the 1990s*. Ithaca: Cornell University Press.

Hennes, M. (1996). "The Reflection Group of the European Union." *Aussenpolitik* 47:1, pp. 33–42.

Henning, C. R. (1994). *Currencies and Politics in the United States, Germany, and Japan*. Washington, D.C.: Institute for International Economics.

Hochreiter, E., and E. Jones (1997). "The Smaller Countries of Europe's Monetary Core: Austria, Belgium, and the Netherlands." Manuscript. Nottingham: Department of Politics, University of Nottingham.

Hughes Hallett, A. J. (1997). "The UK Position on Economic and Monetary Union," in Pisani-Ferry et al. (1997) pp. 72–103.

Hughes Hallett, A. J., and Y. Ma (1992). "East Germany, West Germany and Their Mezzogiorno Problem." *CEPR Discussion Paper 623*. London: Centre for Economic Policy Research.

Hughes Hallett, A. J., and Y. Ma (1995). "Economic Cooperation within Europe: Lessons from the Monetary Arrangements of the 1990s." *CEPR Discussion Paper No. 1190*. London: Centre for Economic Policy Research (June).

Hughes Hallett, A. J., and Y. Ma (1996a). "Changing Partners: The Importance of Coordinating Fiscal and Monetary Policies within a Monetary Union." *Manchester School* 64:2 (June) pp. 115–134.

Hughes Hallett, A. J., and Y. Ma (1996b). "The Dynamics of Debt Deflation in a Monetary Union." *Journal of International and Comparative Economics* 5:1, pp. 1–30.

Inglehart, R. (1990). *Culture Shift in Advanced Industrial Society*. Princeton: Princeton University Press.

Issing, O. (1996). "Europe: Political Union through Common Money?" *Occasional Paper No. 98*. London: Institute for Economic Affairs.

Italianer, A. (1993). "Mastering Maastricht: EMU Issues and How They Were Settled," in K. Gretschmann, ed., *Economic and Monetary Union: Implications for National Policy-makers*. Maastricht: European Institute for Public Administration, pp. 51–113.

Iversen, T., and N. Thygesen (1998). "Denmark: From External to Internal Adjustment," in Jones, Frieden, and Torres (1998) pp. 61–82.

Jacquemin, A., and A. Sapir (1995). "Is a European Hard Core Credible? A Statistical Analysis." *CEPR Discussion Paper No. 1242*. London: Centre for Economic Policy Research.

Jacquet, P. (1993). "The Politics of EMU: A Selective Overview," in Guillermo de la Dehesa et al. (1993).

Jimeno, J. F. (1993). "The Degree of Centralization of Collective Bargaining: The Inflation-Unemployment Trade-off and Macroeconomic Efficiency Revisited." *Working Paper No. 92-102*. Madrid: Fundación de Estudios de Economia Aplicada.

Jimeno, J. F., and S. Bentolila (1995). "Regional Unemployment Persistence: Spain, 1976–1994." *CEPR Discussion Paper No. 1259*. London: Centre for Economic Policy Research.

Jimeno, J. F., and L. Toharia (1993a). "The Effects of Fixed-Term Employment on Wages: Theory and Evidence from Spain." *Investigaciones Económicas* 17:3 (September) pp. 475–494.

Jimeno, J. F., and L. Toharia (1993b). "The Productivity Effects of Fixed-Term Employment: Are Temporary Workers Less Productive Than Permanent Workers?" *Working Paper No. 93-104*. Madrid: Fundación de Estudios de Economia Aplicada.

Jones, E. (forthcoming). "Economic and Monetary Union: Playing for Money," in Andrew Moravcsik, ed., *The Prospects for European Union: Deepening, Diversity and Democracy*. Washington, D.C.: The Brookings Institution for the Council on Foreign Relations.

Jones, E., J. Frieden, and F. Torres, eds. (1998). *Joining Europe's Monetary Club: The Challenges for Smaller Member States*. New York: St. Martin's Press.

Junankar, P. H., and J. B. Madsen (1995). "Unemployment in the OECD: Models, Myths, and Mysteries." *Working Paper No. 278*. Canberra: Australian National University.

Kaufmann-Bühler, W. (1994). "Deutsche Europapolitik nach dem Karlsruher Urteil: Möglichkeiten und Hemmnisse." *Integration* 17:1, pp. 1–11.

Kenen, P. B. (1969). "The Theory of Optimum Currency Areas: An Eclectic View," in R. A. Mundell and A. K. Swoboda, eds., *Monetary Problems of the International Economy*. Chicago: University of Chicago Press, pp. 41–60.

Kenen, P. B. (1995a). "Capital Controls, the EMS and EMU." *Economic Journal* 105:428 (January) pp. 181–192.

Kenen, P. (1995b). *Economic and Monetary Union in Europe: Moving Beyond Maastricht*. Cambridge: Cambridge University Press.

Kennedy, E. (1991). *The Bundesbank: Germany's Central Bank in the International Monetary System*. London: Pinter Publishers for the Royal Institute for International Affairs.

Keohane, R. (1983). "The Demand for International Regimes," in S. Krasner, ed., *International Regimes*. Ithaca: Cornell University Press, pp. 141–71.

Keynes, J. M. (1964). *The General Theory of Employment, Interest and Money*. New York: Harcourt, Brace and World.

Krugman, P. (1991). *Geography and Trade.* Cambridge: MIT Press.

Krugman, P. (1993). "Lessons of Massachusetts for EMU," in Torres and Giavazzi (1993).

Krugman, P., and A. Venables (1993). "Integration, Specialization and Adjustment." *CEPR Discussion Paper No. 886.* London: Centre for Economy Policy Research (December).

Lamers, K. (1997). "Strengthening the Hard Core," in Gowan and Anderson (1997) pp. 104–116.

Laskar, D. (1995). "Union monétaire à deux vitesses: analyse du coeur du jeu." Manuscript. Paris: CEPREMAP (November).

Laskar, D. (1996a). "Accords régionaux: une approche en termes de jeux coopératifs." *Revue économique* 47:3 (May) pp. 797–806.

Laskar, D. (1996b). "Partial Monetary Unions and Openness." Manuscript. Paris: CE-PREMAP.

Layard, R., S. Nickell, and R. Jackman (1991). *Unemployment: Macroeconomic Performance and the Labor Market.* Oxford: Oxford University Press.

Lindbeck, A., and D. Snower (1988). *The Insider-Outsider Theory.* Cambridge: MIT Press.

Lohmann, S., and S. O'Halloran (1994). "Divided Government and US Trade Policy: Theory and Evidence." *International Organization* 48:4 (Autumn) pp. 595–632.

Ludlow, P. (1982). *The Making of the European Monetary System: A Case Study of the Politics of the European Community.* London: Butterworth Scientific.

Marsh, D. (1992). *The Bundesbank: The Bank that Rules Europe.* London: Mandarin.

Martin, P. (1994). "A Sequential Approach to Regional Integration: The European Union and Central and Eastern Europe." *Discussion Paper No. 1070.* London: Centre for Economic Policy Research (November).

Martin, P. (1995). "Free-riding, Convergence, and Two-Speed Monetary Unification in Europe." *European Economic Review* 39:7 (August) pp. 1345–1364.

Martin, P. (1996). "L'importance des exclus de l'union monétaire européenne." *Revue économique* 47:3 (May) pp. 807–818.

Martin, P., and G. Ottaviano (1995). "The Geography of Multi-speed Europe." Working Document No. 95-10. Paris: CEPII (November).

Masson, P., S. Symansky, and G. Meredith (1990). "MULTIMOD: Mark II: A Revised and Extended Model." *IMF Occasional Paper 71.* Washington, D.C.: IMF.

Masson, P., S. Symansky, and G. Meredith (1991). "Changes to MULTIMOD since the July 1990 Occasional Paper 71: Current Model: MULTIAP." Manuscript. Washington, D.C.: International Monetary Fund (11 July).

Masson, P. R., and M. P. Taylor, eds. (1993). *Policy Issues in the Operation of Currency Unions.* Cambridge: Cambridge University Press.

McCarthy, P. (1990). "France Faces Reality: Rigueur and the Germans," in D. P. Calleo and C. Morgenstern, eds., *Recasting Europe's Economies: National Strategies in the 1980s.* Lanham: University Press of America, pp. 25–78.

McCarthy, P. (1996). "Between Europe and Exclusion: The French Presidential Elections of 1995." *Occasional Paper: European Studies Seminar Series, no. 1.* Bologna: Johns Hopkins Bologna Center (January).

McDonald, D., and G. Thumann (1990). "Investment Needs in East Germany," in L.

Lipschitz and D. McDonald, eds., "German Unification: Economic Issues," *IMF Occasional Paper 75*. Washington, D.C.: International Monetary Fund, Chapter 4.

McKinnon, R. (1963). "Optimal Currency Areas." *American Economic Review* 53:4 (September) pp. 717–725.

McNamara, K. R. (1998). *The Currency of Ideas: Monetary Politics in the European Union*. Ithaca: Cornell University Press.

McNamara, K. R., and E. Jones (1996). "The Clash of Institutions: Germany in European Monetary Affairs." *German Politics and Society* 14:3 (Fall) pp. 5–30.

Mélitz, J. (1995). "A Suggested Reformulation of the Theory of Optimal Currency Areas." *Open Economies Review* 6, pp. 281–298.

Mélitz, J. (1996). "The Empirical Evidence on the Costs and Benefits of European Monetary Union." *Swedish Economic Policy Review*.

Moses, J. (1998). "Sweden and EMU," in Jones, Frieden, and Torres (1998) pp. 203–224.

Mundell, R. A. (1961). "A Theory of Optimum Currency Areas." *American Economic Review* 51:4 (September) pp. 657–665.

Nayman, L., and J. Pisani-Ferry (1996). "Elus et exclus de la monnaie unique." *La Lettre du CEPII* (February).

OECD (1989). *Structural Adjustment in OECD Countries*. Paris: OECD.

OECD (1994a). *The OECD Jobs Study*. Paris: OECD.

OECD (1994b). *Employment Outlook*. Paris: OECD.

Padoa-Schioppa, T. (1994). *The Road to Monetary Union in Europe: The Emperor, the Kings, and the Genies*. Oxford: Clardendon Press.

Persson, T., and G. Tabellini (1996a). "Monetary Cohabitation in Europe." *American Economic Review* 86:2 (May) pp. 111–116.

Persson, T., and G. Tabellini (1996b). "Federal Fiscal Constitutions: Risk-Sharing and Redistribution." *Journal of Political Economy* 104:5 (October) pp. 979–1009.

Phelps, E. S. (1994). *Structural Slumps: The Modern Equilibrium Theory of Unemployment, Interest, and Assets*. Cambridge: Harvard University Press.

Pisani-Ferry, J. (1994). "Union monétaire et convergence: Qu'avons-nous appris?" *Document de travail No. 94-14*. Paris: CEPII.

Pisani-Ferry, J. (1995). "L'Europe à géométrie variable: une analyse économique." *Politique étrangère* 60:2 (Summer) pp. 447–466.

Pisani-Ferry, J., and P. Cour (1995). "The Cost of Fiscal Retrenchment Revisited." Manuscript. Paris: CEPII (28 September).

Pisani-Ferry, J., C. Hefeker, and A. J. Hughes Hallett (1997). "The Political Economy of EMU: France, Germany and the UK." *CEPS Paper No. 69*. Brussels: Centre for European Policy Studies (May).

Reeh, K. (1994). "L'Union européenne: de Maastricht à Karlsruhe et au-delà." *Politique étrangère* 59:2 (Summer) pp. 517–536.

Rogowski, R. (1987). "Trade and the Variety of Democratic Institutions." *International Organization* 41:2 (Spring) pp. 203–224.

Rose, A. (1995). "After the Deluge: Do Fixed Exchange-Rates Allow Inter-temporal Volatility Trade-offs?" *CEPR Discussion Paper No. 1240*. London: Centre for Economic Policy Research.

Sachs, J., and X. Sala-i-Martin (1992). "Fiscal Federalism and Optimum Currency

Areas: Evidence for Europe from the United States," in M. Canzonieri, V. Grilli, and P. R. Masson, eds., *Establishing a Central Bank: Issues in Europe and Lessons from the United States*. Cambridge: Cambridge University Press, pp. 195–219.

Saint-Aubin, B. (1995). "Le coût budgétaire de l'adhésion des PECO." *Economie internationale* 62:2, pp. 255–264.

Salmon, M. (1982). "Error Correction Mechanisms." *Economic Journal* 92:367 (September) pp. 615–629.

Sandholtz, W. (1993a). "Choosing Union: Monetary Politics and Maastricht." *International Organization* 47:1 (Winter) pp. 1–39.

Sandholtz, W. (1993b). "Monetary Bargains: The Treaty on EMU," in A. W. Cafruny and G. G. Rosenthal, eds., *The State of the European Community, Volume 2: The Maastricht Debates and Beyond*. Boulder: Lynne Rienner Publishers, pp. 125–142.

Searle, J. R. (1995). *The Construction of Social Reality*. London: Penguin.

Sowemimo, M. (1996). "The Conservative Party and European Integration: 1988–95." *Party Politics* 2:1 (January) pp. 77–97.

Spaventa, L. (1996). "Making EMU Happen: Problems and Proposals." *Essays in International Finance No. 199*. Princeton: Princeton University (July).

Standing, G. (1997). "The New Insecurities," in Gowan and Anderson (1997) pp. 203–219.

Stockman, A. (1987). "Sectoral and National Aggregate Disturbances to Industrial Output in Seven European Countries." *Working Paper No. 2313*. Cambridge: National Bureau of Economic Research (July).

Sutherland, A. (1995). "Fiscal Crises and Aggregate Demand: Can High Public Debt Reverse the Effects of Fiscal Policy?" *CEPR Discussion Paper 1246*. London: Centre for Economic Policy Research.

Svensson, L. (1994). "Fixed Exchange Rates as a Means to Price Stability: What Have We Learned?" *CEPR Discussion Paper No. 872*. London: Centre for Economic Policy Research (January).

Tavlas, G. S. (1993). "The 'New' Theory of Optimum Currency Areas." *The World Economy* 16:4 (November) pp. 663–685.

Thomas, A. (1993). "The Response of Wages and Labor Supply Movements to Employment Shocks across Britain and Europe." Manuscript. London: Centre for Economic Performance, London School of Economics and Political Science.

Thurow, L. C. (1980). *The Zero-Sum Society: Distribution and the Possibilities for Economic Change*. New York: Penguin.

Thygesen, N. (1995). "The Prospects for EMU by 1999—And Reflections for Arrangements for the Outsiders." Manuscript (November).

Thygesen, N. (1996). "Flexible Integration and European Monetary Union." Paper presented at the 1996 EEA Congress, Istanbul, Turkey.

Tietmeyer, H. (1994). "Europäische Währungsunion und Politische Union—das Modell mehrerer Geschwindigkeiten." *Europa-archiv* 49:16 (25 August) pp. 457–460.

Torres, F., and F. Giavazzi, eds. (1993). *Adjustment and Growth in the European Monetary Union*. Cambridge: Cambridge University Press.

Vaubel, R. (1978). "Real Exchange Rate Changes in the European Community: A New Approach to Optimum Currency Areas." *Journal of International Economics* 8, pp. 319–339.

Viñals, J. (1986). "Fiscal Policy and the Current Account." *Economic Policy* 3 (October) pp. 711–737.

Viñals, J. (1994). "Building a Monetary Union in Europe: Is It Worthwhile, Where Do We Stand, Where Are We Going?" *Occasional Paper No. 15*. London: Centre for Economic Policy Research.

Viñals, J. (1996). "European Monetary Integration: A Narrow or Wider EMU?" *European Economic Review* 40:3–5 (April) pp. 1103–1111.

Visser, W., and R. Wijnhoven (1990). "Politics Do Matter, but Does Unemployment?" *European Journal of Political Research* 18:1, pp. 71–96.

Volcker, P. (1995). "The Quest for Exchange Rate Stability: Realistic or Quixotic?" Stamp 50th Anniversary Lecture, University of London (November).

Von Hagen, J. (1991). "Fiscal Arrangements in a Monetary Union: Evidence from the United States." Manuscript. Bloomington: Indiana University.

Von Hagen, J. (1992). "Budgeting Procedures and Fiscal Performance in the European Union." *Economic Papers* 96 (October).

Von Hagen, J., and M. Frattiani (1995). "Banking Regulation with Variable Geometry." Manuscript. Mannheim: University of Mannheim.

Von Hagen, J., and I. Harden (1994). "National Budget Processes and Fiscal Performance." *European Economy, Reports and Studies* 3, pp. 315–418.

Von Hagen, J., and S. Lutz (1995). "Fiscal and Monetary Policy on the Way to EMU." Manuscript. Mannheim: University of Mannheim (October).

Wallace, H. (1990). "Making Multilateral Negotiations Work," in W. Wallace, ed., *The Dynamics of European Integration*. London: Royal Institute for International Affairs, pp. 213–228.

Winters, L. A. (1996). "Regionalism versus Multilateralism." Paper presented at the CEPR conference on Regional Integration, La Coruna, (April).

Wyplosz, C. (1996). "An EMS for Both Ins and Outs: The Contractual and Conditional Approach." Paper prepared for the CEPR-BNL conference on "Monetary Co-Existence in Europe," Rome (February).

Index

adjustment: fiscal, 9, 34; real, 3, 150
Amsterdam Treaty, 165
Andrés, J., 49n1
Austria, 175

Bank of England, 135, 161n31, 182
Belgium, 59–60, 132
Beveridge curve, 26, 51n14
Blair, T., 5, 164
Brandt, W., 165
Bundesbank, 9, 173, 179–180

Carter, J., 166
Castillo, S., 49n1
central banks: independence, 173, 182;
    see also credibility, monetary policy
Chirac, J., 5, 126, 164
competitiveness, 23; Commission White
    Paper, 4, 29; and exchange rates, 66,
    122n19, 136, 151
consumption, 34
convergence: criteria for, 3, 42, 83–4,
    102, 125, 151–152, 167; nominal,
    102, 131, 156; and output/employ-
    ment, 7, 101–102; real 26, 35, 43
core-periphery (see variable geometry)
credibility, 172–175; and fiscal policy,
    34–35
crises, 3, 11n2, 135, 173–174

debt, 88–89, 104–105; default, 107;
    stock-flow distinction, 106–107
deficits (see fiscal policy)

Delors Plan, 163
Denmark, 50n9; expansionary fiscal con-
    solidation, 115; export shocks to, 60;
    veto of Maastricht Treaty, 2, 165
derogations (see Maastricht Treaty)
Dolado, J., 49n1
Duce, R., 49n1

eastern enlargement, 4, 145–146,
    149–150
economic and monetary union (EMU):
    centripetal vs. centrifugal, 138–139,
    151, 157; controversy over, 1, 8, 163,
    184–186; costs and benefits, 36, 42–
    43, 53, 126, 129, 138, 185; joining,
    35, 125; long-term vs. short-term ef-
    fects of, 11, 33, 184
economic geography, 38
electoral systems, 181–182
employment, 4, 49n3; exports and,
    61–62; flexibility, 32
European Institutions, 43, 174; Central
    Bank, 9, 146, 153–155, 180; Commis-
    sion, 38, 151, 154, 187; Council, 1,
    126, 154; Ecofin ,149; Monetary Insti-
    tute (EMI), 10, 160n25
European Monetary System (EMS), 8,
    163, 166–167
exchange rate mechanism (ERM), 3, 21,
    40, 83, 86, 126, 135, 167; ERM2, 155,
    158; see also crises
exchange rate regimes, 38, 54, 66,
    154–155

exchange rates: competitive devaluations, 122n19, 136; determination, 64, 79n2; stability, 128; and stabilization, 17, 40, 55, 64, 66, 132; volatility (see also crises), 7, 55, 69–71

financial markets (see credibility, speculation, crises)
Finland, 6
fiscal policy, 39, 83; bailouts, 84; consolidation of, 34, 89–90, 100, 114–115, 185; correlation across countries, 56, 110; cyclical adjustments, 117; discipline, 83, 103–105; primary budget balances, 106, 122n18, 133–134; sustainability, 89, 105, 120; see also adjustment, interest rates
France: attitudes toward EMU, 9, 169; realignments against the deutsche mark, 86; referendum on Maastricht Treaty, 2–3
free-riding, 8, 146
Frieden, J., 9–10, 49n1

Germany: attitudes toward EMU, 9, 169, 177, 179; exchange rate sensitivity, 64, 69–71; High Court decision, 3, 84; unification, 121n7
Giscard d'Estaing, V., 166
Greece, 138
Gros, D., 6–7, 49n1
growth potential, 35

Hefeker, C., ix
housing markets, 77
Hughes Hallett, A., 7–8

inflation (see NAIRU, NAWRU, prices, unemployment)
interest rates: differentials, 11n4, and fiscal consolidation, 8, 34, 101; see also monetary policy
intergovernmental conference (IGC), 4, 165
International Monetary Fund (IMF), 66, 86, 187
investment, 34

Italy, 7–8, 107, 132, 153, 177

Japan, 25
Jimeno, J., 5–6, 13, 49n1, 54
job security, 31–33
Jones, E., 9–10
Jospin, L., 164
Juppé, A., 5

Keynes, J. M., 10
Keynesian economics, 114
Kohl, H., 5, 126

labor: markets, 29, 40, 46–48, 63–64, 135; mobility, 39, 54, 72–79, 170–171; organized (see trade unions)
liquidity squeeze, 92, 99, 122n14
Luxembourg, 120n2

Maastricht Treaty, 1, 2, 7–8, 83, 152, 165; derogations from, 35, 126, 131; plan for EMU, 164, 167–168, 174; spirit of, 88, 125, 141; see also convergence
Major, J., 164, 172
manufacturing, 38–39, 61, 151, 179
Mateus, A., 49n1
McAdam, P., 7–8
McNamara, K., ix
migration, 39, 73, 76
Mitterrand, F., 2, 166
Modesto, L., 49n1
monetary policy, 36, 40, 85; discipline, 150, 166, 183; relaxation, 100; see also interest rates
MULTIMOD, 7, 66, 84–86, 89, 123n24
multispeed Europe (see variable geometry)
Mundell, R., 53–54

NAIRU (nonaccelerating inflation rate of unemployment), 17, 23, 25, 136, 160n16
Nash equilibrium, 68, 153
NAWRU (nonaccelerating wages rate of unemployment), 136
Netherlands, 137, 173–174

Okun curve, 51n14, 67
Okun's law, 65, 81n14
optimum currency areas (OCAs), 37–38, 41, 53–54, 139, 145, 170–171; assumptions of, 53, 72; testing for, 55–57, 127–129, 158–159; see also shocks
Organization for Economic Cooperation and Development (OECD), 24, 85, 136, 187

Pareto optimality, 68
participation rates, 49n3
Philip Morris Institute, 11n3
Pisani-Ferry, J., 8–9
political culture, 175–178, 186n5
political parties, 181, 183
political union, 168–169
Pompidou, G., 165
prices, 99, 110, 118
public opinion, 175–176; business attitudes, 53, 178–179; exposed vs. sheltered sectors, 55, 178

regions, 179–180; as optimum currency areas, 38, 54, 79n1; specialization, 39
Ricardian equivalence, 114, 117
risk premiums, 35, 106–107, 132, 145, 172

Schmidt, H., 166
Schröder, G., 5
shocks, 6, 20, 186n4; asymmetric/symmetric, 20, 23, 37–38, 41, 55, 81n13, 128; demand and supply, 29, 56, 67, 129; domestic vs. foreign, 54, 56, 68, 159n5; oil price, 26
single internal market, 8, 36, 150, 157
social Europe, 4
Soviet Union, 6
Spain, 18–19, 21, 177
speculation, 145, 172–173
stability pact, 126
Stoiber, E., 5

taxes: increases, 34, 84, 105–106; reaction deficit cuts, 87–88, 121n9; regimes, 91–99, 122n12; see also fiscal policy
technology, 23
Teitmeyer, H., 4
trade unions: attitudes toward EMU, 69; density, 30, 183; insiders vs. outsiders, 31
trade, 23; dependence, 171–172; integration, 129, 146; intraindustry, 38; openness, 66; protection, 151; see also economic geography

unemployment, 5–6, 185; benefits, 32–33; cyclical 25, 27; determinants of, 27–28, 48–49; dispersion, 14–20, 26; European component of, 14, 42, 44–45, 50n7; hysteresis, 25, 27, 34, 37, 51n15; long-term, 26–27, 51n13; political importance, 165; regional, 20, 49–50n6; structural, 42, 135–136; trade and, 57–63; variation in, 19, 22
United Kingdom, 64, 77–79, 125, 145, 160n25, 168
United States, 6, 20–21, 25–26, 30, 37, 56, 73

Vallés, J., 49n1
variable geometry, 4, 8, 125, 139, 156, 171–172, 185; decision rules, 140–141; "ins" and "outs," 148–149, 157
Viñals, J., 5–6, 13, 54

wage bargaining, 30; centralization of, 30, 183; disciplinary effect of EMU, 36–37; insiders and outsiders, 135; and unemployment, 30
wages: and disinflation, 9; flexibility, 39, 64, 74; pressure, 34, 50n11; rigidities, 17, 23–26, 40, 43, 45–46, 54
Waigel, T., 5
Walsh, J., ix
Werner Plan, 163, 184

List of Editors and Contributors

Jeffry Frieden, Department of Government, Harvard University
Daniel Gros, Centre for European Policy Studies
Andrew Hughes Hallett, Department of Economics, University of Strathclyde
Juan F. Jimeno, Department of Economics, Universidad de Alcalà de Henares
Erik Jones, Department of Politics, University of Nottingham
Peter McAdam, Department of Economics, University of Strathclyde
Jean Pisani-Ferry, Ministry of Economy, Finance and Industry, France
José Viñals, Bancoa de España